MAKING A LIVING WHILE MAKING A DIFFERENCE

Possibly the most visionary and integrated body of work in career development literature today ...Melissa Everett has made an enormous contribution to the field. — Ande Diaz, author, *The Harvard College Guide to Careers in Public Service*, and Assistant Dean for Student Life, Princeton University

Melissa Everett is a unique career advisor. If I could have only one book for my career library, this would be it. — Kevin Doyle, National Director of Program Development, The Environmental Careers Organization, and editor of *The Complete Guide to Environmental Careers in the 21st Century*

For soul-satisfying adventure into Right Livelihood, Melissa Everett is the best guide around. In this savvy and exuberant book, she shows us how we can craft our work so that we can follow our heart's desire — to take part in the healing of our world. Must-reading for counselors, teachers, clergy, and all of us who want to come alive to the promise of our time. — Joanna Macy, author, *Coming Back to Life*

Just what you need to take charge of your life and start living your highest vision. — Hazel Henderson, author, *Creating Alternative Futures,* and *Building a Win-Win World*

Melissa Everett has given life and meaning and access to holistic work. — Elly Jackson, co-author, *The New Perfect Resume*

Melissa Everett's *Making a Living While Making a Difference* combines practical advice and thought-provoking exercises with real life stories that touched my heart and spoke to my mind. It is especially exciting to see all the different jobs that people are involved in that — like Melissa herself — are truly making a difference. I highly recommend this book and will continue to refer back to it myself as I continue to reinvent my own life path. — Maureen Hart, author, *Guide to Sustainable Community Indicators*

This is not only the best career guide I have ever read, it is a graduate course in and for the self. Highly recommended for those of us who think we are making a living while making a difference, for those who really do want to, and especially for the hundreds of thousands of exceptional young people who are being 'trained' every day to become entrepreneurs and business leaders without an ecological and social conscience. — Jaimie P. Cloud, Founder and Director, The Sustainability Education Center New York, New York

MAKING A LIVING WHILE MAKING A DIFFERENCE

The Expanded Guide to Creating Careers with a Conscience

Melissa Everett

NEW SOCIETY PUBLISHERS

Cataloguing in Publication Data:

A catalog record for this publication is available from the National Library of Canada.

Cover design by Miriam MacPhail with artwork by by Soren Henrich.

Printed in Canada on acid-free, partially recycled (20 percent post-consumer) paper using soy-based inks by Transcontinental/Best Book Manufacturers.

New Society Publishers acknowledges the financial support of the Government of Canada through the Book Publishing Industry Development Program (BPIDP) for our publishing activities, and the assistance of the Province of British Columbia through the British Columbia Arts Council.

Paperback ISBN: 0-86571-400-2

Inquiries regarding requests to reprint all or part of *Making a Living While Making a Difference* should be addressed to New Society Publishers at the address below.

To order directly from the publishers, please add $4.00 shipping to the price of the first copy, and $1.00 for each additional copy (plus GST in Canada). Send check or money order to:

New Society Publishers
P.O. Box 189, Gabriola Island, B.C. V0R 1X0, Canada

New Society Publishers aims to publish books for fundamental social change through non-violent action. We focus especially on sustainable living, progressive leadership, and educational and parenting resources. Our full list of books can be browsed on the worldwide web at: http://www.newsociety.com

NEW SOCIETY PUBLISHERS
Gabriola Island B.C., Canada

To laugh often and much; to win the respect of intelligent people and the affection of children; to earn the appreciation of honest critics and endure the betrayal of false friends; to appreciate beauty, to find the best in others; to leave the world a bit better, whether by a healthy child, a garden patch, or a redeemed social condition; to know even one life has breathed easier because you have lived. This is to have succeeded.

— Ralph Waldo Emerson

Contents

Acknowledgments

Let me express my heartfelt appreciation to the tribe of friends and colleagues, clients and strangers, who have helped me bring this book to life by sharing their stories, resources, and observations; reviewing chapters and testing exercises; challenging assumptions; and encouraging me to stay with the process.

In particular, I appreciate the feedback and support of my doctoral advisors and fellow students in the Off-Campus PhD Program of Erasmus University; Rona Fried, my editor at www.SustainableBusiness.com, who has given me an outlet for testing key sections of the book; counseling colleagues and clients whose curiosity and candor have helped me begin to understand the psychology of vocational identity and ethics; and the many enterprising spirits I've been able to talk with, who have found ways to create livelihoods that make the world a better place.

Special thanks to my agent, Tim Seldes, and the fabulous team at New Society Publishers ... to the cafés of the Hudson Valley and to the Kingston YMCA, for staying open late in the evenings ... and to family and friends, for handling the usual stresses with more than the usual grace.

Thanks to many organizations that generously gave me access to conferences and libraries, especially the American Management Association for welcoming me to the Executive Forum, "Building Community at Work: Profiting from a Value-Based Corporate Culture."

Contact the author at **melissae@ulster.net,**
PO Box 26, Stone Ridge, NY 12484.

Introduction

Lynne Elizabeth was once a successful graphic designer in Orange County, California, with all the comforts that went with that success. Today she edits a journal called *New Village*, a forum for architects, designers, planners, and others interested in redesigning human settlements so that they are in greater harmony with the environment. To bring the journal to life, she spent a period of time with her belongings in storage, living in a rented room, and has lived through the derailing of a previous publication vision. Today, she earns a decent living. But the organizing principle of her career is much more than the income.

Manna Jo Greene was once a full-time critical care nurse, and still stays connected to the profession by working weekend shifts at the hospital. But eight years ago, her concern for the health of the planet reached a critical level, and she moved into the recycling field. Today, as recycling and education coordinator for a large rural county, Greene touches countless lives — through the job she does directly, through the weekend radio show it allows her to host, and through tireless networking and volunteer environmental leadership in the community.

Karen Clark-Adin used to be a manager in an ordinary manufacturing business. Today she runs a retail store so exciting that tour buses from a hundred miles away make it a routine stop. Anyone Can Whistle is a world music hub for instruments, recordings, drum lessons, and more. The world's largest wind chimes, a player piano, and a circus pipe organ are part of the store's decor. Puppets, mobiles, and all sorts of adult toys grace the place, and music pours into the streets. Clark-Adin is a leader in the local business community's successful efforts to make Kingston, New York's Old Town a happening place. More, she is known for the spirit she brings into a field that more ordinary people handle, well, in ordinary ways. She says, "A few years ago, I had what can only be described as a spiritual awakening. I knew I needed to make some changes. I needed to be in community, because it turns me on. I think that, on a very large scale, that's what's needed in the world. Through this job, I have learned about working at a heart level, just doing whatever I can to help people have a fundamental experience of human value. When people slide into that state of feeling valued and safe, they're able to nurture themselves and others."

I live in the Hudson Valley of New York. My circle of friends is filled with people who have lived through changes like these, and reflect these values. There are lots of mental health types and communicators and environmental professionals. There's a teacher in the local alternative high school for kids at risk, who runs an eco-fashion business out of her home. There's an environmental activist who just got his graduate degree in engineering and went to work for the leaner, cleaner IBM. There's an administrator at the local monastery who is starting a new media company on the side.

These are more or less normal folks today, although many of them are working in ways their parents never heard of. Some of them are in totally new enterprises. Others do time-honored work with new forms of organization. Some of us are specialists with many specialties. Whatever we're doing, we're substantially winging it.

Some of us make a full living doing the work we feel we are on earth to do. Others support their "real" work with day (or night) jobs. Some of us have health insurance, some have supportive spouses with jobs that carry benefits. Some of us have a rental property or two, or successful investments, as a cushion. Some of us are living on the edge.

We do our share of patronizing the strip of malls over on Route 9W, where we occasionally bump into each other in the middle of the night at the 24-hour supermarket with mild embarrassment. We drive our cars to the photocopy palace to reproduce documents about sustainable development. This does not make us happy. Mostly, though, it makes us more committed than ever to building a different kind of economy to live in.

In the early 1990s, our region was the subject of a long, hard look by a group of economic development thinkers, including banks, foundation executives, local and state officials, and planning agencies. In fact, ours was one of several regions to be systematically scrutinized, under the auspices of the President's Council for Sustainable Development. Sponsored by major banks, county governments, foundations, and the like, the resulting report was starkly entitled "Two Futures for the Hudson River Valley." One of these futures, of course, is unconstrained, sprawling development — without attention to its ecological and social consequences. The other is more consciously chosen by the communities themselves, to make human settlements work coherently for people, with minimal disruption of the surrounding lands. Nobody had much good to say about the sprawl scenario. The main debate I've been hearing is only whether it's inevitable, and whether there's anything ordinary people can do. The report urged communities to do serious planning, and citizens to get involved, as many already were. Five years later, the President's Council's National Town Meeting for a Sustainable America, held in Detroit in the spring of 1999, urged citizens and communities to get involved in community change, and provided a rich array of tools in the form of successful models that by then were working around the world.

For most of the people I know, one of the most vibrant opportunities for involvement is the least grandiose, and the most personalized. It has to do with the day-to-day choices we make, to direct whatever economic power we might have into the support of the more sustainable options. In a way that comes naturally when we take our future seriously, we do our best to support the ventures that reflect our values. And so we take all our out-of-town friends to the hippest retail destination in town, Anyone Can Whistle, where they are encouraged to play with the hundreds of drums and whistles and chimes and puppets representing local artisans and a world musical culture. We hold as many meetings as possible in the Tapping Frog Kitchen, our local affordable esthetic healthy gourmet haunt. We are creating an alternative currency, the Ulster Acorn, which will help keep dollars in circulation and businesses healthy in our county. Members of Our Gang have launched a popular Hudson Valley Harvest campaign, encouraging local restaurants to buy from local farms, as a means of bolstering the region's farm economy. Still other friends are working with local youth at risk to teach them business skills, with a socially responsible orientation. Over a glass of wine at night, we blue-sky about creating a fabulous retail outlet for locally produced goods.

My clients' and friends' choices about livelihoods are part of this same fabric. Each in a different way, they are connecting the work they do for material sustenance with the work they do to make their communities more livable. Their work for sustainable development starts with their own lives.

People like these are part of a tribe that is growing in size and self-awareness: those who grasp that we live on a planet in crisis, our communities are in turmoil, and our hearts are in danger of breaking when we pay attention to the darker side of the world we've helped to create. In spite of all this turbulence and uncertainty, they are builders. They naturally reach for opportunities to make positive changes in the world, from protecting and restoring the environment, to reducing violence and poverty, to making society's institutions work. They realize that all the volunteering in the world will not be enough to counter the impact of working lives that have not been designed to take either environmental or human well-being into account. So they are searching for effective ways to be part of redesigning the economy — one organization, one project, one career at a time. They want to devote their working lives to some kind of tangible, positive change. What drives them isn't a sense of duty or guilt, but a spirit of engagement and curiosity and play.

One major national study[1] estimates that the population with these values is 45 million strong, and calls them the "Cultural Creatives." What sets Cultural Creatives apart is a combination of environmental, social, and spiritual values. They are exploring the deep and rich connection between personal development, on one hand, and social transformation on the other. For them, taking care of the environment and solving entrenched social problems are no longer fringe concerns.

Work is not the only arena for this exploration, but it's a major one. As social, ecological and spiritual sensibilities are embraced by a widening circle, it is only natural that our sensibilities about work and livelihood would undergo some fascinating shifts. In 1993, *Working Woman* magazine and the Roper organization surveyed 1,000 working adults on their definitions of success and goals for working. Asked whether they would rather earn a lot of money or earn enough, doing work that makes the world a better place, 86% chose making themselves useful, and 59% said they "agreed strongly" with that outlook. This attitude shift appears to run deep. For example, surveys of graduating MBAs conducted periodically by Duke University have taken a 180-degree turn since the late 1980s. Asked about their primary measures of success, the Class of 1989 cited power, prestige and money. Graduates in 1991 pointed to successful relationships, a balanced life, and leisure time. And the most recent survey's overwhelming response was marriage, health, and ethics.

Deep Economy

"Deep Ecology" is a term coined by Norwegian philosopher Arne Naess to describe the interconnectedness and interdependence of all life on earth. This recognition calls on us all to find new ways to live and work that restore the natural environment and human communities. Deep Ecology is a different environmental ethic than "resource management," which implies that the planet is a resource to manage for human satisfaction rather than a living home requiring stewardship on its own terms. Since at least the late 1970s, a loose network of philosophers, psychologists, educators, and activists has been laboring to translate this value system into a set of educational and therapeutic principles that can be widely applied.[2] My friend Bill Pfeiffer of the Sacred Earth Network in Massachusetts described these educational processes a few years ago as "helping people move out of the mainstream, into the earth stream." Today there's at least a glimmer of possibility that the earth stream is becoming mainstream.

Primary among the teachers and models influencing this book has been Joanna Macy, co-author with Molly Young Brown of *Coming Back to Life: Practices to Reconnect Our Lives, Our World* and named by *Utne Reader* as one of the world's hundred visionaries worth watching. In the late 1970s, Joanna and many colleagues started by taking a look at the peculiar apathy that some of her neighbors were demonstrating when the conversation turned toward difficult ecological and social issues. Nuclear weapons? Ho hum. International terrorism? How tacky of you to mention it ... Toxic dumps in poor neighborhoods? Jeez, will you lighten up?? In search of effective strategies for community activism, they studied the phenomenon of psychic numbing, and concluded that people do not shut down on big-picture issues out of a lack of caring. They shut down because they care too much, and it hurts too much sometimes to look at the mess we are in. It hurts, especially, when we feel powerless to act. Numbing and apathy are directly proportional to the perception of powerlessness. And they deepen that sense of powerlessness by cutting us off from our lighter feelings as well as those of despair. Holding our concerns for the world around us at bay and trying to behave "normally," we begin to feel fraudulent if not crazy. We lose our sense of inner authority.

The antidote to all this is a cluster of very distinctive learning experiences that pulls us out of isolation, lets us feel and speak our own truths about the state of the world and the work that needs doing, allows our voices to be heard to restore our faith in our own perceptions, and then turns attention toward the creativity that is released after repressed emotions are let out.

This happens, for example, through:
- learning to attend to the world with multiple intelligences: emotional, kinesthetic, visual, imaginative, and so on, as well as analytical;
- cultivating a sense of efficacy, or personal power, through a collaborative, co-creative spirit; realizing that nobody can save our communities and the planet alone, but together we may be able to;
- developing fresher, more subtle perceptions of the world and the work to be done in it, and using them to challenge perceived limits about our choices;
- creating and celebrating beauty, in every possible form, to remind us of the sacredness of life and keep us animated.

Not entirely whimsically, I have taken to calling the application of these principles to the vocational quest "Deep Economy." However you name it, this is nothing more than a commitment to organize our working lives with our communities and the earth firmly in mind.

It's doing the right thing, not as a "should," but out of recognition of the enlightened self-interest of preserving our social and ecological life support system. As Naess puts it, "When the social self is well developed, and I understand that I am part of something larger, I no longer want to eat a big cake all by myself. I want to share it with others." So, too, with finding ways to earn livelihoods that maximize benefit to the world around us, as well as being personally satisfying. In keeping with good ecological thinking, *Making a Living While Making a Difference* stresses everybody's right and need to adapt these principles to their own circumstances.

The value-driven career planning program outlined in this book will support your exploration of the ways you can exercise positive impact through your work. It will provide you with information and role models, and a structure for your own individualized exploration and decision-making. It addresses the necessary practical questions such as option-generating, goal-setting, investigating options, self-promotion, and self-defense. But it does so, starting at a fairly intimate level, with questions about who you are and what you most care about; where you draw your inspiration; what futures you see as likely, in your own community and for the planet; how the macroevents and patterns around you affect your sense of the possible and what's important to work for. Above all, it's about freeing up more of our true Selves and bringing them to bear in the work we do. As examples will show, the rewards can put the risks in an entirely different perspective.

Toward Sustainable Livelihoods

Our livelihoods play a major role in defining us, to ourselves as well as socially. But decisions about how to make a living these days are complicated and elusive. We are not only deciding among more options than ever. We are deciding how to decide. What's real? What's essential? What work will make a difference? What institutions are capable of doing it? Where do we place our trust? With respected businesses that show solid increases in stock value? With nonprofits whose mission statements are really compelling? With public agencies that have gotten serious about reinventing government, and are embarked on fascinating experiments in new ways to serve the public? With charismatic leaders? With organizations that show results we care about, or the ones whose cultures and day-to-day operating principles seem most wholesome?

What you will encounter in the pages ahead is a value-driven paradigm for career development, in contrast with most approaches which may address values respectfully but are still driven by considerations of skills. A major school of thought in career development, dating back at least to Thomas Aquinas, holds that we are placed on earth with a particular set of gifts whose fruition will automatically lead to our fulfilling our highest promise. To bring these to light, traditional career development concentrates on identifying skills, and building on past accomplishments. But our talents are not our only gifts. Playing with a full deck also means considering our values and sensibilities, our mental maps of how the world is, and our fantasies about how it could be. The premise of this book is that we become more effective in deploying our skills when our choices are consciously driven by values and life-affirming passions.

This book takes the conversation about values further than some, maybe even far enough to get uncomfortable at moments, by exploring them in context, up close and in detail. It's great to say "I value health." But, for some people, that means "I go to the gym regularly," and for others it means "I want a workplace that's impeccably free of toxics." For still others, it means "I want to work directly in health care." Clearly no one of these is superior to any other, and they fit together nicely. But the choices only become clear in a personally relevant way when we go from the abstract to the specific, and when we consciously make decisions with reference to the well-being of every living thing they affect.

Making a Living While Making a Difference approaches life/work planning in several distinctive ways. The first of these distinctions is in the way we create support systems so that we can achieve our full potential. Conventional career planning teaches useful ways of teasing out support from individuals with whom you may or may not share a shred of common values: the informational interview; the networking lunch, and so on. Here, we look at support as beginning with a strong community that can give all its members a wider range of resources to succeed.

The second distinguishing feature of the program presented here has to do with the challenges of creating what's new, rather than choosing from a menu of preexisting options. We will pay special attention to the art of defining and naming your "ownwork," (to use the term coined by British futurist James Robertson); that is, finding language that communicates not only the functional characteristics of the work you want, but its precise meanings in your life and therefore the specific approaches to the work that will most likely fulfill you.

The third focal point of this program is on the nature of healthy self-discipline, in an era when we are all searching for a solid place to stand, somewhere between addictive commitment and self-pitying paralysis. We will explore the art of healthy commitment in the context of community, self-generation and renewal.

Finally, I am offering you a career development program that's based on a healthy belief in magic, and that encourages balance between planning and surrender.

What does this approach to work look like in action? Often, it looks like a spiral path, inward toward your own center, toward an increasingly clear understanding of who you are as you refine and perform the work that's yours and let yourself be shaped by its demands. I call this approach to work Self-employment — bringing your whole self to work. It is not just about finding or creating work that helps rebuild communities and the planet, although that is sorely needed. It isn't simply the ability to get paid to do something fascinating. It's work that links external contribution with personal development and satisfaction. It's the way paid labor and avocation, relationships and personal growth, study and citizenship all weave themselves together into a life of integrity and contribution.

Consider Ursula Basch, who has a job as groovy as any. She's an environmental ombudsman for New York City, helping small businesses to solve their environmental compliance problems and register concerns about city enforcement. It was an almost effortless move from her environmental engineering job with the city. But the job is not what she regards as her life's distinctive work. She is also a practitioner and teacher of herbal medicine, an interest that overtook her when she saw the power of herbs in reversing her mother's serious cancer some years ago. Her evenings and weekends are given over to a business called Herbal Bear, and her days are filled with useful human interaction that pays the bills. Her life is full, and the elements work together. That's Self-employment.

For most of the people you will read about in these pages, the days are long. The progress is gradual. But there's a gut-level acknowledgment that turning back is not an option. From some inner recess, the strength keeps coming to do work that's often fairly difficult. The source of that strength is the self-expression and personal development that this mode of working calls forth. Without pretending that the issue is black-and-white, they recognize that there really are two kinds of future for all the regions we call home. One is a cookie-cutter economy, the same as anyplace, constrained by the broad brushstrokes of public policy but pretty much imposed on both landscape and communities. With that comes a cookie-cutter vision of jobs and business opportunities. The other is a "custom-designed" economy, growing out of the resources and ideas and human quirks that are indigenous to this place, organized to benefit local communities and the natural environment through the mission and design and strategy of each enterprise and the ways they relate to each other. And within this custom-designed economy there is room for ways of making a living that reflect our values and visions. That's where my friends and I are placing our bets.

When we're contemplating a choice ahead, many of us focus on the risks. How different the same choice can look from the other side, when we can also see the possible gains, and the inner resources we free up by acting on our true values. Among the courageous clients and workshop participants who have reminded me how true this is, one who stands out in my mind is Peter. He was truly twisting on the hook of an idea that had taken over his imagination, but he couldn't figure out how to activate it. He wanted to create an ecological retreat center with demonstration organic gardens, green building practices, meeting spaces, and many other features. One inner voice told him it was a crazy notion. Another voice told him it was his future. During the day, his questions were all about the costs of taking the plunge: reduced earnings, compromised credibility, his wife's uncertainties. Finally, I asked him, "How do you know this idea would be so impractical? How do you know you would earn less than you do now? Have you done a business plan? Have you done market research?"

"No. I've been too scared. I really have no idea," he replied. Just a few months later, Peter sent me a beautiful brochure for the new center, with the next season's program and a note of thanks.

Whatever risks and opportunities you are dancing with, I hope this book will provide a tangible support for breaking out of perceived limits and stepping into a future worthy of your commitment.

PART 1

THE WORK TO BE DONE

Emerging Opportunities to Make the World a Better Place

Chapter 1
Self-Employment

"Never in my 25 years of leadership training has there been a time when principles and pragmatism have converged as completely as they do today."

— Steven Covey

A New Collection of Heroes

I collect stories about mavericks of a particular kind. Let me introduce you to three larger-than-life people who happen to be living coherent and fulfilling lives, even though they fly in the face of cultural expectations. The first is Jon Stocking, who knew for a long time that he wanted to be a chef. Jon dreamed of training in the fine cooking schools of Europe. But he was broke in San Diego, looking for a ticket to anywhere. He heard it was possible to make good money working on tuna boats, so he signed on as a cook. He tells this story of the awakening that followed:

"Three days into the trip, the garbage was piling up on deck. I asked innocently, 'Where's the dumpster?' My shipmates laughed. 'Take your pick. Port or starboard,' they said.

"This was the '80s. Green wasn't the hot topic it is today. I hadn't thought of myself as an environmentalist, but somehow I knew throwing garbage in the ocean wasn't what to do. I said, 'You're kidding.' They said, 'Throw it over or we'll throw you over.' "

Over the next weeks, Jon found himself looking with new eyes at a world that he had once taken for granted. Sometimes he threw garbage over. Sometimes he couldn't do it, and a few times he was thrown into the ocean. But he was a former triathlete. He could handle treading water until he could get the captain's attention. That was the easy part.

What he couldn't handle was the reality of the enormous fishing nets, more than a mile in diameter, pulling in dolphin, sea turtles, tuna, and countless other creatures, all squealing as they were folded into a hydraulic crusher. He was completely unprepared for the high-technology fishing methods that were razing the ocean floor, from the sonar systems to the sticks of dynamite used to disable the big fish. It was his job to set the lines. He vividly remembers the moment his life really shifted:

One day, I looked in and saw this infant dolphin, about 2 footballs long. Without thinking at all, I jumped into the water and took it into my arms, and it relaxed when I held it close. Then I looked around and realized I had to swim through about a mile of this rabid, thrashing sea life to get to the boundary of the net. They were all struggling to escape; they knew they were going to die. I made it through, and turned and released the baby dolphin.

Then, in the net I saw another dolphin, and imagined that this was its mother. Instinctively, I petted it, stroked it, then lifted it over the net to safety. I bloodied it and bit my tongue, and turned to swim back through this mess to the boat. And then I recognized about 30 or 40 dolphins, who all saw that this was the way out. I rescued dolphins all day, swimming in my tennis shoes, until I was exhausted.

Miraculously, Jon was able to slip overboard. without being missed, and to do it several times more. He became adept at cutting the nets without getting caught. He learned to hide his feelings, but they didn't fade. Down by the equator one afternoon, a sailor demanded, "Pick out a shark. We're having shark steak tonight." Jon found one that was already dead, and hauled it ashore. Gutting it and preparing the steaks, he was stunned to find a Budweiser beer can in its stomach, 3,000 miles from any human settlement.

Eventually, they docked in Panama to replace the slashed nets. Jon was given the option to stay ashore there, rather than being drowned at sea later. He found his way to Paris, graduated from cooking school, and realized his dream of being a chef. He was soon running a successful catering business working with movie production companies. But the tuna fishing experience had sensitized him in a way that wouldn't quit. He became a rabid recycler on the movie set, and would wash dishes for 200 at the end of a 20-hour day rather than using disposables.

He married and became a father. When his first daughter was born, Jon Stocking found himself getting still more sensitized to the preciousness of his life. "When you have children, you think differently about putting on your seat belt, getting on an airplane, whatever you're doing. You have an extra reason to stay alive," he realized.

When his daughter was about four, he took a year's sabbatical to spend more time with her. They went to a zoo one day. They were both transfixed at the sight of elephants, shackled, swaying back and forth because this was the only movement they could make. In the car, Jon launched a lengthy speech about endangered species, human dominance, threatened habitats, and the rest. Abruptly, he realized he was talking to a four-year-old. "Honey, that was a little intense," he apologized. "Did you get any of it?"

"Yes, Daddy," she replied. "But I want to know what you are going to do about it?"

The Endangered Species Chocolate Company was born in a hormonal rush in the days that followed. The business deals in gourmet Belgian chocolate, wrapped in packages designed by world-class artists to depict rare species and provide education on ways to stop their decline. Today the company employs a dozen in the Oregon countryside, and gives over ten percent of its pretax profits to environmental groups in the form of chocolate for resale. Chocolate Jon is a well-known figure in the local schools, where he talks to teachers and kids about making their lives count.

I have become an insatiable collector of stories like these — not because I am so adventurous personally by any means. I live modestly, earn modestly, and risk modestly. But I am reassured beyond words to know that people like Jon Stocking are around and able to do what they do.

I heard about Jon Stocking's work from the great biologist and cultural inter-preter Jane Goodall, who spent decades in the African bush learning about primate cultures and forging an absolutely distinctive life through her relationships with the nonhuman world. Jane Goodall now devotes herself entirely to educating people about the impact of human life on animal habitats. In the last five years, she has not spent more than three weeks in one place. She receives the support of the Endangered Species Chocolate Company for her Roots and Shoots project to protect African chimps and their habitat. She is one of many who benefit.

Jane Goodall's powerful slide show about chimps and humans ends with a series of thumbnail sketches of people who give her hope, including Chocolate Jon. Having lived in the wild and been transformed by it, she saw straight into the center of the life-changes experienced by Jon Stocking and many others: "You get to a point where you can't stay on the sidelines anymore. For many people, it happens when you look into the eyes of another living creature and really see them. When you respond to life with all your being. "

I heard Jane Goodall speak while I was involved in a writing project with Gary Hirshberg, CEO of a feisty little yogurt company called Stonyfield Farm. Stonyfield has established itself as a distinctive consumer brand, and the only yogurt with a growing market share, by taking on a broad range of social and environmental challenges. It was one of the first companies to hire an environmental manager, do a "dumpster-dive" to get a grip on its own waste, and take aggressive steps to reduce those wastes. More recently, it has been a front-runner in offsetting its plant's carbon emissions and organizing large industrial companies to reduce theirs. In the middle of New Hampshire, a state not known for its bleeding hearts, Stonyfield has partnered with law enforcement agencies and the business community to promote gun safety by handing out thousands of free trigger locks. Counter to all predictions, the locks were grabbed up in the first 24 hours.

Through Gary and Stonyfield, I was able to deepen my connection with some of the business organizations that reflect these emerging social and ecological values. One of them, the Social Venture Network, brought Jane Goodall in as keynote speaker for its annual meeting. I could keep going, tracing these webs of connection. Right now, let these three stories speak for many.

Not Just for the Maverick Fringe

Every era has its bigger-than-life figures. Your list of the giants who shaped the waning century might start with Andrew Carnegie, Jane Addams, Mother Jones or John Muir. But we are in a time of necessary and creative transition, beginning to envision and design and coax into being an economy that is integrated with ecology and society rather than being at odds. There is a connection between the heroes and models we choose, and the direction we set ourselves on.

New ideas and practices tend to be accepted into a society in waves, starting with the "early adopters" who may be larger-than-life people. Once they have forged the path, however, it's possible for an "early majority" to follow. In turn, people who step out onto this path today can point the way for later waves who need more certainty and reassurance. In this era, a powerful new idea is that we can reconfigure our workplaces and our careers to minimize harm and maximize benefits to all the communities we touch, humans and the rest. At the macro level, this is what Paul Hawken calls a "restorative economy." At the micro level, the principle is "calling" or "right livelihood." For some people, this is obvious. For others, it's an exhilarating new connection.

Not everyone is a former triathlete, a visionary scientist, or a high-voltage entrepreneur. Not everyone needs to be. But the fact that these kinds of creative mavericks are out there, surviving and sometimes thriving, is a sign of the opportunities coming to life for many more of us. A restorative economy doesn't just need the extraordinary heroes. It needs (and they need) accountants, assistants, public relations people, production workers, chefs, receptionists, and the rest. A restorative economy needs nontoxic dry cleaners, natural food caterers, alternative fuel vehicle mechanics, and natural fiber clothing designers, not to mention receptionists and computer repair people and childcare workers for all the visionary new institutions coming on-line. It needs people at all levels, and in every role, who can work effectively while keeping the bigger picture in mind.

Cut Loose, or Set Free?

Things are undeniably weird in the world of work. There is structural turmoil. There is cultural turmoil. And there is a massive transformation underway in the prevailing view of where responsibility lies for your economic future. Career ladders are out the window in a majority of organizations. Government is out the window as a safety net. It is no news that, in the words of outplacement executive William Morin, "You are absolutely, positively, on your own."

This means: whether you are an employee or an entrepreneur or a volunteer or a student, you are in charge of lining up continued work, attaching a compensation package of some sort to it, and positioning yourself to be in continued demand. Whether you are a senior VP aspiring to be CEO in a new media startup, or a home-based craftsperson trying to live as simply as possible, you are the one who needs to take full responsibility for meeting your material needs and turning your talents loose.

In the last couple of decades, most working people in the industrialized world have gotten a massive wake-up call to this effect. As Boston career counselor Cliff Hakim puts it in the title of his on-target book, *We Are All Self-Employed*. Futurist James Robertson calls this creating our "ownwork." Spiritual teacher and religion professor Rick Jarow coined the term "anti-career," to emphasize the importance of decoupling our lives from habitual reward systems and learning to be true to our own ways of thinking about success.

I have floated the term "expanded work ethic" to build on these notions and add one more dimension. I want to go beyond talking about vocational self-determination for its own sake, and examine the opportunity it brings us to take a fresh look at what's most important to work for. We have been functioning in an economy that's been oriented toward a single bottom line of financial goals. As a result, we are living in a world where the vast majority of productive effort has been decoupled from the values and needs of communities.

We are shoulder-deep in social decay. We are shoulder-deep in an environmental crisis. It's becoming more and more obvious that these megatrends are connected.

The notion of Self-employment, then, is about the reintegration of individual vocational satisfaction with an ethic of spiritual development and service — connecting our personal working lives with the work that needs to be done to restore communities and the planet. This is not a new idea. In terms of characteristics of the work itself, nobody says it better than economist E.F. Schumacher in the classic *Small is Beautiful,* who identifies three attributes of what the Buddhists call "right livelihood." First, it offers an opportunity for people to use and develop their faculties. Then, it gives us the chance to overcome ego-centeredness by joining together with others in a common task. Finally, it "brings forth goods and services needed for a becoming existence" — and it's hard to imagine a "becoming existence" separate from livable communities and a healthy natural environment.

This theme was further developed in 1979 by Theodore Roszak in *Person/Planet: The Creative Dis-Integration of Industrial Society*. Roszak speculated that, when people in large numbers started saying no to meaningless work and yes to vocational paths that would stretch

Increasingly, the Great Divide in job opportunities is not between private and public sectors, or between employment and entrepreneurship. We all need to move among these options fluidly and with grace. The Great Divide is between career paths driven by purpose — and especially purpose to achieve something better for those we love — and career paths driven by accommodation and avoidance of risk. This is not a critique of any particular line of work, since they all can be done with worthy motives and in a spirit of service. It's a voice of caution about cynicism and a spirit of inevitability in choices about work. In *Person/ Planet* (1979), Theodore Roszak predicted that the transition from industrial society to the next economy would be characterized by a pull between Right Livelihood and a range of jobs he listed with concern:

Huckstering jobs — inventing, advertising, selling expensive trash to gullible customers;

Busywork jobs — sorting, recording, filing, computerizing endless amounts of data, office memos, statistical figments;

Mandarin-administrative jobs — coordinating, overseeing, supervising clerical battalions and bureaucratic hierarchies, many of which, especially in government operations, exist merely to spin their own wheels;

Financial sleight-of-hand jobs — juggling cash and credit, sniffing out tax loopholes and quick speculative windfalls in real estate, arbitrage, stocks and bonds;

Compensatory amusement jobs — marketing the vicarious glamour and escapist pleasures whose one use is to relieve the tedium and frustration of workaday life: spectator sports, mass media distractions, superstar entertainments, package tours, the pricey toys and accoutrements of "creative leisure";

Cop jobs — providing security against the theft and violence of society's have-nots, policing the streets, hassling the riffraff through the courts, guarding the prisons, snooping into credit ratings, school records, personnel evaluations;

Welfare processing jobs — picking up the economy's casualties, keeping them on the public assistance treadmill, holding the social discontent below the boiling point.

them in the service of community and environment, this would massively shift both material and human resources in the right direction. He dared to suggest that the widespread assertion of "the right to right livelihood" would be one of the prime motive forces for creating a life-affirming economy in the postindustrial future — that is, right about now.

"Right livelihood," by this definition, is not just personally satisfying work. Some people are most satisfied when they are painting their toenails. This is not enough — for them or for the world — choice or not. "Right livelihood," or an expanded work ethic, is about work that provides a meeting ground between personal development and expression, on one hand, and tangible improvement in the world around us on the other. Rick Jarow raises a similar point based upon his work with seekers on several continents who are sooooo ready to shake off external constraints, but still struggle with the need to develop the anchor of internal discipline. "Anti-career" is not just about personal satisfaction, he notes, but also personal ethics and spiritual growth. Coming back from his annual trip to India and checking the e-mail, only to find a flurry of conversation about personal fulfillment on the listserv where his workshop alumni stay in touch, he fired off this reflection:

> What passes for "anti-career" is too often an effort to situate oneself in "heaven" (in terms of the Buddhist six realms), which is not freedom. "Heaven" often translates as "work that I like that pays well too." I am not against this, of course, but the real thing for me is "work that is practice." In other words, my sadhana, my practice of mindfulness, awareness, compassion — whatever way you do it — emerges through my work. My work becomes a vehicle for opening the quality of consciousness, which is a lot more than what most people mean by the "quality of life." If this is not happening in work, it will probably not happen anyplace else.

Anybody ready to crawl under the bed? While all this opportunity for spiritual development and social contribution has a clear positive side — to which I will devote most of the next 80,000 words — it is also bloody difficult. The tension felt by most of us, as we're pulled by all sorts of exciting opportunities and then pulled back by the limits of metabolism and mental capacity, can be exhausting and disorienting. In fact, the level of uncertainty and the range of choices out there is precipitating a bit of a societal identity crisis already. Jon Carroll, writing in the San Francisco *Chronicle*, notes with mixed feelings the passing of the era when Americans brusquely buttonholed each other at parties and demanded, "So what do you do?"

> Now things have changed. Now no one really knows the answer to the question, 'What do you do?' Most people still know where their money is coming from, in a general sense. At least this week. Unless something happens. They understand, in a general sense, what they will be required to do to obtain that money. But what they will do to get that money is often not what they actually do ...
>
> We are all temps now; we are a nation of Kelly Girls. We are all wondering:

Should we get a second career? Should we learn accounting, beekeeping, integrated pest management, computer programming, corporate head-hunting, ATM repair, real estate sales? That stranger in the office — who is he? Are we being bought by the French?

Surreal, yes, but not overdramatized. Because so many organizations and career ladders have come apart so quickly — and quietly, compared to the impact of the change — there is a mismatch, for many of us, between our capacities and the adaptive skills that are required of us. Large numbers of us are swimming in too many possibilities, all of them flawed. We are not just deciding, but deciding how to decide.

In this climate, some of us are learning the art of the shapeshifter: reinventing ourselves as needed to step into new roles, resolving dilemmas with a measure of grace, tolerating a high level of ambiguity, and somehow knowing enough about who we are to say our yeses and noes appropriately. The visionary magazines, from *Yes* to *Fast Company,* are full of role models who are not so badly thrown by changes around them because they are grounded in their own sense of what needs to be done. Barbara Reinhold, head of the Smith College Career Development Office, notes that "people whose anchors are internal do not seem to be falling off the career ladders in large numbers."

At the same time, large numbers of people are barely making it, struggling deeply with the sense that they are being asked to stretch and adapt more than humanly possible. Some of these are highly skilled, highly credentialed, well-connected people with money in the bank and prospects all around. The difference between the two groups doesn't correlate with their external situations. There is a psychological dimension, and it's worth a closer look.

Why Values are Not a Luxury

As we pursue the next gig and wrestle down the next identity to go with it, many of us face a fork in the road in terms of the attitudes, sensibilities, and worldviews we bring to the situation. Fundamentally, we're faced with the need to internalize a new worldview and practice a new set of life skills. At a minimum, healthy Self-employment means taking primary responsibility for:

1. Self-defining (Who have I been? Who do I want to be? How do I want to be seen by others? What kind of legacy do I want to leave?);
2. Self-motivation (setting a direction and moving in it, responding to opportunities and deadlines, producing concrete results; and learning the dance between conscious will and surrender, both in the performance of a given piece of work and in moving from one situation to another during the course of your working life);
3. Self-promotion (getting others to hire you, recommend you, partner with you, and otherwise make your work happen, in ways that are healthy and reflective of your highest values); and finally
4. Self-defense including a well-established routine of self-care (entering into situations with healthy boundaries, high self-esteem, good negotiation skill, awareness of your rights, and a relaxed vigilance to protect yourself from genuine dangers without losing the capacity for trusting relationships at work).

Self-defining, self-motivating, self-promotion, and self-defense are all skills that can be cultivated. These are all built on assumptions about our place in the world, and the sources of our power to take effective action. They are all built on a foundation of self-awareness and self-esteem. And so, it's a matter of survival that we understand ourselves as individuals, and know something about how we are wired as a species. Are we reactive, or can we initiate? Do we see a path ahead that's filled with opportunities to feel like a victim, or with opportunities to create on our own terms? What are the attitudes that can help us move forward?

A few lines of questioning are particularly important to the challenge of healthy Self-employment:

- What conditions and practices give rise to peak performance, helping us to make use of all the inner resources we have?
- What conditions, and what personal practices, help us to handle change resourcefully?
- What conditions and practices help us to be survivors for the long-term?
- What conditions and practices help us to be generous, and able to see how our personal self-interest is intertwined with the common good?

Several parallel strands of social science research have addressed these questions in some depth. One body of literature has been generated by people who want to make workplaces more productive, less toxic in every sense, and more benign in their impacts in the world. Another comes from the study of violence prevention, and specifically group violence and the psychology of resistance. A third major body of knowledge comes from sports psychology — an intriguing source, not only because so much money is thrown at sports, but because there is such precise measurement of stimulus and response in the tracking of athletic performance, giving a certain authority to these findings.

Interestingly, the psychologies of athletic peak performance, workplace transformation, and social responsibility are not so very different. What's good for us in terms of personal effectiveness also seems to hold the key to directing our efforts toward the wider worlds of work and society. These bodies of research all stress the enormous importance of drawing our motivations from powerful private and communal meanings, rather than from somebody else's "shoulds." They all provide strong evidence that personal beliefs and values — and states of consciousness more generally — make an enormous difference in our abilities to initiate action and achieve results.

To take one of the most famous examples of modern history, based on his own experience in World War II, Viktor Frankl wrote about the power of individual meanings in keeping concentration camp survivors alive in the grimmest of times. Management consultant Margaret Wheatley made similar observations in the 1980s and 1990s, drawing on Frankl's theories to argue that personal meanings and values are a lifeline for people who survive with integrity in "crazy" companies.

A similar message comes from Martin Seligman's studies of people who are prone to depression, and others who resist it. This research shows that a major variable is "explanatory style" — that is, how people make sense of experience. In *Learned Optimism*, he reports that people who succumb to depression tend to look at negative experiences and assume they represent a pattern, and take them quite personally, while dismissing positive experiences as an exception or a fluke or somebody else's doing. People who resist depression do not look at a single negative episode and see a pattern; they also avoid personalizing events, instead seeing them less judgmentally as part of wider patterns. States of consciousness, belief systems, worldview, values — these are the underpinnings of humans' ability to survive, cope, and adapt. As Phil Jackson, former coach of the Chicago Bulls, writes in his memoir, *Sacred Hoops*:

> *I've discovered that when you free players to use all their resources — mental, physical, and spiritual — an interesting shift in awareness occurs. When players practice what is known as mindfulness — simply paying attention to what's actually happening — not only do they play better and win more, they also become more attuned with each other. And the joy they experience working in harmony is a powerful motivating force that comes from deep within, not from some frenzied coach pacing along the sidelines, shouting obscenities into the air.*

Do your beliefs affect what you even try to accomplish?

Do you believe that adult development is basically a pedestrian affair, or that big leaps are possible?

Do you believe you are part of a wider web of life that's interconnected and interdependent? Do you live that way?

Do you believe the work that most reflects your values is worthy of decent compensation, clientele, and support?

Do you believe you can lead and inspire others?

Do you believe that the strength of your commitment makes a difference in what you're able to accomplish?

One of the most powerful motivators for human peak performance is a sense of connection — to team, community, environment, and history — an unromantic, even impersonal, sense that the stakes are large and our actions matter beyond their benefits or costs to us directly. Emergency medical people know this. Political campaign managers know this. "Chocolate" Jon Stocking's sudden knowledge that he had to act on behalf of marine life and the oceans, described in the Introduction, came on him so powerfully that it completely overshadowed the impulse toward physical self-protection. And, at the same time, it gave him a level of strength and clear vision that helped him to survive a dangerous ordeal.

The converse is also true. Ignoring the impact of our decisions for those around us — trying to function as though we are in a social and ecological vacuum — leads to a strange kind of impairment in dealing with predictable crises in ordinary functioning. Executives and line workers who do this tend to make dumb decisions, even in terms of primitive self-interest. Going through our days with blinders tends to backfire, as shown in a provocative business study called *We're So Big and Powerful Nothing Bad Can Happen to Us*. Ian Mitroff of the University of Southern California Graduate School of Business studied two categories of companies, "crisis prone" and "crisis prepared." The companies differed in their basic definition of a crisis, because they saw their place in the world so differently:

> *A crisis, for Crisis-Prone organizations, was something that affects them, e.g. their products, their top executives. On the other hand, a crisis for a Crisis-Prepared organization is something that affects not only them personally but also their customers, their surrounding communities, the families of*

their employees, and their general environment. The greatest distinction between these two types of organizations is in precisely this: how they relate to those outside of them, and particularly to those who do not have the same kind of power they have, e.g. the unborn and future generations. For Crisis-Prone organizations, either the powerless tend not to exist or their importance is discounted entirely.

In business and in the worlds of social and environmental activism, ironically, cutting-edge voices are saying the same thing. Maintaining a conscious connection with the wider world is not just an extra-credit activity; it's one of the underpinnings of survival. In *Coming Back to Life: Practices to Reconnect Our Lives, Our World*, Joanna Macy and Molly Young Brown make a cybernetic argument for appreciating the power of humans as open systems who have so much more to gain than to lose from deepening their connection to the wider world.

"My purpose is to live the kind of life that will mean the most to you, to me, to the universe immediately around us, and to some part of the universe that lies a little beyond what we see around us. We've got to stop fooling around and move toward a new way of life. I'd like to get people into the habit of living physically and mentally in such a way that, when they get all through, the Earth could be a better place to live than it was ... Sit back and be comfortable? That's no way to be. Sit up. Move forward. Keep going. I'd like to get out and plant potatoes; cut wood; anything constructive. I would like to live as long as I'm useful."

— Economist and philosopher Scott Nearing, a little before his death at age 100

To the social system, power-over is dysfunctional because it inhibits diversity and feedback; by obstructing self-organizing processes, it fosters entropy — systemic disintegration. To the power-holder himself, it is like a suit of armor: it restricts vision and movement. Narrowing awareness and maneuverability, it cuts him off from fuller and freer participation in life; he has far fewer options for response.

Power-with, or synergy, is not a property one can own, but a process one engages in. Efficacy is transactional. Take the neuron in the neural net. If it were, hypothetically, to suppose that its powers were a personal property to be preserved and protected from the other nerve cells, and isolated itself behind defensive walls, it would atrophy, or die. Its health and its power lie in opening itself to the charge.

Values are not a luxury. They're a fundamental navigational tool for us and our organizations. Social responsibility is not sacrifice; it's Self-interest, when we pay attention to who we are and how we are interconnected with the web of life around us. By opening up to our potential to make a meaningful difference, we also tap into a major source of personal effectiveness, creativity, and resilience, not to mention feedback. Strangely enough, it may be easier to make this leap than to keep pumping our small selves up with the message that things have to go on as they always have.

The research further suggests that people are at their best when they have both a big vision AND a means of breaking it into small, manageable bites on which they can get feedback along the way. This is a key to peak performance. It's also a key to effective social activism. Jerome Frank found this out studying anti-nuclear activists in the 1960s. A study of corporate longevity by two Stanford Business School professors, called *Built to Last*, redis-covered the same principle in the 1990s in a different context: successful, resilient compa-nies, those that re-invent themselves in response to changing times, tend to have "big, hairy, audacious goals" — and flexible, pragmatic, incremental approaches to achieving them.

What works for individuals also seems to work for organizations. Enterprises built on conscious purpose beyond material gain alone are showing themselves to be more resilient and financially successful than ordinary enterprises. Leading with values is a source of business advantage because it builds markets and good will, reduces liabilities, increases esprit de corps in the workforce, and so forth. To cite one of the most detailed and meticu-lous of these studies, Covenant Investment Management grouped the *Business Week* 1,000 companies into top, middle and bottom for social and environmental criteria. Then the researchers tracked stock performance of all the companies over a five-year period. They found that:

- the top 200 stocks had increased 100% in value;
- the middle 600 stocks had increased 92%;
- and the bottom 200 stocks were up 76.6%.

The study further noted that the lagging companies were plagued by poor labor relations, unsafe workplaces, environmental non-compliance, unsafe products, and regulatory problems. This is why more and more people are realizing these costs cannot be externalized.

Going forward with this understanding, appreciating how your power is shaped by interaction and openness, playing with possibilities of who you can be and what you can bring to life — all this will get you much further than all the sober problem-solving in the world. We all know that children learn and develop through play. Should it surprise us to find that adults do too?

Do not think for a moment that this approach means less conflict or complexity. Often it brings more of these, many difficult trade-offs, and a spectacular potential for unintended conse-quences. Consider the story of a friend of mine who began his career as a county planner in New Jersey, with high hopes for work-ing to protect the land and help human beings live in harmony with their environment. He did this by exploring the potential for eco-tourism, 'way before it began to be popular. Looking back with 30 years' hindsight, he speaks with some bitterness:

"In our time, we workers are being called to reexamine our work: how we do it; whom it is helping or hurting; what it is we do; and what we might be doing if we were to let go of our present work and follow a deeper call. We should meditate deeply on Aquinas' theology, learning that it is Providence itself that is calling us to deeper work. I meet many people today who are indeed letting go of their work (as well as their jobs) to find new work, a work in the New Creation."

— Matthew Fox *The Reinvention of Work*

> *We figured that campgrounds would be one of the most benign land uses you could imagine. Campgrounds would preserve open space and generate revenue while bringing people into closer contact with nature. It was win-win-win-win as far as the eye could see. So we built campgrounds. Unfortunately, it did not sink into our minds that the feds were building*

> *highways and the state was encouraging everyone for thousands of miles to vacation in New Jersey, so what we created was the magnet for millions of cars every season, as people from Montreal to Washington, DC, discovered our campgrounds.*

There is no shortage of opportunities for bitterness along this path. The groundswell of interest in "right livelihood" does not come from people who think they will sidestep surprises or be immune to trade-offs. It comes from people who accept a flawed but compelling possibility: that we can consciously design our working lives to minimize harm and maximize contribution, and engage in continuous learning about both. That is the challenge of Self-employment, and the opportunity.

Chapter 2
The Work to Be Done

Healthy Basics

You walk into the supermarket and a luscious red apple catches your eye. It's locally grown. It's organic. And it's affordable. When this happens (or even two out of three of these victories), it is thanks to the work of a long and complex chain of people. The produce manager who made the selection in the store. The distributors and marketing people who built the bridge between orchard and store. The inspector in the state certification program who determined that the orchard land was fit for organic growing. The state assembly staffers who drafted the legislation for the certification program. The citizen activists who showed them the public support for doing it. The county extension agents who learned new Integrated Pest Management techniques to help farmers. The bankers who maintained farm-friendly credit practices. Oh, and of course, the farmers.

There is an explosion of concern about personal health going on, and environmental sources of illness are a major component. These range from sick buildings to unsafe drinking water to unhealthy personal care products to foods produced in ways that are hazardous to people or the environment. The natural foods industry is growing at annual rates between 10 percent and 20 percent, with natural food "stores" appearing under the roofs of many megasupermarkets, because large numbers of people are concerned and becoming educated about the food they put into their bodies. Major national food companies are developing their own organic product lines — for instance, yogurts from General Foods and Dannon — and buying up natural and organic food startups to enter these markets. This trend creates new jobs and alters the nature of others, including those in agriculture, distribution, marketing, regulation and agricultural products and services. And the growth of the natural food industry dovetails with a host of other trends that could be grouped together as "nontoxic living," from carpets without toxic glue to cosmetics without formaldehyde. Finding healthy ways of meeting basic human needs — food, shelter, personal care and health products — is an enormous emerging area of work to be done.

Livable Communities

You are walking down to the corner café at dusk to buy a local newspaper, and you notice: how pleasant it is to have a corner café and to be near it, rather than in traffic, as the sun sets; how reassuring it is to feel safe strolling in your own neighborhood, since you remember years when the streets were less welcoming. Finally, you give thanks that there is a local paper available, owned by people you've met, to give you a flavor of news and commentary not available from the newspaper chains.

"Livable communities" is an intentionally broad category — broad enough to represent the range of concerns that might be important to you, from safety to health to containment of sprawl so that residences and commerce are arranged for a mix of utility and beauty. Writing in the *San Antonio Express* in 1998, Mike Greenberg reports:

> *In the 50 years after World War II, worry about suburban sprawl was the specialty of a small band of architects, critics and other intellectuals, largely on aesthetic and cultural grounds. Suddenly, the anti-sprawl voice has become mainstream. In recent years, voters across the country have passed measures to fight sprawl, rebuild inner cities and protect rural areas from suburban encroachment. Prominent centrist politicians of both parties, notably Vice President Al Gore among the Democrats and Christine Todd Whitman among the Republicans, see sprawl as among today's top issues.*

The coalition of people and organizations working on some version of livability — sometimes marketed as Smart Growth — is enormous, and reflects a wide spectrum of views on how much growth can be smart in the final analysis. New Jersey's Governor Whitman has created an Office of Sustainable Development within the Department of Commerce to preserve land and help a greener business sector come to life through targeted state investment. Worldwide, people working on creating more livable communities may be elected officials and their staffs, employees of regulatory agencies, architects, designers, community and

---

Co-Op America Quarterly, a clearinghouse for alternative businesses and marketplace news, published its ideas on "Fifteen Green Businesses Every Community Should Have" [summer 1996] — that is, businesses that are locally owned, environmentally advanced, community employers and institutions. "Wouldn't it be wonderful," the article asks, "if every time you bought something you supported neighborhood businesses and local farmers; knew you were purchasing from companies that cared about the environment, workers, community and customers; strengthened your community; and contributed to a more sustainable economy?" Co-Op America's suggested short list of community businesses to join, or start:

1. Grocery	6. Clothing Shop	11. Car Repair
2. Restaurant	7. Cleaning Services	12. Bicycle Shop
3. Child Care	8. General Store	13. Bed and Breakfast
4. Body Care Shop	9. Builders' Supply	14. Bank
5. "Wet" Cleaner	10. Lawn Care Service	15. Newspaper

Some of these are once-common local institutions needing to be reclaimed and reinvented after several decades of buyouts and competition from nonlocally owned enterprises. Many can be designed with a special "green edge," such as bed and breakfasts, lawn and car services.

transportation planners, managers of public or private lands, civil servants such as police and court employees working on violence prevention, bankers and venture capitalists, local entrepreneurs and staffers in business associations, labor representatives, or advocates focusing on safer streets, housing, planning and zoning, employment issues, dispute resolution, public transportation, and more.

Planet Protection

While it may be harder to visualize concretely, the global environmental challenges such as climate change, habitat loss and species extinction are also creating a large agenda for human labor to turn around a sobering situation. Here, too, there are emerging specialties and enormous ramifications for new ways of doing work that's already established. There's work to be done by wildlife biologists and their assistants, both in basic research and in consultation with actual biodiversity protection work; rangers and maintenance staff in parks and preserves; land trust professionals and support staff who negotiate and finance land purchases, then oversee wild lands in ways that are consistent with conservation goals; governmental planning departments and private consulting firms; attorneys, advocates, and policy experts who understand the intricacies of the Endangered Species Act, international biodiversity convention, and the like; environmental education and science museum staff who educate the public to build a consensus for conservation; resource economists who figure out how to place a fair dollar value on natural resources lost or preserved; environmental reporters who translate the global picture into locally meaningful terms; and more.

Protecting threatened and endangered species and their habitats is linked by increasingly clear science to a second pressing global issue, climate protection. Starting in

Increasingly, science for environmental protection is concerning itself not only with data but with interpretation, and with advocating for responsible practices. The choice of research topics, as well as the entire approach to reporting and interpreting findings, are being understood as questions of values by more and more scientists. According to the Nature Conservancy's magazine (Jan./Feb. 1999):

Traditional biological research does not necessarily translate to conservation. A biologist may, for example, study grizzly populations without directly addressing their endangerment. Nonetheless, over the past 20 years or so, there has been a movement afoot in biology and ecology to apply the science with an environmental conscience.

"Conservation biology" as an academic discipline came about in the 1980s in response to worldwide environmental destruction being witnessed by field scientists. Conservation biologists, like E.O. Wilson, Michael Soule, Reed Noss, and Thomas Lovejoy, came to reject the time-honored notion of the dispassionate scientist and embraced more of an activist role. "Science must take on an advocacy role with respect to the environment," said biologist Thomas Lovejoy, then of the Smithsonian Institution, addressing a gathering of leading scientists in the 1980s. "It is our responsibility, as those who understand best what is happening and what alternatives exist, to sound the tocsin about environmental deterioration and conservation problems in all their variety."

1998 with the negotiation of the Kyoto climate change convention, the first voices from large US-based industries began to be heard acknowledging that climate change is a real, present issue and calling for conservative responses to reduce human impact now rather than waiting until the costs are higher and the trend harder to reverse. British Petroleum and Shell Oil were the first large oil companies to announce major investments in renewable energy as a way of reducing dependence on fossil fuels — $1 billion and $500 million respectively. This means real work for engineers and technicians in solar, wind, biomass, cogeneration, fuel cells and other low-impact energy technologies. It means roles for research and development groups in universities, industry and government; installation and repair technicians; marketing firms and venture capital companies; trade association staff people and union organizers; vice-presidents of marketing and sales managers; customer service representatives and quality assurance people; wholesalers and retailers — for these large companies and the thousands of entrepreneurial businesses that will sell to them, subcontract for them, and at times compete with them. Most people may prefer not to think about energy when they're not flipping a switch or changing a fuse. But the energy base of a society reveals much about where it is placing its bets for the future, and it drives a great deal of the technological innovations that play out in the rest of the economy. The more business development thinkers chew on this fact, the more they come to grips with the enormous economic potential in creating solutions to a problem of this scope.

Consider some of the heretical thoughts that have been circulating in the financial and business communities in my home state, New York. One is the idea that responding to the challenge of climate protection — conventionally held to be an economic stretch of the highest order — could actually be a catalyst for a healthier economy, smarter technological innovation, and more rewarding partnerships between the environmental and economic communities. In 1998, a task force representing respected organizations like the Association of the Bar of the City of New York and the state's Environmental Business Association carried out an extended study of opportunities to be had by stepping out in front — in their language, becoming the Silicon Valley of climate protection innovation.

While some of us would prefer to create our own regional identity rather than emulating other people's models, at least the Silicon Valley metaphor was being used in the service of something interesting. The vision was of a technological and financial center organized around innovation in energy efficiency, transportation efficiency, urban reforestation, eco-tourism, and the policy tools that would encourage movement in all these directions. From factories producing alternative fuel vehicles in reclaimed "brownfields," to an "energy job corps," the proposal showed the potential of building the new on the existing infrastructure and creating financial incentives for the existing institutional players. Since the Kyoto agreement is built on a system of "emissions credits" that can be bought and sold, providing a financial benefit for early cleanup, the proposal also calls for establishing Wall Street as an emissions trading center — initially for the region, and ultimately for the global economy.

Different readers will be attracted to different aspects of this vision, and will doubtless have their own views about the politics and economics of these options. I offer the whole scenario as an example of innovative thinking at the center of the economic power structure. It shows how far we have come since the era when it was taken for granted that environmental protection was a threat to jobs. It's getting easier to see how environmental initiatives can be as profitable as any other form of problem-solving. How fast the New York scenario (or any other) could be built up to its full potential depends greatly on policy decisions in the overlapping realms of environment, technology, social well-being, and economics. But there is a solid foundation in the form of work being done right now.

Each of these great goals — healthy basics, livable communities, and planet protection — is a priority shared by a majority in the United States and much of the earth's population. And there is a growing movement of towns, counties, cities, and states — as well as the inhabitants of forests, valleys, and deserts who identify with their natural areas more than with political structures — who are taking concerted action at a community level. Starting with their own work, they are beginning to reorient their economies and expand local control of their futures by coming up with economic development strategies that focus directly on the social and ecological benefit that the people value, rather than leaving them to chance.

Mapping the Options

Finding an elegant conceptual order for this diverse range of opportunities is not easy. Each of the issues sketched above is jointly "owned" by the worlds of commerce, advocacy, and government — that is, by the private, nonprofit and public sectors. Researchers, community organizers, fundraisers, pollsters, campaign strategists, and others in the nonprofit sector have devoted chunks of their lives to organizing information, breathing life into a vision, and rallying political and economic power in service of that vision. Technical researchers in universities and nonprofit institutes, innovative farmers and developers, land trust and park managers, and county extension agents have all been part of the picture in developing, testing, and disseminating best practices for natural food production, environmentally sound land use, and the protection of habitat and natural resources. Elected officials, community development and planning departments, and municipal agencies from transit to social services have all been part of creating the local policy climate to realize these three great goals in each community where they are coming to life.

As new forms of work and enterprises come to life, also, it grows clearer that their "social" and "environmental" benefits are not so distinct. Healthy basics that are good for people tend to be good for the rest of the web of life, whether they are methods of food production that conserve water and land, or nontoxic paints and housecleaning compounds. Livable human communities are intelligently designed to preserve natural resources and habitats, as well as promoting conviviality, convenience and culture for people. Planet protection is clearly integral to maintaining livable communities, as every year's storm season makes clearer. Many emerging specialties, by their nature, address the linkage between social and environmental benefits. Consider toxicology, epidemiology, environmental health and safety, transportation planning, and prison garden programs as diverse illustrations of the same principle: that there are positive feedback loops between social and environmental renewal. One of the more obvious benefits of a shift in thinking — from single to multiple bottom lines — is that it leads to the creation of products, services, and entire enterprises that "work" in more varied ways.

All these lines of reasoning, and bodies of innovation, are converging in a new understanding of what the human economy can be: one designed with principles of nature in mind, including the nature and needs of human societies. Underlying and inspiring innovations in industry, transportation, the food system, the built environment, and more, is a body of thinking and practice articulated by such figures as architect William McDonough; Karl-Henrik Robert and Paul Hawken of The Natural Step; Hunter and Amory Lovins of the Rocky Mountain Institute, and a host of others, working both at the level of specific industries and of entire communities. As Robert Frenay describes it in a 1995 article, "Biorealism":[3]

> *Many of our environmental problems stem from structural flaws in the world's economic system. For example, our current system considers it "realistic" to cut down a century-old tree in Alaska, sell it for the price of a pizza, ship it to Japan, render it into snack-chip bags, then ship the bags back to the United States for sale. Such practices are commonplace, but compared with the resilient, economical systems nature has maintained for billions of years, they are far from realistic.*
>
> *McDonough and his associates reject the view that there's an intrinsic conflict between a healthy environment and a healthy business climate. Instead, they're calling for a new way of thinking. As they see it, evolution provides the surest guide to what is ultimately realistic. In his 1954 book,* Survival by Design, *the influential architect Richard Neutra proposed an architecture based on a comprehensive knowledge of biology and behavioral science ... But Neutra was concerned primarily with architecture and city planning. The new biorealists are using nature as a model for reshaping science and industry as well. In doing so, they are going beyond the old romantic notion of living in tune with nature. With the current explosion in knowledge of how nature actually works, today's biorealists have access to deeper and more precise insights as they design new industrial materials and processes. They have also developed a new vocabulary — with terms like* industrial ecology, technical cycles, living machine, dematerialization, throughput, externalization, waste equals food *— which helps simplify and clarify the complex ideas involved. Biorealism is a nascent idea, but its potency as a unifying concept, the quality of the minds it attracts, and its potential for reshaping culture suggest that it could become a guiding theme for the next century.*

Pockets of innovation, in this spirit, are occurring in most major cities and in many rural communities. By their nature, they are usually hard to categorize in terms of a single discipline.

Still, in terms of identifying and investigating opportunities, it is often necessary to think in categories to match the structures that are in the most common use for organizing information. In the private sector, especially, a common point of reference is "environmental industries." The US Department of Commerce's Office of Technology Policy reported in 1998 that "The products and services of the $181 billion per year environmental industry sit at the heart of [US environmental] progress. The economic contributions of the industry – which in 1996 contained more than 110,000 revenue-generating organizations, employed more than 1.3 million Americans, and generated export revenues of more than $16 billion – are significant."

The state of North Carolina is one of the first to conduct in-depth research on its environmental industry, which turned out to be a $4 billion economic player in 1995. The study identified 20 categories of economic activity, covering Environmental Services, Environmental Equipment, Environmental Resources, and Sustainable Products and Services. With over 3,000 private companies employing 43,000 people, the industry was more than four times as large as biotechnology, which had enjoyed considerably more state investment.

And this is only one segment of the work to be done. Environmental opportunities clearly go beyond the environmental industries. The Environmental Careers Organization offers the following, more comprehensive sketch of the terrain:

> *Before 1960, the environmental field consisted primarily of rangers, foresters, and a handful of public health officials and advocates. Today, environmental professionals work for every municipal government in the nation. Each state has an environmental protection agency, and one would be hard pressed to find a federal agency that did not have a variety of professionals working on environmental issues. A great number and variety of environmental consulting firms have sprung up, offering services ranging from hazardous waste management to development of interpretive programs for nature centers. Even small companies are likely to have environmental health and safety staffs; large firms may have environmental personnel at every level from headquarters to plant, including engineers, public relations staff, and laboratory technicians. Nonprofit organizations exist not only in Washington, DC, but also in communities around the country; these organizations engage in public education, research, advocacy, and natural resource stewardship.*

North Carolina's "Environmental Industry" segments:

I. Environmental Services
Environmental testing and analytical services
Wastewater treatment
Solid Waste Management
Hazardous Waste Management
Remediation/Industrial Services
Environmental Consulting and Engineering

II. Environmental Equipment
Instrument manufacturing
Water Equipment and Chemicals
Air Pollution Control Equipment
Waste Management Equipment
Process and Prevention Technology

III. Environmental Resources
Water Supply
Recycling
Environmental Energy

IV. Sustainable Products and Services
Alternative Transportation
Sustainable Agriculture, Aquaculture, and Forestry
Green Building
Green Retail
Eco-tourism
Environmental Education and Programs

Universities and technical schools have expanded or created departments to educate these professionals and are engaged in solving a myriad of environmental problems. Finally, the design and production of pollution control equipment is a multibillion-dollar-per-year industry.

The description provided by ECO covers all sectors: business, government, and nonprofits. And it goes beyond the conventional "environmental" professions to emphasize environmental specialties within the established careers of "accountants, computer specialists, journalists, educators, real estate professionals, lawyers, financiers, entrepreneurs, managers (and more managers), political scientists and librarians."

How far does it go? Is there any line of work that isn't, in a very real sense, part of the needed change? As Rob Day, a research associate with the Management Institute for Environment and Business in Washington, observes, "Some of the most important work to be done to create a more sustainable economy is outside the scope of the 'environmental' or 'activist' professions. If you want to make a real difference, consider going into a company as a product designer or accountant. Be a regular worker, but do your work in new ways."

Rona Fried, editor of the e-zine www.sustainablebusiness.com, makes a similar observation: "We're on the threshold of the environmental age because we have to be. The next 20 years or so will be the transition. It follows that the people who will be most marketable will be those with the skills that can help their employers make the transition, wherever they may work. This includes people who understand sustainable agriculture, nontoxic pest management, green building, energy conservation, and natural products. It also includes people with a wide range of financial expertise — in ecological economics, environmental policy, social investing. For starters."

A tremendous amount of the work to be done is taking the form of new strategies and positions in conventional types of organizations that are willing to become unconventional, and in roles that evolve as work organizations deepen their understanding of their roots in their communities. Much of it, too, will be carried out by people who do not see their jobs as anything special in social or environmental terms, but who are part of the web of decision making and production: the reporters who cover and shape the stories, the planners who use their ingenuity to make human settlements more people — and environment — friendly, the judges who rule on the constitutionality of environmental and social legislation, the health care people who decide whether to explore or ignore the social and environmental backdrop of their patients' complaints. This point is underscored by career counselor Andrea Diaz in *The Harvard Guide to Public Service Careers,* whose premise is that 'Public service' is not a simple field at all, but a value system or ethic that can be defined by each individual and incorporated into many kinds of work."

For example, one of the most effective, attention-grabbing corporate environmental initiatives of the early 1990s — before most corporations were acknowledging the links between business strategy and the environment — came about because a very good marketeer wanted to do something about the flat sales of his product. Bryan Thomlison was Marketing Vice-President for the Canadian subsidiary of Church & Dwight, the makers of Arm and

Hammer Baking Soda. Market share for the product was divided among several corporate heavies, and the situation seemed absolutely frozen. One day Thomlison got a letter from a representative of Friends of the Earth in Canada, inviting the company to consider how baking soda could be promoted as an alternative to toxic cleaning products. Thomlison developed a program which included environmentally-oriented store displays, promotion of environmental organizations in the company's newspaper inserts, and sponsorship of environmental curricula in schools on a large scale. The company's market share increased for the first time in many years.

Soon Thomlison was invited to implement his program nationwide in the US. He was brought in, reporting directly to the CEO, and encouraged to take risks. He reviewed environmental impacts of the company's operations, and discovered some processes in need of improvement — for example, use of cadmium to achieve the brilliant yellow of the packaging. "The supplier can't change it," he was told. "Then tell them we need to change suppliers," he responded. Within two weeks the original supplier had found a much less harmful dye.

Over its life cycle of several years, Thomlison's program not only benefited his company competitively. It brought environmental management into legitimacy inside the company, and brought him invitations to share his methods with numerous corporate audiences. In so doing, he helped to show his industry a new strategic direction — just by being a good marketer and noticing the connection between his industry's existing strengths and one of the era's major trends.

On the small-business end of the spectrum, consider what's possible when you "just" run a restaurant. Judy Wicks, proprietor of the White Dog Café in Philadelphia, has created a restaurant complex that is a springboard for a community forum series bringing in national speakers like historian Manning Marable; Community Service Days in partnership with major institutions like the city's community gardens; tours to sites of interest (whether in Philadelphia or Indonesia); a mentoring and job shadowing program for youth; salons and outdoor movies in partnership with the Drexel University community TV program; a bookstore/craft shop called the Black Cat; and, of course, nutritional education through ecstatic vegetarian experience. Wicks' popular cookbook tells the world about her form of "culinary diplomacy." And the business provides a community base for her true passion, which is building community partnerships to support disenfranchised groups and the environment.

This kind of a business vision also creates a new line of work in community relations. Sue Ellen Klein, the White Dog's Director of Community Programs, has this to say about the way the job found her, and the way many such opportunities are created:

> *My job is taking the message of our vision into the community, and then bringing it back into the restaurant in ways that people can participate in. I have a doctorate in biology. I taught for many years. Then I worked in business in real estate development — a family business — doing human resources and marketing, got involved in affordable housing issues. Then I*

decided that it was time, for very personal reasons, to have a career change. I was fascinated with urban issues, and met Judy because both of us were volunteering on a project at Philadelphia Citizens for Children and Youth. Judy is a legend in the city. Prior to coming here, I worked with the 21st Century League, a leadership group in the city dedicated to promoting the city and improving life here. When they terminated that position, I wrote Judy a letter and the time was right. I have to confess: when I tell people that I work at the White Dog, sometimes I let them think I'm a waitress. The truth is too complicated to keep explaining.

In spite of the difficulties of running any kind of enterprise in these times, a tribe of unusually courageous employers is coming to life. Some, like Wicks and Klein, have a conscious plan. Others seem drawn by intuition, or perhaps driven, to do extraordinary things with ordinary workplaces.

One of the simplest and yet most significant of these approaches is using targeted hiring to contribute to workforce and community development. This can take the form of training programs for adults who may need help in literacy, English as a second language, computer skills, or Workplace 101. Hotels have hired homeless people, with shelter included in their compensation package. Some businesses have actually been organized as projects to employ and develop people and exercise leverage in entire industries. One of the finest examples is Cooperative Home Care Associates of New York, Boston, and Philadelphia. Organized by a Community Development Corporation in the South Bronx, the home-care agency was designed to let workers buy in affordably as part-owners, raise wages even a little over industry norms, and create a stable enough working environment that employees could attend school and otherwise develop their careers. The agency now employs over 300, and has been an influential participant in task forces advising New York State in health care policy.

A personal favorite example of mine is Los Angeles building contractor Baxter Sinclair, who has focused his social vision singlemindedly into one area where he is a wizard: high-impact hiring. Sinclair uses informal referrals from the court system to hire ex-convicts who want to change their lives, and offers them a climate of hard work and support. For him, as a black business owner, it's part of restoring community pride by countering stereotypes and ingrained powerlessness. In the aftermath of the LA riots, Sinclair's company came into the affected neighborhoods and laid 10,000 feet of pipe, using a crew composed equally of black, white, and Hispanic faces. "To make this work, you have to be in partnership with the correctional system, and unions, and the community," Sinclair advises. Since 1979, he has employed some 300 people with criminal records; today, he can vouch for 120 of them as productive, tax-paying, and clean — better statistics than any jail. In spite of all that, he warns, "If you try it, don't think everybody will love you."

The range of constructive and relevant work options available today is vast. They are well represented in the business, nonprofit and governmental sectors. They come in all scales of operations: from feisty startup businesses to multinational corporations; from community organizations to international nonprofit agencies; and from village governments to the United Nations. The work to be done includes emerging industries, and new ways to address the work of long-standing ones. It includes the occupations that have been a backbone of every society, from education to law to governance to food production. And it includes new specialties that are being invented in response to contemporary needs.

Emerging Occupations: Jobs Our Parents Never Knew

Many of the jobs now emerging in response to environmental and social needs are brand new creations. Some industries, such as child care, conflict resolution, and dating services, are social innovations in this era. They formalize — and bring into the realm of paid transactions — services that have historically been part of the voluntary sector. Other occupations have come into being as a result of policies covering previously unregulated ground — for example, job developers in local government, occupational health specialists in industry, and transportation coordinators wherever large numbers of people move into a centralized workplace.

My friend Winifred Armstrong has a penchant for clipping job listings, even though she has a great job herself. Win, a consulting economist for the Regional Plan Association in New York City, got interested in the world of greener jobs when she co-authored a curriculum on ecological economics for middle schoolers called "The Paper Trail." *The final chapter asked, "What are you going to do with this knowledge over the rest of your life?" Her collection of ads offers a taste of the work out there. Take a look at a few.*

Senior Planner
Experienced planner needed to provide project-specific technical assistance and training in neighborhood planning and development finance. MS in planning + 7 years experience in hands-on low-income community development, housing development finance, and related policy issues. Must be familiar with planning and development computer applications. Salary to $45K.

Tree Planting Program
Fortune 500 corporation is seeking ecologist with forestry background and good organization skills to develop our tree planting program in developing and developed countries. Working with local and international environment organization, our company is at an early stage of our work on sustainable agriculture, clean water stewardship, and carbon sequestration.

Broker
Investment/security analyst to build greenhouse gas emissions trading system within corporation and with international partners. Initiative, imagination required. Salary plus commission.

Program Coordinator — Full-time
New York City not-for-profit organization seeks a full-time Program Coordinator to administer and further develop an already successful Community-Supported Agriculture program (CSA in NYC) that connects Northeast regional farmers with New Yorkers at all income levels ... Community organizing experience/collaborative process and people skills/ word processing a must/bilingual Spanish-English a plus.

Laurel Severson is Administrator for Rideshare Services for the giant 3M Company. When any 3M employee on the planet needs help in getting to work, Laurel's phone rings. On the company's home turf, in Minnesota, her major role is coordinating the 25-year-old van pooling program, the first in the country. That means equal parts logistics and diplomacy. "To make an alternative transportation program work, you have to be a really good problem solver, listener, and people person," she says. "I've helped groups iron out questions from who gets picked up first to whether Friday is donut day to whether the van should be fragrance-free." Sometimes, though, her role is mission-critical. When the San Francisco earthquake rained rubble on a mountain pass used by factory workers in a 3M plant, keeping employees on the factory lines became Laurel's nonstop job. At times, some states have experimented with laws requiring employers to provide or finance alternatives to single-car commuting, giving rise to jobs in businesses, and in local governments in the implementation of the policies.

Industries of all sizes have staff titles like Environmental Manager, Vice-President for Environmental Health and Safety, Pollution Prevention Specialist, Vice-President for Community Relations. These jobs are being invented as we speak. And, at the same time, they are filled by real, interesting people. For example, Steve Greska moved out of electronics manufacturing to become a Toxics Use Reduction Planner, a variation on the role of "pollution prevention specialist" as required by an innovative Massachusetts law that has greatly reduced industrial emissions. The Toxics Use Reduction Institute, housed at the University of Massachusetts at Lowell, employs a staff of 25 to provide industrial training and research on safer chemical substitutions. Planners in companies are rewarded when they find ways to prevent pollution.

New lines of work are also arising in response to the climate challenge. In the world of finance, there is much talk and planning for the trading of "emissions credits" as provided by the Kyoto treaty. Trading in sulfur dioxide emissions credits has begun, and much expansion is in the planning stages on Wall Street. In government, too, there is growing emphasis on incentive programs and technical assistance to help businesses clean up, rather than relying solely on regulatory sticks. Controversial though it is, this shift is reshaping established jobs and opening the door to new ones. Myra Flagler of the Dade County Department of Environmental and Resource Management runs a model Urban CO_2 Reduction Program that has been studied by many other cities. The program offers participating industries consultation and technical assistance in cutting greenhouse gas emissions, and provides modest but meaningful rebates when they succeed. With a B.S. in biology and a first career in neuroscience research, Flagler found her way into environmental policy through the regulatory world. "I was always interested in environmental issues, but when I went through school there weren't many of the courses we take for granted now. As new offerings became available, I took night courses, and finally came to DERM in 1989 in a regulatory role. I stepped down, you could say, from a research career to become a lowly field inspector of industrial facilities. But my responsibilities grew to cover the largest sites like the nuclear power plants. Then, when this program was created in the mid-1990s, I was quick to apply to be part of it."

Along with emissions reduction, there is also an upswing in opportunities to compensate for greenhouse gases already released — better known as "carbon mitigation." Leading the way is the Portland, Oregon, firm of Trexler and Associates, which helps companies to offset their emissions through reforestation, environmental restoration, and renewable energy projects. So far, Trexler has been able to bill itself as the largest carbon mitigation firm in the US. "Since we have a staff of seven, that reflects more on the industry than on us," chuckles CEO Mark Trexler. The firm serves as one part management consultant and one part broker, between companies with carbon emissions problems and organizations with cleanup projects that need financing. It has about 150 completed projects to its credit, from reforestation in Guatemala to straw bale housing in China. Over and above its tiny workforce, Trexler is creating work for small nonprofit and private sector climate mitigation projects all over the world by matching them with financing.

Many of these opportunities are in well-established lines of work. "A forester is still a forester, and a solar technician is still a solar technician," says Trexler. "But the new need is for people who can put together climate mitigation and protection strategies for companies and industries, and then implement them. That means people who can understand the technologies, the economics, and the policy issues." Not too surprisingly, there are more and more knowledge workers to match this demand. He observed in early 1999, "This year's graduating class of Master's and PhD students is the first that's coming into the job market with thesis projects on climate protection strategies and technologies."

Giants and Fledglings

Among businesses, at least three major forces are pushing for social and environmental innovation: existing laws, markets, and public opinion. For the largest enterprises, especially publicly traded companies, it is becoming a strategic consideration to manage resources and figure out alternatives to scarce ones, and to build reasonably healthy relationships with stakeholders including customers and communities. And for entrepreneurs on the lookout for a competitive new idea, there are often meaningful market advantages to a greener technology or a business designed to produce community benefits. Frank Mendelsohn, managing editor of the journal *Corporate Environmental Strategy*, observes that "there is a common sequence to the motivations of companies, starting with regulatory compliance, then moving to the search for business opportunities, and finally seeking to respond proactively to public expectations. At this point, many of the major companies are looking at compliance as a baseline, and innovating from there." The Council on Economic Priorities, which tracks and rates the social responsibility and initiatives of larger companies, has recently honored companies including:

- Dollar General, for its strong support of literacy, education, and self-sufficiency training programs for public assistance recipients;
- Avon, for its aggressive promotion of women in leadership;
- British Airways, for its Tourism for Tomorrow program designed to promote approaches to tourism that reduce negative impacts on communities and the environment;
- General Mills, with partners Stairstep, Inc., Glory Foods, and US Bancorp, which created

Siyeza, a Minneapolis facility to manufacture frozen foods, designed to employ community residents and ultimately be handed over to community owners.

Large companies have leverage and budgets. Small companies can be lean and nimble. In terms of change agentry and innovation, there is at least as much potential at the small end of the business spectrum. *In Business* magazine points to an enormous "untapped job creation potential" in small- to midsize businesses designed to meet environmental and social goals, from the 200 member firms of the Northwest EcoBuilding Guild to the 23,000 businesses that were represented in 1995 at the Natural Foods Expo in Anaheim, California. Some are fairly conventional businesses in terms of structure, simply responding to a need that gives rise to a market opportunity. Others are designed as "social ventures," with social and ecological as well as financial objectives as part of the explicit business strategy. The Social Venture Network, a membership group of some of the largest and most successful of these, has grown to over 500 companies.

Lately, SVN's focus has been on the maturing of the social venture — the businesses themselves and the concept behind them. Toward this goal, for example, the network has

---

In a sustainable economy, what would the work look like? The North American Regional Consultation on Sustainable Livelihoods was convened by the Society for International Development in 1996, with the participation of some 50 organizations, to wrestle with this question. As they fleshed it out, the term "sustainable livelihoods" refers to a more ecologically sound and humane economy overall, and to the efforts of advocacy and innovation needed to get us there. They proposed the following definition:

"Sustainable livelihoods provide meaningful work that fulfills the social, economic, cultural and spiritual needs of all members of a community — human, non-human, present and future — and safeguards cultural and biological diversity."

Participants identified, as key features of sustainable livelihoods, that they:

· Promote equity between and among generations, races, genders, and ethnic groups; in the access to and distribution of wealth and resources; in the sharing of productive and reproductive roles; and the transfer of knowledge and skills;

· Nurture a sense of place and connection to the local community, and adapt to and restore regional ecosystems;

· Stimulate local investment in the community and help to retain capital within the local economy;

· Base production on renewable energy and on regenerating local resource endowments while reducing intensity of energy use, eliminating overconsumption of local and global resources and assuring no net loss of biodiversity;

· Utilize appropriate technology that is ecologically fitting, socially just and humane, and that enhances rather than displaces community knowledge and skills;

· Reduce as much as possible travel to the workplace and distance between producers and users;

· Generate social as well as economic returns, and value nonmonetized as well as paid work.

· Provide secure access to opportunity and meaningful activity in community life.

---

launched a "standards project" to help companies create meaningful measures of social and environmental performance and the payback of investments to improve them. Many of these companies went through honeymoon phases of nearly limitless expectations and some self-congratulation, followed by sobering episodes like *Business Ethics* magazine's highly publicized 1994 exposé of The Body Shop for a range of breathtakingly ordinary flaws. Today, the social ventures surviving have established for themselves a common ground where financial, social, and ecological goals can coexist and cross-fertilize, and an image of considerably greater humility than in the early days.

In many cases, initial failures have led the same entrepreneurs into new phases of business development, bouncing back just the way single-bottom-line businesspeople do. For example, biologist Lisa Conte founded Shaman Pharmaceuticals as a way to preserve rainforest economies by sustainably extracting plants with medicinal value, drawing on the wisdom of native healers as a source of competitive edge in identifying promising new drugs, and paying substantial royalties in exchange for that wisdom, thus helping to equalize power between indigenous communities and the industrialized world. The company moved several vaccines down the product development pipeline, and became an attractively growing employer in the San Francisco Bay Area, with high hopes riding on the idea that the shaman's edge would help bring products to market faster. Eventually, though, the Food and Drug Administration's demands for new levels of clinical trials exceeded the company's financial capacity, leading Shaman to shelve several of these efforts in late 1998. But Conte did not give up on the initial vision. She shifted the focus of research and development from the highly regulated world of medicines to the less stringently controlled turf of nutritional supplements, and the enterprise continued.

There is enormous work to be done to protect human health, ensure livable communities, and exercise stewardship of the planet. Some of it looks like jobs. Some of it looks like business opportunities. Some of it looks like efforts that have to be made by somebody, somehow, using any combination of paid and volunteer labor that gets the work done. Along with these needs comes a second level of work: bringing new industries and occupations more fully to life: building their financial base, creating industry standards for performance and pay, creating associations and networks, launching communication vehicles. Also on the list of necessary work is education and advocacy to level the playing field for sustainable industries. This takes place in settings from trade associations to grassroots coalitions to law firms. This means policy supports and the removal of subsidies like those now supporting pesticides, fossil fuels, and corporate migration. Over and above the direct service it provides, advocacy along these lines is a prime reason for the existence of the nonprofit sector, currently about 8 percent of the US economy.

Nonprofits, fundamentally, are organizations designed to promote innovations that are too speculative to have a clear bottom line attached to them. With special tax status to allow financing through donations, memberships, grants — and often contracts and modest profit streams as well — nonprofit institutions are a varied and essential component of the economy and especially the "innovation sector." Despite stereotypes about low pay and chronic dysfunction — which in my experience are no more prevalent than in the private and governmental sectors — nonprofit organizations are an amenable home to many people working for social or environmental change. According to *Nonprofit Times'* 1997 annual survey of salaries and working conditions,[4] CEO salaries averaged $82,000 per year (i.e. including college presidents and other high-ticket people). Salaries for Program Directors, a mid-level professional position, averaged $48,000. Benefits packages are becoming competitive with the private sector after a widespread return to the drawing board, to figure out how to retain good employees. *Nonprofit Times* reports an "accordionlike expansion and contraction" of employment opportunities, as well as high regional variation, for a number of reasons including a high proportion of campaign-oriented work with natural beginnings and ends, and ongoing experiments with technologies to replace complex human functions.

The nonprofit sector can be credited with a great deal of effective behind-the-scenes work to promote more humane and sustainable business practices. Well before the US Department of Labor got into the act, the groundswell against sweatshops and child labor in the global garment industry was spearheaded by nonprofits such as the International Labor Committee for Worker and Human Rights, which conducted tours for fashion executives to see Central American working conditions; and the Council on Economic Priorities, originator of the HR9000 certification for workplaces meeting minimum standards for worker health and safety and human rights. Large environmental organizations like the Environmental Defense Fund are well known for their partnerships with major corporations to develop waste reduction strategies, one of the best known being EDF's work with McDonald's to reduce packaging. Increasingly, nonprofits receiving the support of businesses have been reaching for new levels of creativity in framing partnerships for mutual benefit. These begin with marketing partnerships like the one between Timberland and City Year, which have yielded respectable returns for both parties but come nowhere close to meeting the social needs addressed by the nonprofit. Recognizing this, a few major companies have been going much farther. Rosabeth Kanter reports in *Harvard Business Review*[5] that the "social sector" is gaining credibility as a "beta site" for developing and rigorously testing new products and services:

> *Today several leading companies are beginning to find inspiration in an unexpected place: the social sector — in public schools, welfare-to-work programs, and the inner city. These companies have discovered that social problems are economic problems, whether it is the need for a trained workforce or the search for new markets in neglected parts of cities. They have learned that applying their energies to solving the chronic problems of the social sector powerfully stimulates their own business development. Today's better-educated children are tomorrow's knowledge workers. Lower unemployment in the inner city means higher consumption in the inner city. Indeed, a new paradigm for innovation is emerging: a partnership between private enterprise and public interest that produces profitable and sustainable change for both sides.*

Among the companies moving beyond social responsibility into social innovation, Kanter cites:

- Bell Atlantic, whose Project Explore installed computers in Union City, New Jersey, schools and gave hardware to 135 students and their teachers to use at home. Besides turning the troubled school system into a national role model, the company found new ways of handling data transmission, sharpened its goals for video on demand, and found itself a new market in distance learning.
- IBM, whose Reinventing Education initiative similarly tests out communication tools such as technologies for letting parents view children's homework remotely; scheduling software that allows the creation of a year-round high school; and a voice recognition tool to teach reading.
- Marriott, whose Pathways to Independence program, running in 13 cities, hones life-skills and job skills for welfare recipients and guarantees them a position when they finish the program.

While there is always a need to pay attention to the risks of partnerships involving such inequalities of power, the ability to show business benefits for social initiatives is undeniably opening up fresh thinking about the range of possibility in corporate community relations.

Finally, government as an employment sector should not be overlooked. No matter how much government may devolve, there will always be a large role for federal, state, regional, and local agencies in implementing current policies and building the next generation's policy framework. Working in governmental programs usually involves a mix of policing and promoting positive behavior change by working closely with members of the community, from businesses to neighborhood associations and even households. Many of these jobs are heavy in community relations and marketing in order to build public acceptance of new policy tools that may face initial skepticism. In the words of Dennis Church, principal of the consulting firm EcoIQ in San José, California, "You have to have the communications skill and savvy to overcome the natural mistrust that may occur when you say, 'I'm from the government, and I'm here to help.' "

There is lots of work to be done by expanding the definitions of current jobs, industries, and organizations. But that expansion is very much a work in progress, and there is constant tension between the work to be done and the configuration of actual jobs. In the words of Kevin Doyle, Director of National Programs for the Environmental Careers Organization: "Where the jobs are, and where the cutting-edge problem-solving needs are — these can be very different. People interested in really innovative work often need to straddle two worlds. On the one hand, they need to take a very locally-specific look at the work to be done to build sustainable communities, and find ways to do that, while realizing that the actual infrastructure of jobs hasn't progressed far past the paradigm of pollution control and resource management. If your local government doesn't have a position called 'bicycle transportation coordinator,' find a job in a related agency where people are open-minded, do your job, and make a project of the innovation you want to see."

This is true for two major reasons. First is the fluid nature of social and environmental policies, and markets, in all the areas described above. The second reason is the sea change we are living through in the economics of labor and the structure of work. William Bridges' *Jobshift* makes the case that the job as a unit of packaging work is fading with the industrial era, and that we will all need to learn more fluid ways of defining our economic potential. Jeremy Rifkin's *The End of Work* argues that technological changes, corporate consolidation and globalization are creating a long-term prospect of "jobless growth" on a scale the world has never known. The unknown factor in this analysis, of course, is what kinds of work opportunities and structures are being created, or can be. As an indication of how far these trends have progressed, a 1997 study by the Economic Policy Institute found that 30 percent of US workers were employed in "nonstandard" jobs, including part-time jobs, independent contracting, employment through temporary agencies, contract or on-call work, day labor, or self-employment.[6] According to the US Department of Labor, wage and salary worker employment will account for 94 percent of the workforce's growth. But the number of self-employed workers is expected to increase to a not-shabby 11.6 million by 2006.

The mismatch between opportunities and stable jobs may require some of us — those capable and willing — to consider "hybrid" careers, for example, with one kind of income-producing work subsidizing another that is too inspired to let go. In the present moment, we cannot know how much of the cutting-edge work that attracts us is on the way to economic viability, and how much will always have to be supported by a separate income stream. This economic instability adds to the list of reasons why entrepreneurship is beginning to look like a social movement in its own right, although not one that works for everyone and not a solution to the erosion of the conventional employment contract. This flux has also given rise to an international movement that calls itself "New Work," which urges people to take the initiative and design their lives with multiple sources of security and expression, through personalized hybrids of jobs, business ventures, barter, and simpler living.

How far all these developments go depends greatly on collective political will. Do we care about our communities and the environment the way we have cared about the Olympics, the space program, national security? Do we have what it takes to translate that caring into action in one of the most challenging, and promising, arenas of our lives, the ways we earn our livelihoods? Today's challenge demands a great deal more personal engagement than these previous ones have. It isn't enough to endorse the efforts of scientists, athletes, or the military on our behalf. This time, the work to be done is for all of us. And one of the most direct and tangible ways for every one of us to affect the larger society's agenda is through our choices about where we will bring our talents to bear.

Chapter 3
Headlines We'd Like to See, I: Work that Protects and Restores the Environment

1. Natural Heritage: Food and Forests

The Food System

A NEW GENERATION FINDS WAYS TO MAKE FAMILY FARMING WORK
ORGANIC ACREAGE EXCEEDS CONVENTIONAL IN US
MAJOR FISHING NATIONS REACH SUSTAINABILITY PACT
FOOD'S TRIP FROM FIELD TO TABLE IS SHRINKING FAST
TOP CHEFS RECOMMEND ORGANIC WINES

There is vigorous debate on what constitutes a healthy food system, but increasing agreement about some things that stress it: overuse of pesticides, herbicides, preservatives, petrochemicals, and water; too much distance between producer and consumer; irradiation and genetic modification of crops; unsustainable harvesting practices, whether depleting the ocean with overfishing or the fields with monoculture crops. The complex of businesses and public sector enterprises that work together to put the food on your table is vast, and so are the opportunities to reduce the distance between farm and table, increase the safety of food and equity of access to it.

According to Holly Givens, a spokesperson for the Organic Trade Association, there are approximately 5,000 certified organic farms in the US, and "all kinds of work, from raising crops to data analysis of organic sales." Generalist or specialist, you can manage a farm designed to reflect your values and the strengths of your bioregion, from produce to specialty cash crops like medicinal herbs and gourmet goodies, all the way to nonfood crops such as corn for ethanol production, soy diesel fuel, and kenaf as a fast-growing alternative paper source. According to *In Business* magazine, "The US Department of Agriculture estimates that $30 billion could be added to farm income each year through the development of new farm and forest products. Commenting on these figures, US Small Business Administration counsel Thomas P. Kerester said, 'I think we've hit on the place to begin the revitalization of rural America.' He added, 'If we are going to successfully develop a biobased products industry, small companies must be the leaders.' "

For better or worse, farms are diversifying to stay in business, sprouting bed and breakfasts, hayrides and cultural programs, museums, craft shops, greenhouses, and more.

They're experimenting with new forms of investment such as the popular Community-Supported Agriculture model. While political and scientific battles rage as to what constitutes "appropriate" farm technologies, farmers are experimenting with everything from computer-based Geographic Information Systems to biodynamic methods of soil enrichment. A promising business strategy for small and medium organic farms is vertical integration. Farms like Walnut Acres in Pennsylvania, which combine production, processing, and marketing, illustrate the variety of career paths that are possible within one growing organization.

Choosing a career as difficult as farming, and then choosing a way to farm that reflects your values and holds some promise of survival, is an act of bravery and a path of experimentation. Consider Andy Radin, proprietor of the Community-Supported Agriculture program, And-Sow-On. The idea of the CSA — a partnership between farmers and people who eat — came to life in response to the farm crisis of the 1980s and '90s, to help small farmers finance operating expenses by collecting customers' payments for a season's worth of produce in advance. From May through October, weekly pickups of produce double as a social watering-hole, with appetizers on the grill, recipes handed out, and the occasional strumming of a musical instrument.

Andy is a kinetic guy who tried to be an academic biologist but couldn't stay away from the soil. He did farm labor in the summer while getting his master's degree in entomology, then started renting cropland with friends and learning to grow vegetables. The venues changed. The community-supported model seemed like an obvious win. He began teaching people about farming because he needed helpers. "I love to teach, and I find that people get incredibly stimulated when placed in a situation where first-hand learning can take place," he notes. The network expanded, and expanded, and expanded. From work-exchange volunteers to chefs up from New York for the weekend, the farm became a hub of activity that gave people a chance to work and play close to the land. What happened here has happened in many CSAs: not only does the community support the farm, but the farm helps to reignite the spark of community. Says Andy: "I didn't set out to create a place for people to experience personal growth while doing horticultural work therapy. It was nowhere near that conscious. But this work setting creates openness, and a sense of rootedness, and people get to be whatever flavor they are. So they like it. So they come back."

Stacie Edick is an outreach and education specialist with an agricultural research project whose goal is to develop a new fuel source — biomass from fast-growing willow. In western New York State, she works with farmers to get them interested in growing willow themselves or leasing their land to the project. Funded by the US Department of Energy, this large-scale effort is being undertaken by a consortium that also includes the utility Niagara-Mohawk, the State University of New York's Department of Environmental Science and Forestry, and the regional Resource Conservation and Development Agency, which is Edick's direct employer.

"This did not happen according to any great plan," she says. "My background is in early childhood education. I taught Head Start in this community, then reached a point of looking for ➔

"Farming" usually refers to agriculture, but the term is increasingly relevant in the world's waters as well. With 69 percent of the world's fish populations in decline and the world's population growing at 80 million per year, aquaculture, or fish farming, is being heralded as "the blue revolution" in the spirit of the last generation's "green revolution."[7] Now a $36 billion industry providing about a quarter of the world's fish — and widely touted as a sustainable alternative — aquaculture has moved into an industrial mode that has brought a variety of ecological ills including depletion of aquifers, pollution of downstream waters with wastes and antibiotics, risk of spreading disease from nonnative species into wild populations, and a massive drain of protein in the form of fish meal fed to big carnivorous fish like salmon. At its best, however, aquaculture can be designed for ecological soundness, for example, by using "closed loop" systems to recycle wastes, ecologically sound pond maintenance and water recirculating technologies. Just the same as with land-based farming, there is much work to be done in developing, testing, and commercializing sustainable methods, setting standards, and building markets.

Within the mainstream food industry, one of the highest-profile ethical dividing lines has been between dolphin-safe tuna producers and the rest. And here is an encouraging story about a few large employers that appear to be choosing the high ground. Even though relaxed federal standards on dolphin-safe tuna have been proposed (and are pending at press time), the CEOs of the three major US tuna importing companies (Chicken of the Sea, Bumblebee, and Star-Kist) announced in early 1999 that they would voluntarily continue to abide by the more stringent standards. Every time a major enterprise raises the benchmark for environmental and social performance, it breathes a little more life into the possibility that human competitiveness might be channeled in a positive direction. Commonly cited national companies producing healthy products and exerting leverage on their industries include Newman's Own (with its recent expansion and organic lines), Ben & Jerry's (dairy), Odwalla (juices), and Muir Glen Organics (sauces and juices).

You can find out about hundreds of others, and the industry as a whole, by consulting *Natural Foods Merchandiser* and its companion publication, *Natural Foods Investor*. The marketplace for natural and organic foods is a spectacular growth area, with more than a little Wild West atmosphere. You can now choose between a natural food supermarket, including large national chains such as Whole Foods, Wild Oats, and Fresh Fields; the natural foods section in your local supermarket; a privately-run health food store; and your local co-op. Employees, too, have this range of choice. And, of course, the range of work being done goes beyond direct customer service and shelf — stocking to include marketing, purchasing, training, finance, and management at the store, regional, and national levels. Depending on your values and talents, you could end up managing an organic greenhouse supplying a natural food superstore with fresh salad greens, or an e-commerce program for a fast-growing retail chain such as Wild Oats. A key element in the marketing of organic

→ something new ... " Edick had good local connections through her teaching and because she had started a community garden. Her boss at the agency invited her to come in to replace an educator who was on maternity leave. She completed several projects and was making a good impression, when the agency's involvement in willow biomass began to expand. She was asked to work on the project part-time.

"As the project grew, so did our role," she explains. "Now I'm on it full-time. I work with farmers to get them involved. I also do public education about the project, such as attending conferences. I love it so much that I'm now doing a master's degree through Empire State College, an independent-study program for adult learners. This thing has just captured my imagination." ❖

produce is certification of croplands, currently involving over 45 agencies in the US. OTA's Givens predicts growth in this area, especially in the need for field inspectors.

One of the most obvious ways to work in the food business, of course, is to get involved with a restaurant. Whether or not you are in a position to spring for dinner at the top of the World Trade Center in New York, there's a message in the fact that the chefs there have made it a priority to find produce from area farmers' markets. The same strategy in more down-home style has been a draw for Clyde's, in Washington, whose eight branches have signed a contract with city farmers for deliveries, allowing them to advertise "produce picked today."

People in the food business can help not just by what they serve, but whom they serve. Thousands of chefs have participated in Share Our Strength community banquets against hunger, brought together by the Washington-based nonprofit of the same name, to finance nearly a billion dollars of anti-hunger philanthropy.

As complex as the politics of food and farming is the politics of agricultural research. But, from federal and state agencies to higher educational institutions to community-based organizations, a lot of people are working to figure out more politically viable, ecologically and economically healthy ways to produce food and other farm products, and help consumers make informed choices. Research and teaching in organic farming has begun in schools of agriculture such as Wilson College in Pennsylvania and the University of California at Davis. Agricultural extension agencies at the state and county level vary widely in their interest in alternative food production methods. On the positive end of the spectrum, New Jersey's extension agents have been heavily involved in the creation of a regional system of farmers' markets.

Besides healthier farming methods, work toward food security and healthier living overall has brought renewed interest in urban and suburban food production. In the US, according to the National Gardening Association, 25 percent of all urban and suburban families or 11 million people grow some of their own food. That means gardening supplies, non-genetically-altered seeds, classes and books are a business niche. According to Jack Smith, president of the Washington, DC-based Urban Agriculture Network, urban gardening is a growing source of part-time work and expense reduction. "The full-time work is mostly in finding a niche — be it mushrooms or chickens — that benefits from being close to your market."

Doing its best to bridge rigorous ecology with pragmatic operational guidelines, the Institute for Sustainable Forestry has identified Ten Elements of Sustainable Forestry — the basis for its own action plan in the Pacific Northwest:

1. Forest practices will protect, maintain and/or restore the esthetics, vitality, structure, and functioning of the natural processes, including fire, of the forest ecosystem and its components at all landscape and time scales.

2. Forest practices will protect, maintain and/or restore surface and groundwater quality and quantity, including aquatic and riparian habitat.

3. Forest practices will protect, maintain and/or restore natural processes of soil fertility, productivity and stability.

4. Forest practices will protect, maintain and/or restore a natural balance and diversity of native species of the area, including flora, fauna, fungi and microbes, for purposes of the long-term health of ecosystems.

5. Forest practices will encourage a natural regeneration of native species to protect valuable native gene pools.

→

Forests and Forest Products

TIMBER INDUSTRY GROUPS RENOUNCE CLEARCUTTING
MATERIALS REUSE CURBS MARKET FOR VIRGIN TIMBER
URBAN YOUTH LAUNCH REFORESTATION EFFORTS

Deforestation has reached crisis proportions in many developing countries, and globally is a factor in climate change. In the Pacific Northwestern US, only four percent of original old-growth redwoods remain. Sustainable forestry — using biological sophistication and appropriate technologies to extract only what the forest can spare — is far more complex than simply replanting some kind of trees when you cut others down. While media attention has been grabbed by confrontation between environmental and timbering interests, quiet and creative behind-the-scenes work has begun to build a new approach to accessing forest resources while protecting forest ecosystems.

In 1995, the Rainforest Alliance of New York and other groups reached for the high ground of sustainable, community-friendly forest economics by developing the SmartWood certification program for harvesting sustainably managed woodlots. Because forestry is a global industry, and sustainably harvested logs from Oregon or Maine have to compete with clearcut ones from Indonesia, the certification was designed to be applicable to imports as well as US products. The program concretely helps participating companies by providing a marketing support system, which has proved especially attractive for small businesses. Fairly quickly, a network of timber companies, processors, wholesalers, and end users has crystallized to endorse, and learn to practice, a more sustainable form of forestry.

"A lot of the work going on now is restoration," according to Jude Wait of the Institute for Sustainable Forestry in northern California. She adds: "The companies that brought in highly mechanized forestry are now leaving. The cut levels are down in response to the draft federal plan for the Pacific Northwest. But the jobs that remain are less standardized, more varied. There's work for foresters, resource managers, planters, wildlife biologists, loggers, transportation people, and then of course the milling and production. People are responding to the situation with portable sawmills, their own woodshops, lots of cottage industry. What we hope to create in the next few years is an economy of scale through slightly larger production, by certifying and supporting a new generation of sustainable forestry enterprises."

Increasingly common employers are small, carefully developed model enterprises like Wild Iris Forest Products, a prototype

→

6. Forest practices will not include the use of artificial chemical fertilizers or synthetic chemical pesticides.

7. Forest practitioners will address the need for local employment and community well-being and will respect workers' rights, including occupational safety, fair compensation, and the right of workers to collectively bargain, and will promote worker owned and operated organizations.

8. Sites of archaeological, cultural, and historical significance will be protected and will receive special consideration.

9. Forest practices executed under a certified Forest Management Plan will be of the appropriate size, scale, time frame, and technology for the parcel, and adopt the appropriate monitoring program, not only in order to avoid negative cumulative impacts, but also to promote beneficial cumulative effects on the forest.

10. Ancient forests will be subject to a moratorium on commercial logging, during which time the Institute will participate in research on the ramifications of management in these areas. ❖

processing facility in the Northcoast Region of the US. Wild Iris started up in the summer of 1998 as a model of efficient milling and processing, creating high-quality lumber and flooring out of low-grade tanoak sawlogs. Other employers moving ahead with more sustainable forestry techniques include some of the giants that have been involved with the maturing and the struggles of timbering in years past, including the Canadian giant MacMillan Bloedel, which made a high-profile commitment to end clearcutting in the Pacific Northwest. This sustainable forest economy consists of more than the forestry and logging sector. It also includes companies like the furniture maker Ikea that purchase certified wood on a large scale.

And then there is paper. What was once taken for granted is now a subject of intense research and innovation, from recycled content to bleaching and dyeing methods to commercializing alternatives to wood pulp such as kenaf and hemp. Paper recycling technologies continue to develop, creating work for engineers and for innovative niche businesses in general. So do markets, creating marketing opportunities in both private sector companies and governmental programs.

More and more, the ecological economics of forestry is revolving around the spectrum of biological products that can be produced by the intact forest, and the management sciences for optimizing yields while preserving long-term health of the forest and surrounding communities. In this issue like many others, progress has been sparked by a blend of impassioned advocacy and deliberate, low-key dialogue. Demonstrating the potential role of higher educational institutions as consensus builders, the Yale School of Forestry and Environmental Studies has supported the quest for solutions through its Yale Forest Forums, bringing together multiple stakeholders, from environmentalists to major timber companies.

2. Human Enterprise and the Built Environment

Industry

TOXIC SOLVENTS FIND SAFER REPLACEMENTS
INDUSTRIAL NATIONS ADOPT CLEAN PRODUCTION STANDARDS FOR OPERATIONS WORLDWIDE
DESIGN FOR THE ENVIRONMENT MOVEMENT TRANSFORMS CONSUMER PRODUCTS

We've been hearing for decades now: manufacturing is where the jobs aren't. It is certainly one of the zones where technology and mobility have moved routine work out of the more industrialized world, and in some cases out of existence altogether. But this massive sector has by no means vanished. Within it, you can discern opportunities that are widely varying degrees of green, and the greenest ones are interesting indeed.

Pollution prevention and waste minimization have become mainstream operating principles for companies that see value in recovering raw materials and in reducing the toxic outputs to be contained or cleaned up later. The notion of "extended product responsibility" means that, not only will Xerox take back your empty copier cartridge; it will take back your run-down copier itself for disassembly and remanufacturing. Ford will do similarly with much of your car, and Volkswagen will do it more completely.

Triggered in some cases by regulatory pushes and in other cases by strategic vision, major industrial companies including Hewlett-Packard and Monsanto have declared war on specific hazardous chemicals and classes of chemicals, from ozone-depleting chlorofluoro-carbons to greenhouse gases to toxic solvents and cleaners, and have devoted major research and development efforts to putting safer systems in place. In grappling with compound after compound and process after process, many companies have realized that the wisest strategy is to move far upstream and "design for the environment," rigorously identifying nontoxic materials, processes that minimize waste, and design options that allow for aggressive reuse and/or recycling using a life-cycle analysis. Because some of the largest companies are those with the most resources, and the financial ability to implement changes when they want to, genuine improvements like these often coexist with entrenched problems and highly contro-versial activities. An example of the latter is Monsanto's notorious lines of seeds with the "terminator" gene that prevent the seedstock from being used to plant new crops, thus ren-dering farmers more dependent on agribusiness companies. These paradoxes can create extremely tough career dilemmas.

Some impetus for all this innovation has come from within companies seeking long-range advantage or avoidance of regulatory sticks. Some has come from companies in response to invitations from government to be proactive. For example, Rochester Midland's development of a major line of safer industrial cleaning agents was prompted by outreach from employees at the US Environmental Protection Agency's Region 2 office in New York City. They, in turn, were driven less by regulatory enforcement zeal than by discomfort in sniffing cleaning residues when they came in to work in the morning.

A great deal of the toxic pollution from industry and small business comes from a minority of industries, such as printing and dry cleaning. Targeted government funding on alternatives, and technical assistance to help small businesses adopt them, has begun to result in cleaner practices. Alternatives have even begun to crop up in the form of franchises such as EcoMat. This illustrates the principle that "many of the innovations that displace established industrial practices actually come from outside them, often from the next gener-ation of entrepreneurs," according to Nicholas Ashford of MIT, a specialist in industrial innovation. Startup enterprises galore coexist with more established businesses in state and national Environmental Business Associations.

There is not a clear correlation between the growth of environmental sensibilities and the emergence of environmental job roles within industry, except in very general terms. There is a trend toward creating specific positions in environmental management — which may be oriented toward regulatory compliance, technological innovation, market share, community relations, or a mix of these. However, there is a countertrend, at least as power-ful, toward integrating these responsibilities into existing jobs, from engineering to law to marketing. Environmental management positions as such have been subject to another cycle, resulting from the export of significant portions of large companies' businesses with high environmental impact, to nations with less stringent regulations — so says Kurt Fischer, co-founder of the Greening of Industry network. This trend in the US parallels Europe's, as described in a 1995 research report by Joyce Miller.[8] She observes:

Analysts estimate that more than 2 million people will be employed in the environmental industry within the European Union by 2000 as a result of new policy initiatives and continuous public pressure to clean up the environment. While interest in working in the environmental field is at an all-time high, it is important to recognize that:

Expectations regarding future career opportunities need to be grounded in the reality of how companies are actually utilizing their environmental expertise.

Demand is growing mostly for those who can play integrative roles within organizations with respect to environmental ethics.

As environment becomes more integrated into traditional business activities, working in this area can become a route to general business management.

Within a context of eco-efficiency which aims to operationalize the concept of sustainable development on the part of companies, environmental employment, as such, may ultimately disappear.

Training is emerging as one of the largest needs and is a tremendous area of opportunity for the future.

Building Design and Construction

REUSE OF BUILDING MATERIALS AT ALL-TIME HIGH
TOWN PLANNING BOARDS SHOW PREFERENCE FOR GREENER BUILDINGS

A good number of the eco-design visionaries at work today are architects, civil and mechanical engineers, builders, materials developers, and others in the trades. The healthfulness and economics of shelter are a dimension of sustainability that touches everyone's life. US consumers use more resources than any others, including an estimated 20,000 pounds per year per person of "active" materials such as virgin forest products, fuel, steel, glass, cement, and plastics. According to a 1992 study by the Office of Technology Assessment, 90 percent of this stream is converted to waste within a year.

Green building includes minimizing impacts on land through siting and natural landscaping; adopting the healthiest possible materials, including reused and recycled ones wherever possible; minimizing water and energy use. For many greener designers, the esthetics of green building has been a highly effective calling card for residential, commercial, and industrial clients, as well as communities grappling with the broader questions of what healthy development might look like. This trend goes together with building deconstruction, a gentler approach to demolition that recovers the reusable resources in a structure and sends many fewer tons to landfills.

The interconnected fields of architecture, design, and the building trades provide a powerful example of how individual innovators can begin spreading good new ideas through professional associations and standards. A prime mover is the American Institute of

Architects, whose 4,000-member Committee on the Environment has now been part of high-profile projects like the Greening of the White House Initiative. AIA is part of a consortium of major builders, developers, and financing agencies backing the US Green Building Council in San Francisco, which is developing standards and models for building materials and designs. According to Managing Director Kristin Ralff-Douglas, "All the work involved in green building follows a normal career development path, with a sharpening of focus. You do the same things, but more creatively. Historically, the building industry has approached its work in a linear mode: the client hires an architect who hires a builder, and so on." In contrast, she says, green building takes into account the full life cycle of products and of decisions, so "the mode of thinking has to be integrative. Everyone involved needs to be around the table together."

A front-running community in green building is Austin, Texas. A push, starting in the 1970s, by a group of architects and designers known as the Center for Maximum Potential Building Systems, to educate and inspire builders, architects, materials suppliers and others, has resulted in a greener building stock for the city, a Green Building project with Habitat for Humanity, a Green Buildings directory, and a staff position in the city government called Office of Green Buildings. Larry Doxsey, head of the Green Buildings Office, remembers a tragic but educational fire in a green building project for low-income housing. Chatting with the fire marshal as the blaze was being fought, Doxsey asked, "Notice anything different?" "Of course," said the fire marshal, "no toxic fumes."

The marketing of more sustainable buildings is growing easier as awareness spreads about environmental health and the toxins that permeate traditional building materials. According to Trudy Mason, Vice-President for Public Relations at EcoSmart Healthy Properties in New York City, "Buildings pollute more than automobiles, when you take into account what comes from the materials through off-gassing." Developer Barry Dimson created the EcoSmart Building Center in the heart of New York's financial district after attending a lecture at the Audubon Society's headquarters, designed by prominent ecological architect William McDonough. EcoSmart provides resources and consultation to the real estate industry, and maintains a "permanent trade show" — in Trump Tower, no less — featuring air conditioners designed to minimize climate impacts, paints with no volatile organic compounds, and kiosks of "grid-core," a synthetic material made from agricultural wastes.

Dimson has also developed the art of marketing green development projects. With several partners, he recently did a $20 million renovation to create Philadelphia's first eco-hotel, the Sheraton Rittenhouse Square. Appeal to the public stresses elegance, flexibility, and a high-tech flair provided by high-speed Internet connections in every room and a video conferencing center for guests and others.

More and more major institutions are creating the position of Environmental Coordinator or Environmental Manager to address the spectrum of concerns about resource stewardship, pollution prevention, and environmental justice. For example, Kurt Teicher became Environmental Coordinator for Brown University's large urban campus in Providence, Rhode Island, by doing what he knew how to do, but expanding the scale.

Teicher had been on the staff of a visionary nonprofit called New Alchemy Institute on Cape Cod, where ecological technologies such as the Living Machine for wastewater treatment were developed. He knew about windmills, solar technologies, intensive gardening, and recycling — and about facilities management and education. When he began feeling restless in the intimate environment of New Alchemy, Brown provided the opportunity to do much more of the same — while dealing with the added challenges of conventional New England building stock and a diverse urban population.

Hand-in-hand with architecture and building goes planning. Planners in towns, counties, regional and state government, consulting firms, and in economic development agencies, translate ideas about human settlements into concrete designs. At its most noble, the planning profession aims to mediate tensions between people, social groups and the natural environment by creating an orderly process for determining common values, shared priorities, and elegant principles for transcending conflicts. Therefore planners may find themselves caught in some of the most challenging political crossfire to be found. But they also have the opportunity to educate many sectors and communities. Sarah James, a planner who works as an independent consultant in the Boston area, has developed an educational slide show on sustainable development which showcases the region's most promising home and community designs and new businesses — from an aquaculture venture employing handicapped adults to an eco-industrial park almost off the drawing boards. James has developed a specialty in conducting and teaching participatory planning processes, a challenging and critical aspect of sustainable development.

Creating environmentally benign and socially coherent human settlements also involves preserving open space, and one means to this end is the legal device of the land trust. The Land Trust Alliance reports that, in the last decade, the number of trusts has increased from 743 to 1,213, and land under protection through trusts has increased to equal the area of the states of Connecticut and Rhode Island.[9] Administrative, legal, fundraising, and educational professionals work with land trusts, as do hands-on managers who must balance ecological health with social benefits such as unobstructed views and recreational access. Urban land trusts may contain real estate and be settings for varied social programs.

Travel/Transportation

**US EXCEEDS CO2 REDUCTION GOALS PLEDGED AT KYOTO
ENGINEERING SCHOOLS ATTRACT NEW POPULATION: THE ECO-NERD
TELECOMMUTE CENTERS TAKE OFF IN MAJOR CITIES
IMPROVED CARDIOVASCULAR HEALTH, SAFER STREETS, LINKED TO
INCREASED WALKING, BICYCLING**

Let us not waste any breath moaning about how we're all hooked on our cars, and how ambivalent we are about this. Let's talk instead about the enormous benefits to be had in even moderately reining in this habit and making use of transportation alternatives, in terms of environmental improvement, social and health benefits. In the months leading up to the Kyoto climate protection negotiations, the US Big Three automakers entered a phase of fierce competition to bring alternative fueled vehicles to market, pitting themselves against competitors like Toyota's RAV-4 and Daimler-Chrysler's prototype fuel cell car.

But technologies alone are unlikely to solve the problem. In a 1995 essay, Hal Harvey, president of the Energy Foundation, notes that the last few decades' advances in fuel efficiency and alternative fuels have been more than cancelled out by the spiraling increases in vehicle-miles traveled by the average US adult. Metropolitan sprawl has led to an increase in the developed area of Los Angeles of 300 percent, while population only grew by 45 percent. Every year, over 43,000 Americans die in auto accidents, according to the Center for a New American Dream, and transportation is the second highest household expense after shelter itself. The automobile in its present form was simply not designed with environment or community in mind; it was a novelty that took off. As John DeCicco and Martin Thomas note in their *Green Guide to Cars and Trucks Model Year 1999,* "Environmental impacts start when an automobile is made, continue throughout their life on the road, and don't even end when the vehicle is scrapped, since waste disposal creates pollution too."

To get closer to the root causes of air pollution, sprawl, and other downsides of the car culture, a vibrant coalition of alternative transportation advocates — from high technology firms to city planners to state governments — has been crystallizing. You can find them, for example, at an annual megaconference called RailVolution, where stories and strategies are exchanged on the many concrete successes in developing metropolitan light rail, bikeways, telecommute programs, and other strategies for helping individuals increase their range of transit options. This coalition overlaps with another, known as New Urbanism, that is working to make human settlements more livable and less sprawling.

"Transportation" is an enormous multidisciplinary undertaking, one that brings together technical and policy people in settings as diverse as local and state agencies, workplace telecommute programs, engineering departments and firms, nonprofit community educators and advocates of more sustainable lifestyles. Some transportation jobs carry more of a mandate for innovation than others, but everyone working in transportation has opportunities to do social and ecological good — even the maverick cab driver who turns off the engine between fares and encourages others to do the same.

Power Generation

SMALL WIND GENERATOR USE EXPECTED TO QUADRUPLE IN NEXT FIVE YEARS
LAST NUCLEAR POWER PLANT SET TO CLOSE — RETRAINED WORKERS
EXPRESS HIGH SATISFACTION

Fossil fuels pump carbon into the atmosphere, and are rarely obtained without environmental compromise. Nukes do not strike too many people as a good idea anymore. With a proposed 1999 budget containing large-scale funding for energy conservation and renewable energy technologies, the Clinton Administration helped keep alive the possibility of shifting the US energy base in our lifetime.

Although it isn't something we usually have to think about, the way we obtain our energy has a profound impact on the environment, economics, and the distribution of political power. This awareness is catching on. In *Factor Four*, Amory and Hunter Lovins of Rocky Mountain Institute and Ernst Weiszacker of the Wuppertal Institute in Germany make a compelling case that millions of dollars can be freed up by manufacturing companies, utilities, and the building trades by embracing a "new efficiency revolution." Instead

John Shafer is founder and CEO of RealGoods, a mail order business that deals in alternative energy hardware and know-how for the homeowner and small business. RealGoods' vision of solar living — off the power grid — is both technologically and politically sophisticated, but growing more practical every day. The company estimates that over 18,000 households now live off the grid in the US alone, using solar, wind, hydroelectric, biomass, and other renewable energy sources. "We're in the midst of a major shake-up in the industry," Shafer said in mid-1999.

"*BP Solar just bought Mobil Solar. There's talk about putting up some giant photovoltaic plant in Nevada that would cost 5 cents a kilowatt-hour. We're talking about a deal to put up a power plant now and sell cleaner power jointly with Green Mountain Energy, a producer of cleaner power which has captured 12 percent of the market share in Pennsylvania in just three months. Overall, deregulation is causing prices to come down. I believe the oil industry is seeing the writing on the walls. Add to that the Clinton Administration's Million Solar Rooftops initiative, and you begin to see renewable energy moving into the mainstream. The wind industry has been growing at 35 percent a year, solar at 20 percent. At the same time, old Mom and Pop operations are being swallowed up by conglomerates, now that the economics are beginning to be demonstrated long-term. But there are interesting and viable companies on the landscape now at every scale, from micro-enterprises to giants.*"

of fixating on labor efficiency, as industries have been doing — at times to the detriment of workplace relationships and working people — shift the focus to energy and materials efficiency. Drawing on the work of ecological economists around the world, and the models of several Scandinavian countries, they suggest taxing inefficiencies to send the proper price signals and to generate revenue in the process. *Factor Four* not only tells the story of what works, but reveals some of the major corporate employers that are taking these lessons to heart (as well as others that have not).

Some forward-thinking public utilities have begun to recognize that they have painted themselves into a corner by defining themselves only as energy suppliers, and are beginning to seek niches as energy conservers. "Demand-side management," also known as conservation, is about helping consumers of all kinds (residential, industrial, municipal, etc.) make smarter use of energy. This idea had wide currency in the 1970s, resulting in visionary programs in many states. Many have been dismantled in the devolution of government. Others are embattled. But some have been sustained, and in some regions both private utilities and governments are placing their bets on the cost-effectiveness of conservation.

An overarching context of the world of energy conservation and innovation is the process of utility deregulation. Sweeping state laws in California, Pennsylvania, New York and elsewhere, repealing or sharply cutting back regulations on the marketing and pricing of electric power, have created a wide-open and radically uncertain playing field in the production and distribution of energy. Among other things, they allow utilities to sell power anywhere in the US, not just in prescribed service areas, setting the stage for unprecedented competition. A few companies — such as Doug Hyde's Green Mountain Power of Vermont — are placing their bets on the consumer who is socially conscious, economically OK, and willing to pay a little more for electricity from "green" sources. Green Mountain has developed several "electricity products," from sources ranging from clean natural gas to renewables, and is ramping up its renewable generating capacity to prepare for expanding markets. In a year, it was able to capture 12 percent of the residential electricity market in Pennsylvania, where much of the energy supply has been coal and nuclear power.

The field of energy production, distribution, conservation, and policy employs scientists and engineers, advocates and educators, economists, managers, marketeers, administrators, and — in some regions — the utility or local government employees trained in energy conservation technologies, who bring energy audits and energy-conservation hardware to your door. Even as the Kyoto climate protection negotiations were taking place in 1998, the first companies were breaking from the pack and acknowledging that the danger is real enough to demand a response. In addition to the massive investment of British Petroleum and Shell Oil, the Houston-based giant Enron has become a major player in renewable energy projects. The Big Three automakers have all unveiled alternative-fuel vehicles, and the *Wall Street Journal* in March 1999 announced that "the race is on" among them to commercialize fuel cell powered cars.

Fuel cell development is employing a growing number of scientists and engineers at companies such as Plug Power of Latham, New York; Ballard Power Systems in British Columbia; and H-Power in New Jersey. Feeding the effort are groups at the Department of Energy, the national labs, universities such as Stanford; many private consulting firms; as well as such companies as DuPont and W.L. Gore, who have been developing and refining the proton exchange membranes that make the cells work. As the technology nears the marketplace, it has begun to employ builders of demonstration projects such as a fuel-cell-powered house in Latham and a vehicle, the Sunrise, developed by Solectria Corporation of Arlington, Massachusetts.

3. Quality of Life: Being Human While Preserving the Planet

Fashion, Beauty, and Personal Care

SPRING COLLECTIONS RELY ON ECO-TEXTILES
HEALTH AND SAFETY PRESSURES MOVE COTTON GROWERS TO ORGANICS
TEXTILE UNIONS LAUNCH ENVIRONMENTAL HEALTH CAMPAIGN
US CONSUMPTION LEVELS FALL SHARPLY, PREFERENCE FOR ECO-
PRODUCTS EMERGES

Humans have adorned themselves for millennia, and currently pour billions of dollars into personal care products. Consumer health and environmental concerns in recent years have included the petrochemical base of many cosmetics; the dyes, preservatives, and other ingredients which slip through labeling requirements as "trade secrets"; animal testing; packaging; biodegradability of products; and, for the many who still care, the images of women that are used in marketing these items. On all counts, innovative options are available for shoppers, employees, and entrepreneurs. Many famous, pioneering social ventures have been in the realm of personal care products for a simple reason: you can make 'em in your kitchen.

The Body Shop International is emblematic of this business, and social ventures in general, for its bold founding vision, stormy adolescence in full view of a critical press, and maturation as a more humble but still ambitious organization.

The textile and fashion industries also have enormous environmental impact. For example, cotton constitutes 3 percent of the world's crops, yet uses 26 percent of the world's pesticides by weight. Other environmental and social issues facing the fashion and fiber industries include water use, soil protection, competition for cropland, toxic dyes, and worker health and safety, especially for many thousands globally working in marginal conditions in the garment industry.

Worker health and safety concerns have been a focus of both international campaigns and enforcement by the US Department of Labor's "no sweat" initiatives. Levi Strauss led the industry a few years ago in devising and implementing a progressive "global sourcing code" for its branches and subcontractors around the world, which lays out concrete standards for all the global company's subcontractors and suppliers in the areas of worker health and safety, child labor, and environmental practices. Levi's was the first to implement annual environmental health and safety audits of suppliers, and has rejected on average 15 percent per year for violations of the sourcing code.

Out of these concerns, an "eco-fashion" sector has begun to emerge, seeking ways of doing business that are smarter and gentler for the earth, consumers, the workforce and the industry itself. The linkage between environmental protection, on one hand, and worker health and safety on the other, makes this industry one of the most visible zones of opportunity for cross-fertilization between the "environmental" and "social" aspects of making a difference.

One of the best known eco-fashion innovators is Sally Fox, a geneticist and weaver who noticed the occasional colors creeping into her raw cotton. Applying ancient and simple techniques, Fox began breeding plants for this trait. Painstakingly, she developed natural cottons in green, brown, rust, and blue shades that, unlike dyed fabrics, grow darker with each washing. FoxFiber, based in Arizona, produces its distinctive natural cottons for Esprit and other clothing manufacturers, and also makes a line of fine papers from the production "waste."

Major industrial players have discovered markets in "eco-fibers," notably Wellman, Inc., whose Eco-Fleece made from recycled plastic bottles addresses multiple environmental problems profitably and with elegance. Lately, Wellman has engineered a Master Apprentice Program, an annual showing of high fashions made from 100 percent recycled soda bottles. Designers have included Oscar de la Renta, Tommy Hilfiger, and Diane Von Furstenberg. Co-sponsors, logically enough, are Pepsi-Cola and Teen People. The company has pledged five years' worth of scholarships to aspiring fashion designers.

Also on the horizon are myriad small businesses such as the high-fashion Blue Fish Clothing of New Jersey, which markets distinctive hand-painted clothing using natural dyes. Because the textile and fashion industries are among the most thoroughly globalized, the economics of making an eco-fashion business work in the industrialized world are tricky.

Blue Fish has had its greatest successes on the socioeconomic high end, doing great education and commercializing a distinctive look but struggling with mass marketability. A low-tech variation with an interesting strategy for impact is the Recycled Trash Company of Solana Beach, California, which addresses multiple issues by using "recycled" cotton fabric reclaimed from production processes, rescuing up to 40 percent of cotton that would otherwise end up in landfills and using it to make naturally-colored t-shirts, sweatshirts, polos and tote bags. They also mix marketing with philanthropy by offering wholesale prices to nonprofit groups seeking fundraiser products.

Some of the changes in the fashion business are a result of entrepreneurial inventiveness. Others have come about through the efforts of advocates working with industry decision-makers in a concerted manner, such as Businesses for Social Responsibility's Fashion Industry Working Group. According to staffer Deborah Weiner, "Most of the big fashion labels do not do their own production, so there's a sense in the industry that they don't have much environmental impact." They may understand office energy and waste audits, but Weiner and her colleagues had to do some work to gain acceptance for the idea that a major product brand could influence the production process of its chosen suppliers. The groundwork done by Levi's helped. So did Weiner's own background in the industry.

Weiner was a successful clothing store manager in southern Maine, but the volume of solid waste generated by her store and parent company worried her. She filled in field staff feedback cards galore and wrote polite letters to headquarters, to no avail. A course on environmental management for businesses caught her attention, and she offered to attend on her own time if her schedule could only be adjusted to make it possible. The request was denied. Weiner wrestled with her options, but not for long. Within two weeks, she had politely resigned and taken the Graduate Record Exams. After getting a master's degree at Yale School of Forestry and Environmental Studies, she has come full circle to work in the fashion industry as an environmental advocate. Weiner and a small team work with major fashion labels on ways to improve environmental performance on sourcing, fiber selection and design, manufacturing process, and, of course, waste reduction.

Tourism/Recreation
MOST PEOPLE PREFER VACATIONS CLOSE TO HOME, STUDY SHOWS
REGION ADOPTS ECO-TOURISM AS ECONOMIC DEVELOPMENT CORNERSTONE

Tourism is a top global industry and a cornerstone of economic development thinking. It moves people around. It creates infrastructure. It brings cultures into contact with each other. It stirs up commerce. For all these reasons, the direction taken by a tourist industry can be a mirror of the society and a catalyst for change.

One of the simplest aspects of healthy tourism is the world of camping. The 3,200 member camps of the American Camping Association are a subset of the world of specialty camps, conference and retreat centers that lift humans out of their ordinary lives and place them closer to nature (whether a little closer or a lot). Camp counseling is the quintessential summer job, and a growing number of colleges now have associate — and bachelor's degree programs in camp administration. Camps, like any other facility, can be designed as environmental showplaces, as illustrated by the YMCA's Frost Valley Camp and Conference Center in the Catskill Mountains, an environmental education center using greener building materials, solar hot water, and food waste composting.'

The CERES (Coalition for Environmentally Responsible Economies) Principles of Environmental Responsibility (http://www.ceres.org/), signed by over 80 businesses, nonprofits and public agencies:

By adopting these Principles, we publicly affirm our belief that corporations have a responsibility for the environment, and must conduct all aspects of their business as responsible stewards of the environment by operating in a manner that protects the Earth. We believe that corporations must not compromise the ability of future generations to sustain themselves.

We will update our practices constantly in light of advances in technology and new understandings in health and environmental science. In collaboration with CERES, we will promote a dynamic process to ensure that the Principles are interpreted in a way that accommodates changing technologies and environmental realities. We intend to make consistent, measurable progress in implementing these Principles and to apply them to all aspects of our operations throughout the world.

Protection of the Biosphere
We will reduce and make continual progress toward eliminating the release of any substance that may cause environmental damage to the air, water, or the earth or its inhabitants. We will safeguard all habitats affected by our operations and will protect open spaces and wilderness, while preserving biodiversity.

Sustainable Use of Natural Resources
We will make sustainable use of renewable natural resources, such as water, soils and forests. We will conserve nonrenewable natural resources through efficient use and careful planning.

Reduction and Disposal of Wastes
We will reduce and where possible eliminate waste through source reduction and recycling. All waste will be handled and disposed of through safe and responsible methods.

Energy Conservation
We will conserve energy and improve the energy efficiency of our internal operations and of the goods and services we sell. We will make every effort to use environmentally safe and sustainable energy sources.

Risk Reduction
We will strive to minimize the environmental, health and safety risks to our employees and the communities in which we operate through safe technologies, facilities and operating procedures, and by being prepared for emergencies.

Safe Products and Services
We will reduce and where possible eliminate the use, manufacture or sale of products and services that cause environmental damage or health or safety hazards. We will inform our customers of the environmental impacts of our products or services and try to correct unsafe use. ➔

Especially in pristine areas with an interest in preservation, a more evolved idea of eco-tourism is gaining attention as a basis for sustainable development. Depending on the context, this can mean everything from camping and hiking to cultural tours to guided trips visiting ecological spots of note. At its best, eco-tourism can generate jobs for local guides, interpreters, managers, and guardians of protected areas; create revenue streams to fund wildlife preserves in developing countries; and generate commerce for local communities.

CERES Principles *(continued)*

Environmental Restoration

We will promptly and responsibly correct conditions we have caused that endanger health, safety or the environment. To the extent feasible, we will redress injuries we have caused to persons or damage we have caused to the environment and will restore the environment.

Informing the Public

We will inform in a timely manner everyone who may be affected by conditions caused by our company that might endanger health, safety or the environment. We will regularly seek advice and counsel through dialogue with persons in communities near our facilities. We will not take any action against employees for reporting dangerous incidents or conditions to management or to appropriate authorities.

Management Commitment

We will implement these Principles and sustain a process that ensures that the Board of Directors and Chief Executive Officer are fully informed about pertinent environmental issues and are fully responsible for environmental policy. In selecting our Board of Directors, we will consider demonstrated environmental commitment as a factor.

Audits and Reports

We will conduct an annual self-evaluation of our progress in implementing these Principles. We will support the timely creation of generally accepted environmental audit procedures. We will annually complete the CERES Report, which will be made available to the public.

These Principles establish an environmental ethic with criteria by which investors and others can assess the environmental performance of companies. Companies that endorse these Principles pledge to go voluntarily beyond the requirements of the law. The terms may and might in Principles one and eight are not meant to encompass every imaginable consequence, no matter how remote. Rather, these Principles obligate endorsers to behave as prudent persons who are not governed by conflicting interests and who possess a strong commitment to environmental excellence and to human health and safety. These Principles are not intended to create new legal liabilities, expand existing rights or obligations, waive legal defenses, or otherwise affect the legal position of any endorsing company, and are not intended to be used against an endorser in any legal proceeding for any purpose. ❖

For example, a women's cooperative at Costa Rica's Monteverde reserve grosses about $50,000 per year selling homemade souvenirs to eco-tourists.

At the same time, however, eco-tourist experiments have brought grave risks. Twenty years ago, almost no tourist lodges existed in Nepal's Annapurna region. Now, approximately 50 lodges cater to the tourist trade. The demand for wood to heat the lodges and prepare meals has lowered the forest line by several hundred feet. In his study of the trade-offs, *Handle with Care*, Scott Graham adds that "in the Nepalese village of Ghorepani, which sees an average of 18,000 trekkers in nine months, food and lodging costs have soared, creating inflationary prices for the local people. And yet, without the tourist trade, Nepal would be in dire straits."

No matter how environmentally concerned the participants may be, the hotels, resorts, roads, harbors, airports, and other chunks of infrastructure that accompany tourism have dramatic physical impact on land, waterways, and habitats. For people in the developed world who are considering work in the travel or tourism industries, the guiding question is clearly "How much restraint is enough?" But another question is emerging next to this one: "How much positive impact can a well-designed tourism project have?"

One of the most visionary approaches to that question comes from Stanley Selengut, a New York civil engineer and developer who has found a stimulating new life running a "research resort" called Harmony in the US Virgin Islands. Powered by sun and wind, off the local electric grid, the facility is advanced in esthetics as well as engineering. The multicolored roof tiles are made of crushed glass. These, and the floorboards of recycled newspaper, are made in local workshops. Rainwater caught on the roofs is channeled into solar showers; composting toilets make septic systems unnecessary. Features like these make a sustainable resort much less expensive than a conventional one to construct, and therefore more profitable. Selengut is also researching ways these ecologically advanced construction methods can be creators of local jobs. He comments:

> There are real opportunities for win/win solutions in this business, providing you can control greed and don't leverage yourself at such a level that one mistake will bring you down. Resorts of this type, with individual units, can start small and expand. You can assess environmental impact and carrying capacity as you go.
>
> Most hotel management is like making cookies with a cookie cutter — it's all the same. This work is site-specific and much more interesting. Your palette is all the indigenous assets, natural and cultural. The challenge is to bring people into an environment, and into communication with each other, in a way that opens them up to new ideas.

By combining high tech and low impact, Selengut has attracted some powerful partners for assistance with materials and monitoring, including the US National Park Service and Sandia National Laboratories. He is convinced that "there are tremendous entrepreneurial opportunities" for sustainable architecture and design, and for travel destinations where people can sample the state of this art. Selengut shows the possibility of a fresh start for engineers, technicians, and others whose prospects in large organizations may be dimming but whose talents and vision are more needed than ever.

In his guidebook, *EcoJourneys*, Stephen Foehr suggests some questions for the traveler to ask a tour company. These can also be posed by the job-seeker to tourist ventures more generally:

- How do they contribute to the local economies of the places they visit?
- Do they hire local guides and staff?
- Do they buy local supplies as much as possible?
- Do they contribute to or otherwise support environmental organizations, especially those in the host country?
- Do they make a conscious effort to inform about the environmental and cultural issues of the places they visit?
- How do they show respect for the local culture, people, and wildlife?
- Do they provide information on products that should not be purchased, such as those made from sea turtle shells; reptile skin or leather; ivory from elephants, whales, walrus, or narwhals; bird feathers or skins; or fur?

Chapter 4
Headlines We'd Like to See, II:
Work that Protects and Restores
Our Communities

INFANT MORTALITY SHOWS SHARP DECLINE
COLLEGE GRADS SCORE RECORD HIGHS IN ECO-LITERACY AND
    COMMUNITY INVOLVEMENT
GANG-LED PEER TUTORING PROGRAMS LEAD CITY IN SAT SCORES
INDEPENDENT LIVING BY SENIOR CITIZENS AT ALL-TIME HIGH
HEALTH, HUMAN SERVICE BUDGET EXCEEDS MILITARY

Many of the fields of work geared toward social well-being are caught in tensions similar to those on the environmental front. There is push-and-pull between public and private provision of services; between responding to crises and devising more preventive approaches; and between containing costs and doing what's needed. As a result, the work opportunities are distributed among the private, public, and nonprofit sectors in ways that defy logic; there is enormous diversity in work structures and philosophies; nearly every organization believes it is on the side of the angels in reforming its industry; and the work is being continuously reinvented.

Health

Health care is an enormous sector that can make copious uses of skills in medical arts, business, technologies, communication, caregiving, and advocacy. The *American Health Professions Education Directory* lists 45 separate professions (audiology, dentistry, epidemiology, nursing, etc.), each of which can be practiced in many ways, with many specialties, and at many levels of expertise. As the structure of the industry continues to be in flux, the practice of healing arts involves a mix of healing the patient and healing the system. Out of the turmoil, though, has come a wealth of inventive career directions: MDs who have given up on the managed care system and are developing individualized specialty practices; nurses who are exploring the potential of entrepreneurship and intrapreneurship (i.e. innovation within a workplace); paraprofessionals finding or creating their niches; and practitioners of healing arts that are understood as partly or completely outside the traditional health care system.

More than half of US adults say they've used some "alternative" health care methods, whether herbs or shiatsu or hands-on healing. There is growing research support for "complementary" medical approaches — that is, those that can work along with conventional medical options — and the first accredited training programs such as Dr. Andrew Weil's at the University of Arizona's Health Sciences Center, as well as programs New York Presbyterian Hospital, California Pacific Medical Center, Beth Israel Deaconess Medical Center in Boston, the State University of New York's teaching hospital in Stonybrook, the University of Pittsburgh Medical Center, and the Health Alliance of Greater Cincinnatti.[10] In Britain, alternative medicine is penetrating the mainstream to the point that 62 percent of practicing acupuncturists are physicians. In the US, there is some degree of integration. The National Institutes of Health now operate a Center for Complementary and Alternative Medicine, which researches a vast range of healing modalities and provides a militantly neutral information clearinghouse. A good simple mapping of the territory is provided by the Center's seven categories:

1. Diet-nutrition-lifestyle change;
2. Mind-body intervention;
3. Bio-electromagnetic applications;
4. Alternative systems of medical practice;
5. Manual healing such as Therapeutic Touch and Reiki;
6. Pharmacological and biological treatments;
7. Herbal medicine.

Among the richest areas of innovation, for physicians and many kinds of paraprofessionals, are the ends of the lifeline, birth and death. Hospice workers may come from the worlds of medicine, social work, clergy, advocacy, and many other backgrounds. The many specialist roles connected with childbirth and parental support include preconception and fertility counselors, maternity fitness instructors, midwives, breastfeeding instructors and advocates, infant first aid and safety instructors, and more.

In addition to their direct services, medical practices are discovering several other levels on which they can make a difference. As advocates, people in the medical community bring unique credibility to issues of public and environmental health. For example, one of the prime movers in creating the US Postal Service's "Stamp Out Breast Cancer" campaign was a physician, Ernie Bodai of Kaiser-Permanente in California, who devoted two years to getting the educational and fundraising partnership up and running. Initially facing skepticism from breast cancer groups, the Postal Service, and even stamp collectors, Bodai persisted and touched such a chord in the public mind that 33 million stamps were sold in the program's first two months.[11] Across the country, Dr. Joseph DiFranza of Worcester, Massachusetts saw too many deaths from smoking and too many cigarettes marketed to teenagers, and declared a personal war against Joe Camel by helping to form a national anti-smoking organization, "Doctors Ought to Care." Says DiFranza, "We're too cautious sometimes, treating diseases one case at a time. If you think preventively and get a big enough idea, you can save millions of lives."

At the level of the practice, too, health care is finding new ways to define its mission more expansively. Catholic Health Care West is a massive practice, with 48 facilities for acute care and a total staff of 38,000. The organization, a signatory to the CERES Principles for environmental responsibility and disclosure, has taken a holistic look at its mission and services. This led to a strong focus on the root causes of illness such as poverty, domestic and gang violence, environmental dangers, and drug abuse. Catholic Health Care West operates a program of community grants for organizations working to eliminate these root causes, as well as an alternative investment strategy to put its financial muscle behind health-promoting enterprises. This thinking is replicable by any health care practice, large or small.

Health care institutions are also developing alternatives to animal research and the use of live animals in teaching, spurred in part by the work of Physicians for Responsible Medicine. At a number of medical schools including the University of Florida's, medical student activism has replaced the use of live dogs for surgical training with audiovisual tools oriented toward human anatomy.

Finally, a wide coalition of environmental and health care organizations has come together to promote Health Care Without Harm, a national initiative to find safer replacements for toxic elements like dioxin, mercury, and polyvinyl chloride, and to help medical facilities reduce their waste incineration as much as practical. Beth Israel Medical Center in New York City, a participant, saves $900,000 a year through product purchasing and disposal changes including reducing, reusing, and recycling.

Helping People Thrive: From Social Services to Community Development

Mental health and social services help every community to take care of its own, including providing safety nets for children, elders, and people needing care or protection such as victims of violence or witnesses in criminal trials. Child and elder care, hospice care, prevention of suicide and domestic violence, substance abuse prevention and recovery all fall into this category. Service providers are also natural advocates and policymakers.

Psychologists, social workers, counselors, trainers, and professionals with many other titles assist people with personal development and healing. They work in private practices, managed care settings, institutions including schools, hospitals, prisons, and businesses. There is a nearly infinite range of schools and modalities to consider, with corresponding variation in educational and licensing requirements. Psychiatrists with medical training, and PhD psychologists, are still sought after, especially when clinical expertise is combined with management skill and other specialties. However, managed care systems have led to the replacement of many generalist psychologists with clinical social workers who bring less strenuous but still solid training, yet command more modest salaries. Social workers also find niches in corporate Employee Assistance Programs, helping employees with the spectrum of issues that affect performance, from family stress to substance abuse.

The Age Wave cannot help but create new areas of work in service, advocacy, information, and more. Margaret Newhouse of the Harvard Office of Career Services, who offers workshops on finding work you love in the second half of life, observes, "There are, of course, the social service positions in agencies and employee assistance programs, helping aging adults and their children who may be working full-time and need help sorting out the maze of services available. There are social workers focusing on independent living and others focusing on hospice care. But there is also a wealth of opportunities focusing on older adults who are thoroughly active and constitute a major market . These include, for example, consumer advocates; Elderhostels and other lifelong learning programs; tours and retreats; workplace empowerment programs like Boston's Project ABLE; advocacy groups like the Grey Panthers. "To start networking in this area," Newhouse recommends, "visit your local Council on Aging, join the National Association on Aging, and visit Web sites like www.ThirdAge.com."

Over the generations, psychologies have expanded their perspective from a central focus on the intrapsychic to a recognition of the relationship between individual well-being and the social and environmental context. Family, group, social, community, political, and ecopsychologies have developed in the twentieth century in recognition of this systems view. Within social work, the field of "macro practice" provides a framework for psychologically sound intervention in whole systems, from organizations to towns to political movements. Shirley Jones, Distinguished Professor of Social Welfare at the State University of New York in Albany, defines macro practice as the realm where "social workers work with large systems and focus on social issues" — for example, applying a social systems perspective in roles as diverse as "legislative assistant, planner, manager of an agency or corporate program, community organizer and economic developer."

In the 1980s, psychologists took on a key role in working with communities to recognize and address environmental concerns and the dangers of the nuclear arms race. In a similar spirit, in 1998, the American Psychological Association stepped up to the plate on the issue of school and community violence. APA partnered with MTV to deliver a national special about violence prevention called "Danger Signs" — with training of community-based psychologists to work in-depth with schools and parents to implement the show's recommendations. The work of psychologists on social issues has also contributed a legacy of new methods for group communication and dispute resolution. Principles of family therapy have been finding their way into dialogue processes on public issues such as abortion, thanks to the work of the Cambridge Family Institute in Massachusetts and other groups.

While many psychologists with individual and family-oriented specialties find ways to use their professional skills in community settings, the field of community psychology itself is coming of age. Linda Silka, trained as a community psychologist, runs the Center for Work, Family and Community at the University of Massachusetts in Lowell. An action-teaching nucleus for the community, she works with stakeholder groups on projects that bring them together, teach skills, and build institutions of value to this multicultural community.

> *A central idea of community psychology is you can't do it alone. University people can't. Businesspeople can't. Neighborhoods can't. The way we're successful is by brokering relationships and doing partnerships that bring together different skills and let groups see what's in it for them when they work together.*

The Center's River Ambassador Program involves high school youth teaching other kids about environmental and social issues connected to the Merrimac River. Says Silka, "It's a growth of community strength because the kids learn that they are potential role models, not to mention future environmental scientists and community leaders." She teaches graduate classes that include grant-writing and program evaluation, but their organizing principle is community projects so that "students can see firsthand the complications of the role you're in, ethical and strategic issues like when to share data about a community with the community." The essential skills of the community psychologist include everything an individual psychologist needs, plus a strong systems outlook.

> *You have to have a real strong knowledge base, to know the literature and best practices and so forth. But, more, you must have the flexibility to look at things in multiple ways. You'll have experiences where you don't do it quite right and you look at that, watch groups argue and succeed and fail and you're a part of it all, and it's not exactly working but it's moving along. You learn to draw on your knowledge base in unusual ways, because life doesn't organize itself the way the literature does.*

Another of the interesting opportunities to blend the micro and macro levels of human development is ordained ministry. In this role, you can move from individual and family counseling to organizational development to community projects, while attending to the more conventional roles of education and ceremony — not to mention building maintenance, fundraising, dishwashing, and more. Ministers, rabbis and other faith leaders, through councils of churches, can exercise considerable influence on the policies, services, and programs of a local government.

An entire division of the American Psychological Association is devoted to community psychology. But some of its most intuitively effective practitioners are self-taught. One of these is Onaje Benjamin of Woodstock, New York. He says: "I'm a consultant, a workshop facilitator, sometimes I use the term 'social justice educator,' which addresses a range of different issues." With the Upstate Center for School Safety, he works in 30 school districts. Teams from the Center provide a three-day workshop to train school safety teams that consist of school personnel, community members, parents, teachers, and students. The teams gather data and assess their schools' indicators of risk, hot spots, teacher training needs, and student needs. That allows for data-driven decision-making, which empowers the community. Benjamin, an independent learner who has studied through Goddard College, Empire State College, and other learner-driven programs, has evolved a very clear and marketable approach to helping communities reduce violence:

> *I do two or three types of violence prevention. The most effective is a systems approach, not just targeting kids but getting a lot of the stakeholders around the table. Usually, when you find a child who's aggressive, there's more than likely causation behind it, from individual abuse to systemic issues such as poverty, racism, and so on. I've evolved a counseling model called 'empathic accountability,' recognizing the causal factors in anti-social behavior but keeping the focus on how the young person can change. A kid might be selling crack cocaine and say, 'Well, I can't get hired in the white world,' and I'll say, 'So what are you doing to reclaim your power and change that?'*

My passion is working with marginalized communities that are looking for skill enhancement in becoming more empowered. As a 50-year-old, I find it necessary to apologize to young people as a representative of the elder class: "We left you a real stacked deck here. You can't drink the water, and we haven't gotten that nonviolence thing down." Cornel West talks about "black nihilism," and I think that's even more severe among the young. There have to be mature elders who take on the responsibility of stewarding young people through the waters of adolescence.

Increasingly, I'm also doing rites of passage and initiatory mentoring with young people. I borrow from cultural anthropology, the psychology of Franz Fanon, indigenous cultures, all over. I'm doing more and more training of staff who work with at-risk kids, drawing on these traditions. For instance, when I do workshops for substance abuse professionals on their own anger, I bring up the archetype of the wounded healer. Or I get them to look at the relationship between gangs and ritual, or adolescent body piercing and the archetypal curiosity about initiation.

Law enforcement and corrections are among the highest-stress professions in existence. I respect them, and at the same time I think there's a need for a much more systemic approach.

Within the world of law enforcement, too, there are moves toward more systemic approaches, some of them under banners such as "community policing" and "value-centered leadership." Lorne Kramer had been a cop for 28 years, most of them in Los Angeles, when the beating of Rodney King by his fellow police shocked the nation. "I already had feelers out to make a change, but it's true that timing is everything," he reflects. "I had been proud to be in Los Angeles, but did not sense that we were taking as progressive an approach to doing our jobs as I wanted to. We were a traditional large department, and as I traveled and talked with senior people in law enforcement, I realized a lot of us were concerned with the direction being taken by traditional large departments."

Today he is Chief of Police in Colorado Springs, a sprawling city of 360,000 where he has implemented a series of culture change initiatives to improve community relations, discipline and cohesion within the Force, using the methods of quality management and community-based policing which today are being tested in several hundred cities and towns. As he explains it, "Community-based policing boils down to two things: better, more constructive partnerships with neighborhoods, so that people are able to take more ownership of problems at the street level; and problem solving to develop solutions to chronic problems."

Initially Kramer expected, and got, some rumbles of resistance by community members who saw him as "this Nazi from LA" He lost no time in attending community meetings throughout the city to build relationships firsthand. At the same time, he began the process of culture change with a year-long pilot project in one division, emphasizing the strengths in the Force and experimenting with ways to build upon them. He says, "I knew I couldn't dictate a culture change, so I gave a lot of latitude to the practitioners who knew the job best to design how the job ought to look."

Part of the new mode was a formal problem-solving methodology, and an examination of the true indicators of success. "We used to think that how fast our cars got us to the calls and the number of responses was everything. Now we opened it up to ask how many crimes were solved, how much property was returned, how the community perceived our effectiveness. It was an eye-opener." The other dimension was a natural outgrowth of this: bringing officers into contact with Neighborhood Watch and other civic groups for cake and coffee and discussions of how the police were viewed in the neighborhoods.

Today, Colorado Springs is one of a number of cities working with the National Institute of Justice and the International City Managers Association on a research partnership called Standards of Service. As Kramer describes it, "Are we really measuring what matters? Is an increase or decrease in a specific crime truly indicative of the sense of fear or safety that a typical citizen has in a neighborhood?"

Lorne Kramer's path through life gave him a perfect blend of ordinary and extraordinary experiences to make this latest step possible. As he tells it, "I played baseball for a few years after high school, and never aspired to be a police officer, but there I was. I was fortunate and was promoted very fast, and got my higher education as a police officer — in the 1960s. When I sat in classrooms, and had to step back and look at issues of brutality and racism and discrimination and police abuse through the eyes of other disciplines and people, that really did broaden my perspective. I know law enforcement people to be extremely dedicated and valorous. I also know that their view of the world is really unique."

He found Colorado Springs at a time when the city's police force needed a change. "This was a good department when I came here, but there was an identified leadership crisis. The previous chief had left. The people were ripe for someone to come in and say "let's go in a new direction." They too were listening around the country.

"When I interviewed, I told them that I had a vision of how law enforcement ought to be delivered, some of the things I thought we should do. You have to take personal control and responsibility of your career. Mentors are important. Formal and informal education are too, and looking for ways to really stay in touch with what is evolving in your profession."

Economic Development

The work of economic development is not only about bringing some economic activity into a community and hanging onto it, but about weaving that activity into a vibrant, coherent economy whose benefits are felt and whose hazards are contained. People do this working for local agencies including planning departments, economic development bureaus, and departments of commerce; nongovernmental organizations including unions and community development corporations; for the community relations staffs of larger businesses; for chambers of commerce, private industry councils, and other business groups; and for non-profits concerned specifically with sustainability. They may specialize in business attraction and retention, financing, planning and zoning, entrepreneurship, citizen participation processes, environmental management, or economic policy. Combining all these kinds of expertise is a challenge, although this is one of the fields where a knowledgeable and gutsy generalist can do enormous good.

One of the primary reasons people get involved in economic development is pure, appropriate self-interest. Mary Ann Kristiansen became the proprietor of a local crafts market because she was a craftsperson, and outgoing, and was dismayed at the difficulties of her fellow craftspeople in organizing to sell their wares. The availability of an empty Woolworth's building in her home town of Keene, New Hampshire, became the impetus for the formation of the Hannah Grimes Marketplace. With active support of local economic development agencies and a grant from the Farmer's Home Administration, several dozen artisans set about renovating this landmark building to create a cooperatively run crafts market and tearoom that would become a magnet for revitalization in a town that was beloved but a bit run down. Things did not happen according to plan; environmental toxins were found in the building. But the team stayed connected and determined. The market opened up in early 1998.

A popular blend of community psychology and economic development is the movement to teach and support youth entrepreneurship, some of which integrates social and environmental values with vigor. While some programs, such as Junior Achievement, are run in high schools with faculty guidance, many are sprouting their own nonprofit agencies or becoming attached to established business incubators. This makes it possible for customized programs to spring up in response to a community's needs and make use of a community's resources. Trainers and program developers may come from business, nonprofit management, or casework with youth, or simply step forward and gain the skills to meet the need.

Consider the West Philadelphia Enterprise Center, a true community resource proudly housed in the former American Bandstand broadcasting station where the historic dance floor is still intact. The center runs hundreds of interested city teens every season through a Boot Camp on entrepreneurship, weaving in an extra social dimension with presentations from socially responsible businesses and nonprofits like City Year. With a growing census of established eco-businesses, including the White Dog Café and the Sheraton Rittenhouse Square Hotel, Philadelphia is home to a wave of experimentation to find low-tech sustainable enterprises that can be run by youth and by disadvantaged city residents.

Some of the most inventive and promising of these turn out to be the most holistically designed as they mobilize underutilized human capital to create profitable businesses that meet local needs. For instance, Rosalind Johnson, the visionary director of a nonprofit called Sea Change Resource Center, organized the cleanup of a troubled half-acre in North Central Philadelphia. With the help of agencies from Temple University to the Horticultural Society, she created an oasis of raised-bed gardens and tree saplings. Her vision was nothing short of "a web of profitable businesses focusing on food security issues and food production from abandoned urban land." Food-related startups include a

Community-Supported Agriculture project and crops of herbs and hot peppers for local restaurants, as well as a project to study the feasibility of urban aquaculture. A quest for a cost-effective, ecologically sound power source led the agency to create a fuel cell research partnership involving local businesses, government and universities. The emerging vision is turning into an urban "ecobator."

As an aspect of economic development, trade is an opportunity to change the conditions under which goods are produced, and to organize consumers in support of more equitable approaches. Pueblo to People, a Houston-based mail order catalog, links up cooperatively owned and managed craft producers in Central America with consumers in the United States. Even on a small scale, ventures like this need management, marketing, finance, and "sourcing" or purchasing. With sourcing comes setting standards for social, environmental, and quality criteria. These partnerships provide opportunities for business-building that can greatly increase social stability in an area.

ForesTrade is an international business with 30-some employees, that trades in high quality certified organic and sustainably harvested spices, essential oils and coffee. Founders Sylvia Blanchet and Tomas Fricke spend part of their time in their Brattleboro, Vermont, home base, and part traveling to production areas in Southeast Asia and Central America. Married when they both worked in sustainable agriculture in Guatemala, the couple never expected to work together. Fricke had a long involvement in sustainable agriculture, ultimately working for the World Wildlife Fund, looking for ways to protect a major parcel of rainforest in Sumatra and the communities living on it. "This wonderful natural resource was being carved up and permanently diminished. There were farmers squatting where the trees had been, clearcutting leaving steep slopes, erosion washing down into the river below. Everyone could see the devastation. Everyone wanted a solution."

The solution he proposed, creating a buffer zone for the cultivation of nontimber cash crops that can be sustainably harvested, is gaining a global following thanks to numerous experiments. ForesTrade now grows cardamom, pepper, vanilla, coffee, and other valuable cash crops organically, using a network of small farmers, indigenous organizations and local businesses. Blanchet, trained as a social worker, never expected to be running a global business. Her interests had centered on helping people who had experienced violence, addiction, or abuse to recover from deep trauma, which led her to study the methods of indigenous healers. But a family business linking Vermont and the rainforests of Asia and Central America seemed to her like a ticket for rich cross-cultural experiences. Blanchet finds that her skills in social work and counseling come into play on a daily basis in managing an international business, both in one-on-one relationships and in understanding the growing business as a human system.

In general, economic development and organization-building are rich fields for determined and knowledgeable people to "play hardball with soft skills,"[12] as Lawrence Gross illustrates. He helps other people do economic development in his role as co-chair of one of the more interesting new on-campus programs, in Regional Social and Economic Development at the University of Massachusetts in Lowell. A PhD in American Civilization who couldn't find a more conventional teaching job and couldn't face law school, Gross followed his bliss into a job at the Textile History Museum in the era when Lowell was doing its best to get past its identity as "declining mill town" and redefine itself. He was hired to learn about the generations of technologies, but refused to decouple it from an interest in the human side of millwork and the labor issues involved. He published a study of the local mills, *The Course of Industrial Decline*, in 1993.

By that time, the community was redefining itself. Refurbished mills became offices for the US Fish and Wildlife Service and for various university departments. Lowell began attracting southeast Asian and Hispanic entrepreneurs. Gross became interested in healthy enterprises and healthy communities. That led him into an exclusive contract to document one of the late twentieth century's most honorable business models: the nearby Malden Mills, which rebuilt after a tragic fire in the early 1990s and kept the entire work-force on the payroll during the reconstruction. With just a classic useless history degree and an insistence on looking at the whole picture, Larry Gross represents an emerging breed of community-based action researcher who brings multiple disciplines into the work of healthi-er economic development.

Nonprofits as well as universities are bases for economic development research and innovation. At Chicago's Center for Neighborhood Technologies, David Chandler runs a program called Connections, which is pioneering "transit-based development" in the city and its suburbs. The program is working with underemployed city dwellers wishing to become entrepreneurs, partnering them with franchise opportunities in lines of business that belong in a human-scale downtown: groceries, cafés, children's stores, hardware, bak-eries, wet cleaning (less toxic than dry), reused goods, and more. The program's goal is to create synergistic business clusters near transit centers, reducing the automobile reliance of entire communities. Chandler learned his skills through a series of powerful on-the-job training opportunities, starting with a degree in anthropology and a stint as a social worker. He started up and ran a major food bank, then spent 11 years with Francorp, a major fran-chise development consulting firm.

Economic empowerment has found a new tool with the proliferation of local cur-rencies, or Local Exchange Trading Systems, which keep resources in a community and add to the purchasing power of those with the least money. Susan Witt works at the center of the international movement to build up community exchange networks, microlending, and other forms of neighbor-to-neighbor economic support. Majoring in English and caring about the wider community, Witt decided that storytelling skills were the key to creating an economic renewal project that would be genuinely attractive to her neighbors and others like them. She became Executive Director of the E.F. Schumacher Society, founded by Bob Swann in the 1970s after he read Schumacher's *Small is Beautiful* and realized the need for high-quality, long-term economic education for citizens and policymakers alike. The Schumacher Society, in the Berkshire Mountains of western Massachusetts, has a 7,000-vol-ume library and meeting rooms for conversations about breathing new life into local economies by building cooperation, local accountability, and pride. Ideas springing from the Schumacher Society have been tested in towns like Great Barrington, which has used local currencies to focus community investment on businesses that will offer real payback to the town.

These experiments embody some sophisticated economic principles, most of which most people don't want to know a lot about. More to the point, they foster community and restore the linkage between the economic and the social levels of experience. Drawing on the Great Barrington experiments, local currencies are alive in over 60 communities in the US and more globally. Ithaca has its famous Hours. Burlington, Vermont, has Bread, with the currency unit called the Slice. The Pacific Northwest has (Puget) Sound Dollars. They're all locally controlled — of course — but Susan Witt serves as a mix of technical consultant, coach, and chronicler of these campaigns, and of the broader movement for local self-reliance.

Education and Training

Every town has schools. Many have private and alternative schools, charter schools, Waldorf and Montessori schools, homeschoolers. There are adult education and community learning centers, language and literacy programs. There are childcare franchises with educational packages. There's high school equivalency training and college test prep. And, beyond delivering, administering and marketing the services, there is development of curricula and evaluation of their effectiveness — not to mention education and training for people who do all of the above. Education, by its nature, makes a difference. Within this vast field, there are enormous variations in philosophies and strategies as well as educational content, not to mention in the health and financial well-being of workplaces.

Environmental education has expanded considerably in the last generation, with some states having mandated programs and many teachers appreciating the power of the subject to engage students. But Kevin Doyle of the Environmental Careers Organization sounds a cautionary note: "Environmental education is increasing, but it doesn't always translate into more hands-on opportunities for environmental educators. Often conventional teachers find themselves faced with a mandate to integrate environmental offerings into the curriculum, and go looking for off-the-shelf resources to help them do that."

Institutions of higher education have begun to realize what riches they are sitting on, in terms of providing incubators and demonstration sites by applying knowledge to produce real-world change. The University of North Carolina's Keenan-Flagler Business School, the Oberlin College Environmental Studies Center, and the Penn State Science, Technology and Society Program are among the leaders in meshing curriculum, physical construction, and community involvement projects to green both campus and surrounding community. At Penn State, a project representing several academic departments has helped the community to develop "sustainability indicators" against which future projects can be evaluated. At the University of North Carolina, business graduate students learn about the strategic advantages of getting out in front by embracing sustainable economics. At Oberlin College, a world-class architectural demonstration project is underway to create an environmental center that will model green building techniques including photovoltaic cells, passive solar design, and a Living Machine system for metabolizing organic waste into nutrients.

Several dozen business schools now offer "green" or sustainably oriented MBA programs, as well as programs in nonprofit and public sector management and in business with a community development orientation.[13] These are generally developed in close collaboration with businesses and integrate environmental considerations into the ordinary processes of manufacturing, finance, marketing.

The vision of a greener, more community-friendly campus is gaining adherents. Conferences like "The Greening of the Campus" at Ball State University in Indiana draw hundreds of student, faculty, administration, and staff representatives from around the US annually to share progress reports and strategies. Internationally, the first Greening the Campus conference was held in the spring of 1999 in Lund, Sweden. Many of these efforts

---

Susan Canali — Organizer, International Environmental Conference for Youth

After much roaming around, my family settled in Harvard, Massachusetts. There I enjoyed year-round backpacking, camping, and orienteering. I did my undergraduate work at Colgate University in upstate New York, English Literature and Fine Arts (BA 1983). My junior year was in Florence, and I visited much of Europe, the Middle East, and the Soviet Union that year.

Next I volunteered two years in Appalachia, mainly teaching English /reading to teenage juvenile delinquent boys in a group home school. I also helped out with a teenage girls' program, elderly home visitation, and Christmas baskets. I saw parts of Kentucky that I don't think exist anymore — so rural, poor and "out of the loop."

I went to graduate school at Indiana University in Bloomington, and got a Master's in Special Education (1986). I had a variety of part-time jobs working with handicapped adults and teens in residences, plus working with teenage girls who were victims of rape or incest. I continued my studies for a PhD in Instructional Systems Technology (1991). I like the creative, but sometimes exacting, design of instruction. My dissertation was an 18-month study on new technology use for the School of Education. At the time, I worked on an AT&T-funded project to identify the technology needs for

our new Center for Excellence in Education which was subsequently built. I often had CNN on in the background while writing my thesis, because my father was commanding the foremost field hospital in the Gulf War.

My work experiences shifted to designing an interactive videodisc for teacher training on instructional clarity, developing software for public school use, and researching user requirements for IBM's in-house training involving multimedia. Carlo and I kept running into each other playing soccer at IU He was getting his PhD in Theoretical Physics. He is from Milan. We married in 1992, and left for London that March.

I continued to work for IBM. Then we lived in beautiful old Trieste, Italy, and I taught English to some lively Italian businesspeople. Moving on to Sweden, I spent two years attending language courses and getting used to a new land.

I was glad to find my current work at the International Institute for Industrial Environmental Economics, because it is a very good fit. I work full-time on a project basis developing a distance education course for the Global Environmental Youth Convention planned for June 2000. We expect hundreds of young people. It is a little quiet here at the Institute, but there is a flow of international visitors who bring me news of the wider world.

---

have been catalyzed by organizations like Second Nature and University Leaders for a Sustainable Future, and by the 1996 Campus Earth Summit, which produced a *Blueprint for a Green Campus* built on the following principles:

1. Integrate environmental knowledge into all relevant disciplines.
2. Improve undergraduate environmental studies course offerings.
3. Provide opportunities for students to study campus and local environmental issues.
4. Conduct a campus environmental audit.
5. Institute environmentally responsible purchasing practices.
6. Reduce campus waste.
7. Maximize energy efficiency.
8. Make environmental sustainability a top priority in campus land use, transportation, and building planning.
9. Establish a student environmental center.
10. Support students who seek environmentally responsible careers.

For every vision of educational reform, there is a market in materials to help implement it. For example, Donna Nichols-White of Redmond, Washington, is a home-based entrepreneur and the mother of two teenage boys. Early in their lives, she became a practitioner of home-schooling and an advocate for it. At the hub of a network of black families who believe in the power of self-directed learning and the need for culturally diverse learning materials, she now runs a business, Drinking Gourd Book Company, and publishes *Drinking Gourd: Multicultural Home Education Magazine*. Both help parents and others to assess kids' skills, needs, and interests, then to prospect for educational resources that support customized learning programs. "This is Self-employment in a big way," she reflects. "I work about 60 hours a week, at home, with my children in tow. Having received no business education myself, I've decided to learn my business through trial and error, failure and success, in full view of my children. I'm showing them that families can work and learn together."

Along with education, but distinct, is the field of training. If good education pro-motes understanding and principled choices, training promotes skill and reliable behavior. Imagine if just about all the facilities managers of airports, hospitals, universities and shop-ping malls knew how to use nontoxic cleaning materials, paints, varnishes and carpeting. Imagine if all the cab drivers in your home town had gotten into the habit of never idling their engines between fares. In all these cases, the technologies exist to reduce environmental harm greatly. Helping people to learn specific new behaviors is called training. Both private and nonprofit training organizations are helping to promote systematic change in the ways we do business. Environmental practices are one of many examples of a field that also includes cross-cultural communication, diversity, mediation, and business ethics.

Chapter 5
One Step Behind the Headlines:
Catalysts for Change

It should be clear by now that the work of restoring the environment and healing society is being done by a vast and diverse workforce. Some of it is in specialized new fields or on the "sustainable edge" of existing industries. But a great deal involves simply doing ordinary jobs in the context of emerging needs, in occupations like these:

Communication

Information ecology. Cultural environment. Call it what you will, the messages being transmitted on both commercial and noncommercial media are powerfully shaping everybody's sense of the possible. You can put your presence behind your values by means of the media you choose, the audience and scale you choose from local to global, and the ideas you voice. A generation ago, environmental reporting was just coming to life; today major newspapers and broadcast media have specialists on these beats. Journalism is not a growth field, and its principled practice is plagued by the concentration of ownership of media outlets. But good people still get good stuff into print and onto the airwaves.

Although it's a battle, at times good people are gaining control of media or creating their own. Consider Envirolink, described by *E Magazine* this way:

> *Six years ago, 18-year-old Josh Knauer envisioned the Internet creating a global community of activists — students, volunteers, anyone willing to work for a better world. He set out by linking environmental Web sites to one another, eventually creating Envirolink, a grassroots online community which grew from a small Web site with environmental links to one which now links the sites of 130 countries and supports activists with services like daily action alerts, searchable databases and congressional updates.*

The application of new media and Internet technologies for social change has become a life-work for any number of small nonprofits and entrepreneurs, including idea-tanks like the Institute for Global Communications in San Francisco, which manages the activist PeaceNet, LaborNet, EcoNet, and RTKNet (covering Right to Know laws in communities and states).

With the growth of socially responsible business and social marketing comes a new thrust in the public relations industry. PR firms may work with clients that have been on the wrong side of public controversies on how to clean up their image, and — sometimes — in the process, clean up their act. For instance, the New York firm Ruder-Finn has experimented with an environmentally-oriented marketing program, helping client companies listen to consumer and citizen concerns and figure out how to change in response.

One of the simplest and most popular strategies for doing this is called cause-related marketing: tying product profits to a popular charitable goal. Carol Cone, CEO of the Boston-based Cone Communications, is a pioneer in these methods. She has worked with the women's athletic shoe company Ryka on campaigns against domestic violence, and with Levi's on ethical standards for subcontractors in its global factories. Cone conducts annual surveys on consumer approval of cause-related marketing and attraction to socially responsible businesses, both of which are growing. Just over five feet in height, Cone has been known to open talks by saying, "I used to be six feet tall. This is really hard work."

Most major public relations firms have some involvement in public interest campaigns, in many cases facilitated by the nonprofit Advertising Council. Founded during World War II as a government information outlet, the Ad Council has brought the world Smokey the Bear, McGruff the Anti-Crime Dog, and other bread-and-butter public interest images. More recently, the Council has worked with the US Environmental Protection Agency, Natural Resources Defense Council, and Japan Ad Agency on a major water pollution awareness campaign.

The work of providing and protecting community access to media (for example, cable TV) involves professionals as diverse as attorneys, organizers, community access TV producers and trainers, and the technical staffs who build and run the stations.

It's easier than ever to be a freelance communicator, but as competitive as ever to make a complete living at it. On the plus side, the 18-year history of the National Writers Union has helped to challenge norms in the communications industry to the point that freelance journalists can have some expectation of contracts and payments on schedule. The communications world is embattled, with struggles for ownership of individual businesses, control of technologies and public accountability.

The world of communication also includes the book trade, which is one of the most competitive as the major chains consolidate and position themselves to take each other on. Only a few proud socially-oriented independent bookstores remain as community institutions — Hungry Mind Books in Oakland, California, and New Words in Cambridge, Massachusetts, to name two.

At the same time, independent magazines are proliferating, many with humane values and fresh ideas. Consider *Who Cares?* by and for activist young people; *Valley Table*, a regional magazine about the food and farm culture of the Hudson Valley; *Pos,* a journal of healthy living and advocacy for HIV+ people; and the immensely popular *Fast Company*, a watering hole for people in growing businesses who are interested in innovation, communications technologies, progressive social values and building community.

Libraries

The world of libraries is diverse, and much of it is specialized. A public librarian may be a specialist in urban or community issues, information systems, youth services, or another area. Public libraries make a difference just by existing, and some of the most inspiring cases of librarians' activism revolve around keeping their own facilities funded and functional. Libraries on special topics, or for special audiences, are found in government agencies, trade associations, museums, hospitals, prisons, businesses, and nonprofit organizations.

The American Library Association's divisions and conferences offer a hint of the breadth of this field and the specialties that are well established: intellectual property, intellectual freedom and censorship issues, access to libraries, diversity issues, literacy, information technology, service to business, and more. The ALA's 1999 conference in New Orleans featured a spirited workshop on "civic librarianship." A respected voice in the politics of governmental information classification and the public's right to know, the Association has been heavily involved in lobbying in support of public access to information.

Recently, the Association's Office for Literacy Outreach hired a Literacy Officer to spearhead national programs. An example of the service careers that are possible in the world of libraries, Dale Lipschultz started in the field of children's literacy development in the mid-'80s, and moved on to working with teachers and paraprofessionals in an after-school program through Ericson Institute of Child Development in Chicago. She developed a parallel track of working with technology and telecommunications as a tool to improve children's literacy development, and developed trainings for adults, "moving the circle ever-outward." She also worked in a pediatric literacy program at LaRabida Children's Hospital, in which the doctors and nurses gave books to children and talked to them about the importance of reading. Then she went on to direct whole-family literacy programs. This led Lipschultz into a position with the Illinois Resource Development Center, working in partnership with ALA on a project funded by Lila Wallace Readers Digest Fund, called Literacy in Libraries Across America. She supported 13 library programs across the US. She was working in collaboration with the ALA when the position of Literacy Officer opened up. Her job is to support and enhance local programs, which may be run by librarians, educators, and others. She says, "I'm really developing ALA's internal and external focus and agenda for literacy. Our goal is to launch a significant literacy initiative in the twenty-first century, and I am going to do all I can to help that to happen."

Information Systems

Managing information and communicating it in useful form will continue to be an important area of work for people in many occupations, and there is a rise in the designation of people in medium- to large-sized organizations as "Chief Information Officers" to keep up with the flow. Designing and maintaining databases, generating and applying demographic information, and using the new media tools such as geographic information systems (GIS) are specialties with wide currency. GIS, in particular, can be used to link up the information systems of many users to facilitate sharing, as the San Diego Association of Governments and many others are doing. It can be used to make a city's neighborhood resources and features accessible to citizens. It can facilitate services such as ridesharing, as the city of Seattle demonstrates. Programmers, system managers, analysts and technicians are all needed, as are people who integrate these skills with others like planning or information science.

Detroit's Randy Raymond shows the potential of GIS as a tool for teaching and community empowerment in the hands of a visionary educator who likes to work in partnership. Raymond was teaching GIS at the Detroit Country Day School, but was restless for an opportunity to work in a more urban setting. When a position opened up at the largest high school in Michigan, Cass Technical High, he jumped on it and created a program to involve students in an underutilized community resource, the Belle Island Nature Center. Soon the kids were doing natural resource inventories and computerizing the information, as well as being trained as guides to welcome others to the Nature Center.

Building blocks of a bigger vision came from that experience. One was the educational power of involving learners as teachers of others. Another was the integrating potential of the technology. Soon teams of high schoolers were doing environmental education for elementary school kids, and in the process "noting the horrible environmental conditions in parts of the city, which of course the kids wanted to do something about." Since then, Raymond has involved teenagers and younger kids, with corporate and government partners, in community research that ranges from inventories of vacant and abandoned buildings to international marketing with Ford Motor Company. In this "constellation model" of shared learning among schools, neighborhoods, and the city's major institutions, the kids are in a lead role. They are paid for their time through grants, and are becoming highly employable in the process.

Philanthropy

Thousands of philanthropic foundations are in the business of giving away money. Some are private or family run. Others are publicly incorporated. Still others are under the auspices of a corporation. Although they vary widely in terms of budgets, strategies and individual impacts, collectively foundations are a significant power source in setting the agenda for social activism and policy.

The smaller foundations may be little more than trustees who have other sources of income, with a bank account, a brochure and an answering machine. But there are thousands of foundations of significant size and means — from community foundations with a few million dollars' endowment up to the giants of Ford and Packard and Rockefeller. Foundations employ program officers, who bring expertise in an issue such as literacy or women's economic development, and who interface with projects through the application phase and when they are funded. Research staffs, field evaluators, and financial and administrative staff, and managers of the foundation's assets are also part of the workings of a major funding enterprise.

Among larger foundations, many are questioning how to be truly effective partners with nonprofit organizations in creating fundamental change. One promising strategy was tested out by Stephen Viederman, president of the Jessie Smith Noyes Foundation, for bringing the foundation into a grassroots campaign as more than a passive funder. Working with the Southwest Organizing Project in New Mexico to challenge the environmental practices and community relations strategies of the computer giant Intel, the Noyes Foundation found a powerful tool to accompany its grantmaking, the presence of Intel stock in its investment portfolio, which soon led Viederman head-to-head with Intel as a shareholder activist.

At the other end of the financial spectrum, Boston educational consultant Jamie Coats shows the possibilities that can be brought to life by creating a foundation with a relatively modest amount of money and a clear design for distributing it. As of mid-1999, Coats' organization, Kids' Energy, was giving $24,000 to 2,000 children in a pilot project in the schools of Portland, Maine, with just three rules:

1. The money can only be spent by kids for kids' goals.
2. The money flows through schools, and collaboratively the adults and children have to design a process whereby the funding is connected to educators' goals.
3. Kids have to tell the world about it.

Coats brings extensive experience in building business-community partnerships, first with Business in the Community in his native Britain, and then at the Center for Corporate Community Relationships in Boston. Kids' Energy is built on a vision of partnerships that link up community leaders and children, give resources to children and celebrate what they do — coincidentally riding the wave of educational and communications technologies such as simple web page design which can be used with great effectiveness by children. Complementing the vision and experience is a particular talent which Coats has learned to recognize in himself and rely on: "I have a particular skill in helping two different sectors or parties take down their defenses, and use the resources that used to be devoted to defending themselves to collaborate on something of value to them both."

On the business side, too, there is room for innovation in philanthropy and community relations. It is becoming common for businesses to go beyond simple philanthropy to work in partnership with nonprofit organizations, in the interest of specific community changes. Timberland's partnership with City Year in New England is well known. Starbuck's Coffee has had similar links with the development agency CARE, earmarking a percentage of profits from specific coffee plantations for nearby development projects such as wells and irrigation systems, and involving local residents as managers in the projects to provide a training ground for business skills. In the Pacific Northwest, the Outdoor Industries Conservation Alliance takes this thinking to a higher level through a partnership between makers of outdoor equipment, on one hand, and local groups protecting the outdoors on the other.

Advocates

Here is a cluster of professions for highly results-oriented, strategic and very social people. Among the people who are paid to influence others directly, three major categories are political party staff, lobbyists, and organizers (who might focus on labor, consumers, or other citizen populations). There are advocates on issues, and also advocates for individuals such as nursing home residents, hospital patients, victims and witnesses interfacing with a court system, and so forth.

Some of the most compelling advocates for advocacy itself come from the "turn-around generation," young people who recognize that they are inheriting a world with serious work to be done. Heather McLeod, Chloe Breyer and Leslie Crutchfield founded a

Who Cares? magazine right after their Harvard graduation in 1993, as a rallying point for young people with a social vision and a practical outlook. The magazine provides dependable and articulate one-stop shopping on public sector management and leadership, community service, philanthropy, community organizing, and other dimensions of making the world a better place.

The labor movement ("the people who brought you the weekend") is alive and in a good many places, well. "Union Summer" in 1997 re-created much of the high energy of Freedom Summer in the 1960s, bringing 1,200 college students into organizing internships across the country. Union organizers build support for union representation and engage in ongoing education and advocacy. An organizer is usually, but not always, a practitioner in a trade who also has skill in communication, administration, consensus building and strategy. Shop stewards, who generally hold full-time industrial or trade jobs and double in this role, act as advocates for workers or workforces when there's trouble. Some union positions are elected, and others are competitively hired. At the state, national, and international levels, union research staffs, pension fund investors, and other professionals create organizing strategies and service packages to support the workforce, both while it's on the job and after retirement. The investment of union pension funds, one of the largest pools of concentrated capital, is becoming recognized as a force with major potential to affect federal and state policy.

The world of union organizing can be somewhat nomadic, but a coherent path can be forged by attaching oneself to an issue or a constituency. For example, John Wilhelm, who led the pioneering Yale clerical and technical organizing drive in 1984, is now president of the Hotel and Restaurant Employees International union.

As technical, administrative and professional workforces adapt to the new world of work, professional unions such as the National Writers Union are making a mark. Many professional societies, like the American Association of University Women and National Association of Social Workers, fight hard as advocates for their members on bread-and-butter issues. Professional and trade associations — such as those in mental health, alternative health care, and natural food — are on the lookout for legislation that stands to influence members' choices of methods, and their ability to be compensated for their work; for example, they watchdog controversies over labeling laws designating nutritional supplements as drugs and licensing requirements for alternative health modalities. The larger associations have national staff that provide member services (such as health benefits), publications, research, and direct lobbying.

Mediation

The *Wall Street Journal* announced a few years ago that it had figured out why Rome wasn't built in a day: "No facilitators." Beneath the coy headline, though, was a respectful article about teamwork and communication trainings in the building trades. From ordinary confusion and insensitivity among co-workers, to rough waters between collaborating businesses, breaches in labor-management relations, and disputes involving many stakeholders, most of us have experienced the paralysis that comes from workplace conflicts. Mediation, negotiation, and related skills are gaining wide respect.

Leah Haygood's path illustrates where a mediator can go by focusing on a set of issues. With background in renewable energy projects, she entered Yale School of Forestry and Environmental Studies interested in mediation in the early 1980s. There wasn't a lot of coursework available, so she got to create her own through internships. She settled on a one-year internship with Resolve, a mediation program developed by the Conservation Foundation (and later spun off as an independent organization). This led to a full-time job as a mediator there, which kept her happy and busy for five years. But she "started feeling an itch, and some nonprofit burnout."

Haygood was recruited by Waste Management, Inc. where she spent seven years developing the company's public environmental reporting and other programs to implement its ambitious environmental policy. During that time, her skills were put to work as a facilitator for internal process improvement teams. She also started a family, and began looking for ways to create a more flexible work schedule. When a corporate reorganization eliminated her position, Haygood was able to create a freelance career in project development and mediation, working at home two days a week and retaining both Resolve and Waste Management as major clients. Soon Resolve hired her back on a part-time basis to develop new projects.

On the field of mediation, she observes, "It's growing. There are always predictions that it will explode, but what's actually happening is steady growth using mediation in a variety of areas. Most court systems have programs. Labor-management and family issues are major. Two growth areas that especially interest me are commercial applications and mediation programs in the schools." Breaking into the field requires commitment, and sometimes ingenuity, in creating those first experiences. Haygood also notes that the opportunities to mediate go far beyond the obvious: "For every person with a full-time job in mediation, there are many more who do it as part of a planning commission, or on the board of their cooperative, in many different settings."

Every time a major social issue or policy initiative comes to life, opportunities for mediation come with it, whether it's youth violence or the Americans with Disabilities Act. Fields making major use of mediation include law, business management, public administration, labor relations, community organizing, and much more. For example, Peter Shapiro runs a landlord counseling program for the Cambridge, Massachusetts city government. He helps mostly small- to medium-sized landlords deal with tenant difficulties in ways geared toward reducing the risk of eviction. His tools include structured training on the business of landlording; one-on-one problem-solving assistance; and direct mediation. A master's degree in urban planning plus a certificate from the Harvard Program on Negotiation led Shapiro into this role, to which he brings the added credibility of being a landlord in the three-family building where he lives across the river in Boston.

Law

Most, if not all, public controversies have legal dimensions. As a result, the range of legal specialties that can be practiced from a public interest perspective is vast. Consider homelessness and poverty, community redevelopment, environmental issues, election law, bioethics, immigration, substance abuse, and trade issues — for starters. Most lawyers work for the people with most money, and many lawyers are unhappy with their careers. Seventy percent of lawyers responding to a California survey said that, if they had the opportunity to start a new career, they would take it; 73 percent said they would not recommend a legal career to their children. The institutions and networks of public interest law are being sustained for the long haul by lawyers, paralegals, and support staff who think these trends are connected and see the necessity to help lawyers expand their horizons in the public interest. This is the spirit behind the move by Ralph Nader's Harvard Law School class to establish Appleseed Centers for public interest law around the US, to address systemic problems and improve local and state policy. "There's a lot happening out there when you start looking," counsels Elissa Lichtenstein of the American Bar Association's Public Services Division, "and once you find out about a few opportunities, it mushrooms."

Ronald Fox's valuable book, *Lawful Pursuit,* surveys the terrain of public interest law, beginning with national organizations whose mission is to litigate in the public interest. These are not numerous, he notes, but "While there are only about 3,300 lawyers in such positions, many have achieved some spectacular results and are held in high regard by the legal profession and society in general." Because test cases or class action suits filed by major organizations have the power to affect entire demographic groups, there is high impact to working with organizations like the Children's Defense Fund, Native American Legal Defense Fund, Lambda Legal Defense and Education Fund (gay and lesbian rights), National Organization of Women's Legal Defense and Education Fund, NAACP Legal Defense Fund, American Civil Liberties Union, and Natural Resources Defense Counsel, to name some of the most prominent. But statewide coalitions and community projects also offer a wide range of opportunities for high-impact legal practice. The smaller the organization, often, the greater the variety of work available to anyone in it. The practice of public interest law can include litigation itself, research, training community advocates and citizens, teaching in a law school, writing and publication, negotiating, and much more. Law firms, companies, nonprofits with legal departments, specialty clinics in law schools, government agencies and private practice are some of the venues for practicing law in the public interest. With a strong enough focus, you may identify a need and create a practice — or a project — to fill it.

Sanford Lewis, an environmental lawyer in Boston, has tapped into this entrepreneurial spirit as founder of a national initiative called the Good Neighbor Project for Sustainable Industries. He tells this story:

> *Early in my career, I was a lawyer for the Massachusetts Public Interest Research Group working on legislation, and particularly on "Right to Know" laws giving workers the information they needed about the safety of chemicals they came into contact with. I was very much involved in lobbying and hated it. I'm not a schmoozer. But I put a lot of effort into this. And, as the state law was negotiated, I came to believe that the real influence was wielded at a level higher than mine, through the negotiations of players like unions and the governor's office.*

Meanwhile, I was doing some stuff I liked more, which was negotiating the language of legislative and regulatory provisions. But it was so abstract and removed from the real problems people had in real neighborhoods. I concluded that I needed to move away from that whole lobbying arena to more grassroots level.

Under the auspices of another nonprofit, the National Toxics Campaign, Lewis ended up crafting an approach to bringing community coalitions into direct negotiation with local industries to work out agreements on issues of concern, from chemical safety to corporate migration. He recalls,

My first intensive contact with a grassroots group was positive in a way that really turned my life in a new direction. It was in Worcester, Massachusetts, in the neighborhoods around the chemical plant Lewcott. I was working with absolutely mainstream Americans, a school bus driver, the mailman, the policeman, the gym teacher, helping them to profoundly empower themselves to the point that they got this company to sign an agreement as to a schedule on when it would move out of the neighborhood. We did a brainstorming exercise on the question, "How can we gain power in this situation?" and we literally filled a living room's walls with newsprint. I followed up with coaching on the phone, but it was the community people who implemented the strategy and brought the company to the negotiating table. They became, in the process, a really cohesive, empowered neighborhood. I loved it.

Today, Lewis directs the Good Neighbor Project nationally from his home office in the Boston area. The concept has taken off to the extent that he devotes most of his time to training others in local areas, and coaching them — still on the phone. His hardest struggle is to hang onto that sense of spark that comes from direct work with communities. Sometimes he does this by getting out into the field, and sometimes by schlepping his computer and cell phone to the local café where home-based professionals with cabin fever seem to gather. His innovation has led to a career that's satisfying but not without frustration — and one that he continues to reinvent every season.

Banking, Finance, and Investment

The banking industry has had its share of struggles with both communities and regulators, leading some banks to target funds for community economic development while others run in the opposite direction. The same is true for environmental businesses. Chicago's South Shore Bank is a recognized leader in community investment. Ecotrust, in the Pacific Northwest, is a think-action tank on building a sustainable economy. They teamed up with a long-range vision that has recently come to fruition. First, they pulled together some money, through South Shore Bank's FDIC-insured EcoDeposits option for customers. Then they created a new financial institution, Shore Trust Bank, in Willapa Bay, Washington. Focusing on commercial lending to targeted businesses in the Pacific Northwest coastal rainforest,

*Tammy Newmark works for the
Nature Conservancy, managing a large investment
fund that backs economic development projects in
environmentally sensitive areas of Latin America.
The fund targets partnerships between ecologically
sound, for-profit businesses and community organizations that receive a percentage of the venture's
profits, thus promoting economic and community
development in tandem. This is her story:*

When I was first out of Wharton with my MBA, I
said "I want to get into international development." I talked to a woman who said, "Well,
honey, what does that mean?" She sat with me
patiently until I honed it down.

I always had an interest in developing countries
and microenterprise. I had started my career on
Wall Street. I tried to move directly into economic
development work and was told it was too competitive without an advanced degree. So I got the
MBA but then went back to Wall Street, and
began meeting a lot of people who had done
international work. Many were involved with
women's programs. While working at Chase
Manhattan Bank, I organized a big program. Sixty
or seventy women met every two months and
brought in speakers from agencies like Accion
Internacional and the Women's World Bank. So I
made contact with top executives who were bringing about change in this market. I was so intrigued
that I had to get involved.

While I was in business school, I saw a little ad in
the Wall Street Journal for exactly the work I wanted to do. They were a two-person shop, and they
didn't hire me, but they kept my resume on file.
Then, when the first environmental venture fund
was started, this resume got passed around and I
was hired by the Environmental Enterprise

Assistance Fund. I stayed there 6 years. I moved
into a business advisory group assisting community businesses in developing countries. I found there
was capital out there, but nobody to do the hand-
holding for the startups, nobody to help them
write business plans, establish linkages, get their
products to market. I moved on to a company
called TechnoServe, and spent two-and-a-half
years working on starting advisory groups for
small environmental businesses.

I had been in the field in different capacities for
nine years. So when my current program needed a
head person, they knocked on my door. The small-
to medium-sized enterprise is clearly the key to
economic growth for Latin America and the
Caribbean. By incorporating an environmental
mandate, while making money by better management, we show it's possible to allow a resource to
be preserved over time. My job is to create models
that will bring other investors and financial actors
in, and get business leaders more involved with
nonprofit agendas.

To be in this field at this level, you need the energy, enthusiasm and patience to be able to push
the mission. You also need the technical skills to
actually do the business, not to mention a good
gut feel and business acumen. We're dealing with
entrepreneurs who face a lot of risks, from basic
business problems to political risks. We have to be
in there with them.

I find this the most creative and fun. It's a passion, and it definitely has its own lifestyle. I'm
from Burlington, VT, and I hope eventually to
spend half the year in Burlington and half the year
based in the region. Right now, we're fundraising.
So, if I have to be in Washington or New York a
lot, that's where I'll be.

this bank is doing no more than what (we like to think) old-fashioned local banks did: targeting for investment those businesses that will serve the community's long-term interest. And it's an idea that can be replicated in every community.

If sustainable economics is about forging a linkage between social values and financial returns, then there's an outrageous possibility of real money to be made by supporting, or participating in, enterprises that serve the common good. It's no longer a new idea that plenty of investors want to vote their values with their dollars. This idea has given rise to a generation of socially screened investment portfolios, socially responsible stockbrokers and financial advisors, and national organizations such as the Social Investment Forum to promote this arm of the industry. Early innovators, mostly in smaller firms, have done the difficult groundwork needed to make the concept practical by developing solid enough measures of both social and financial performance to give investors competitive returns. Lately a new level of investor interest has prompted Wall Street to take a fresh look at these upstarts.

Lisa Leff is a portfolio manager for the Socially Aware Investment Fund of Salomon Smith Barney Asset Management, a fund she has helped to grow from an embryonic level. Back in 1991, Leff was an idealistic graduate of the Wharton School of Business. She thought of using her marketing background in "helping some groovy startup figure out what messages to put on their packages," but found that none of the salaries in those startups would cover her student loan repayments. She spent a year working with the Council on Economic Priorities, a highly regarded research and education organization, managing a research program on the social and environmental practices of major corporations. But she confesses, "I came in as Ms. Hotshot MBA, and got restless really fast wanting to do everything. Not necessarily cool in a nonprofit environment." Phone contact with the major brokerage firm of Smith Barney led to an invitation to create a social investment program there. She said no a few times, then finally surrendered.

When Leff took over the project, the company managed $150 million in socially screened investments for some 700 investors. Today it's worth over a billion dollars, and represents more than 4,000 accounts. Smith Barney has since merged with Salomon Brothers, and Leff is sitting on the only major socially screened portfolio program on Wall Street. She works in a team of seven with another portfolio manager, a couple of social researchers, account administrators, and investment analysts who cover specific sectors. She observes, "It's exhausting. We have grown so fast. Being part of a large, publicly traded company means you are part of a strict cost-cutting environment, you have to battle for resources no matter how well you do. Even though I would argue that this approach to investment is really more prudent — minimizing risk exposure and waste, just for starters — it takes energy to make that case when people are used to thinking about a single bottom line and not taking these factors into consideration."

Still, she has been able to create a major ripple effect by being at the international center of this program. That gives her the freedom to reach out to the company's 500 offices and 10,000 brokers in the field with a simple proposition: "Every time a client walks into your office, and you see that some of their charitable giving goes to Defenders of Wildlife or

NOW, just ask them if they want to make sure that their investments are consistent with their values. Just ask them."

As that question has made the rounds, demand for socially screened investments has grown, creating opportunities both elite and ordinary. To speed up the educational process, though, Leff began working with the New York Society of Securities Analysts, the industry's main association. Together, they developed a seminar series and annual conference to get to the heart of the question, "What do we attach value to, and why?" Companies with proactive social and environmental policies have been eager to speak to the investment community, and the dialogues continue.

Parallel to the growth of socially aware investment, there is an embryonic but growing population of venture capitalists, management consultants, technical advisors, and others available in the world of institutional investment to guide dealmakers in evaluating social and environmental impacts of business ventures they are financing. Linda Descano has created a fascinating job for herself as Environmental Officer in the investment banking firm of Salomon Brothers, now merged with Smith Barney. In many finance-related fields, the standard job description for an environmental professional is to make sure the print shop is not spewing anything hazardous, and to deal with recycling, energy efficiency, and other office management considerations. But Descano recognized that these things would come to nothing if the company were to run aground of major environmental disaster in one of its investments. She saw her job as a way to bring environmental due diligence into the normal process of analyzing a prospective deal. She explains:

> We've been working to understand how environmental trends shape the competitiveness of the companies we work with, as a research function, so we can improve our capacity to reduce risk as a lender or in underwriting securities, improve the performance of securities and know who's ahead of the curve by understanding the environmental drivers of business performance. As the trend toward sustainable development takes off, shifting the industrial focus from end of pipe to pollution prevention — which is a question of corporate strategy — the company that can anticipate and factor these things in will be more competitive. If you think about climate change and the processes that affect it, you see that this issue transcends countries and markets, and can reshape an entire industry.
>
> There are always environmental actions that will be a cost of doing business. It would be simplistic to say that they can all be business opportunities. But, increasingly, issues of environment — not to mention racial and gender equality — are becoming more integral to a company's market share, brand integrity, ability to access new markets, maintain existing market share, and be competitive in terms of operating costs.

A geologist with strong coursework in communications and public policy, Descano has been "used to seeing any issue holistically, across the range of impacts." Hired as an environmental consultant, she had a chance to work with companies that were paying the price for environmental short-sightedness. She knew that banks lend money for real estate and that, under Superfund law, they can incur liability for toxic surprises. The linkages between environment and finance became clear in her mind "over the years, interacting with people from other banks." She began talking with upper management about the value of anticipating issues and providing more diversified services to clients, and gives credit to the company's "visionary management" for listening to her pitches to create something new.

> *Wall Street is a very challenging crowd, and with all the consolidation underway it will only get more challenging. They're critical. They question everything. Innovation requires very thick skin and very good data to make a point so that it's attractive to my culture.*

As companies formalize the notion of multiple bottom lines and environmental accountability, there is also a growing need for ecological economists and a rising appreciation of this role. In fact, it's flagged as one of the 25 hottest careers by *Working Woman* magazine in 1996, which noted that "Between 1980 and 1993, cleanup costs for air, water and solid waste in the US rose $13 billion, to $89 billion. That's why there is more demand than ever for environmental economists, who assess the costs of cleanup and find environmentally friendly solutions that won't break the bank for taxpayers and businesses." The University of Maryland has a pioneering PhD program in this field, with senior faculty including Herman Daly, author of several seminal books and formerly of the World Bank. Governments at all levels, banks, private companies, and nongovernmental organizations all employ ecological economists, with entry level salaries around $30K and senior compensation above $100,000.

Ethics Officers

Although born of corporate scandals, the business ethics movement has matured and grown more sophisticated and substantive as companies recognize the motivating power of authentic values — and the disarray and risk exposure that comes from disregarding them. Michael Hoffman and Dawn-Marie Driscoll of the Center for Business Ethics in Boston report on the high cost of ethical violations:

- Texaco was fined $176 million for racial discrimination after tape recordings of improper conversations among top executives were released;
- Archer-Daniels-Midland paid a $100 million fine for price-fixing;
- Laboratory Corporation of America paid $187 million in fines and penalties for health care billing fraud; and
- Louisiana-Pacific paid $37 million for customer and environmental fraud.

Added to the wake-up call of pure expense has been the 1991 Federal Sentencing Guidelines for Organizations, which impose heavy fines and strict probation conditions mandated for organizations convicted of federal crimes. The Guidelines contained a brilliant incentive to develop meaningful ethics programs. They decreed that fines could be cut, and prosecution avoided, if companies could show that they had created such programs as a good-faith effort to prevent violations. Very quickly, the high-level position of Corporate Ethics Officer came into being in a majority of publicly held corporations. Their professional society, the Ethics Officers Association, now has a membership of 500, and sponsors conferences, research, education, and a certification program.

John Ferraro, Ethics Officer for Orange and Rockland electric utility in New York State, holds a position that has been designed by building on lessons learned in other companies. Ferraro does not report to the CEO, but to the chair of an independent audit committee on the board — "an essential feature to give me the autonomy to do my job." Often, his job deals with issues as ordinary and yet challenging as employee conflicts of interest and sports gambling on the job. And his path into the position is also growing more common. He was chosen not for any specialization in ethics, but for his strong networks and credibility in the company, gained through his previous job in building design.

If you hold a title like Chief Ethics Officer or Vice-President for Corporate Ethics, your role will likely include helping to build an internal consensus on ethical standards; crafting a code that is understandable and, hopefully, inspiring; running it by lawyers, top executives, union and shareholder representatives, and others; training the workforce in the code itself and in expectations about how they will make decisions; providing some kind of low-risk way for employees to report abuses and get help in handling dilemmas; and evaluating the effectiveness of all you have created.

There is a growing body of research that employee retention, morale, and productivity are positively affected by a culture that employees regard as "values-based." Maybe for this reason, Hoffman and Driscoll believe, "global managers are now exchanging ideas about values programs, rather than just compliance programs."

Government

As government devolves, more and more of the work to be done in implementing policies is at the local level: through elected officials, political appointees, and their staffs. Consider the range of roles that are arising as communities take a fresh look at their priorities and innovative ways to achieve them.

June Holte gets paid to do exactly what she loves: helping people redesign their own lifestyles to use fewer resources, free up time, and add spark to their daily existence. Holte is a program manager for the Community Lifestyle Campaign of Kansas City, Missouri, a partnership between the city's Office of Environmental Management and the nonprofit Global Action Plan of Woodstock, New York. Before she and the city found each other, Holte's career path had included community organizing for an energy-conservation program, energy education for junior high schoolers, mediation, managing a co-op, transit advocacy, guiding cave tours, waiting tables, and construction demolition. She sold herself, in part based on her eclectic mix of skills, and in part by being the most enthusiastic candidate. For the city, this step was a natural outgrowth of a program called Clean Sweep, where neighborhood teams match "sweat equity" with city services to help clean up vacant lots, plant community gardens, maintain parks, and generally make their neighborhoods more livable. Clean Sweep itself was born out of the reinvention of government — the need to provide more services with fewer resources. In many cities and towns, this process means a new openness to innovative programs.

More and more environmental protection decisions are being made at the local level, from the delivery of municipal services to land protection to transportation policy to industrial development decisions. As a result, local governments are employing recycling coordinators and market developers, bike trail developers, water conservation educators, planners, and many other specialists. There might be a dozen of these in a small town, and a hundred in a major city. But with 17,000 cities, towns, counties and other local entities on the US map, the opportunities add up.

According to Dennis Church of EcoIQ, who has helped design these programs for such cities as San José, California, "Local governments have always had a primary responsibility for environmental quality. They, after all, plan land use and transportation systems, adopt and enforce codes, run local water and sewer utilities, pick up the garbage and recycling, and so on." He outlines three categories of local jobs. The first is designing programs to meet these environmental goals — and keeping the municipality in compliance with federal and state regulations. The second is enforcing local law and policy. The third, and often most creative, is working proactively to help businesses, homeowners, and others find greener ways to do what they do.

Government jobs can be local, state, federal, international, and regional, as well as hybrids of these. Regional associations and councils of government are formed to address social or environmental problems that are larger than a community but do not fit neatly in state boundaries, such as air quality, immigration, or trade. Many government jobs require a mix of technical, conceptual and political skills that doesn't come easy for everyone. For the same reasons they're challenging, though, they can provide a base for experimentation and a surprising degree of mobility. One of the most spectacular examples of "local-government-as-springboard" is the saga of Jeb Brugmann, whose path started in Cambridge, Massachusetts, and has led to a top job as founder of a global agency. This story is convoluted but glorious. During the 1980s, Cambridge was heavily involved in Sister City programs and in an embryonic movement known as "municipal foreign policy" — one part serious populism and one part tweaking the federal government. Brugmann helped start a Cambridge Peace Commission and served a term as its first chair. Then he took a personal sabbatical at the John F. Kennedy School of Government at Harvard. On graduating, he steeped himself in environmental issues to prepare for a hot state job that fell through. He ended up as Field Director for the Center for Innovative Diplomacy, a national nonprofit aimed at helping local governments to make their voices heard in setting national priorities and shaping international relations. The issue that grabbed him was air quality.

The year was 1989. The big issue was ozone protection. Brugmann was key in pulling together 30 local governments to sign a treaty with each other to phase out chlorofluorocarbons in compliance with the Montreal Protocol. This treaty hit the news — with aggressive local media outreach in 30 cities to fuel the national story — just as the Bush Administration's weak Clean Air Act was proposed. "The press had a field day with the David-Goliath story." Noel Brown, head of the United Nations Environment Program, tracked down Brugmann and crew. Brown offered them access to local governments through

UN channels to create something broader, an umbrella organization called the International Council for Local Environmental Initiatives. Headquartered in Toronto, ICLEI helps its over 150 member municipalities to create and implement "Local Agenda 21" plans for sustainable development. In every one of those cities, there are at least dozens of jobs focusing more on community and environmental benefits as a result.

Artists

Among the most powerful catalysts for claiming and living out new visions are the world's visual and performing artists, and the wider community of choreographers, stage designers, conductors, gallery owners, curators, art teachers and others — professional and amateur — who keep the spark alive. The high profile of struggles with arts funding in recent years may mask the fact that people do make a living in the arts. Susan Togut's work came to my attention when she displayed a series of exquisite 'Healing Mandalas' at the Women's Wellness Center in Kingston, New York. She sketches her career path this way:

> I trained as painter, and did sculpture. Gradually my work became more dimensional. I moved into what's called environmental art — creating installations designed for particular places or themes. Through this, I realized I was interested as much in the space between objects and people as I was in the objects themselves. Thus, I was exploring transparency, color, and light, in installations that were very ephemeral, about the connection between private and communal worlds.

> By the mid-80's, following a master's degree in fine arts, I became a 'public artist' in New York City, focusing on installation work. I started competing for opportunities, grants, and funding to facilitate large-scale projects. One thing led to another, and soon I was heavily involved in inner city, community revitalization work. Initially, on a creative level, I was most interested in developing indoor and outdoor, environmental installations. This kind of work is well suited for downtown areas, waterfronts, parks, and so on. Simultaneously I became more aware of my love of nature. In the process of mounting public art projects, which I created for and with diverse communities, I realized I had a natural awareness or instinct for working with people — and public art is very people-oriented work. Throughout this period I was teaching in schools and community centers to supplement my income. My educational work, focused on empowering individuals and groups, became naturally entwined with my public art work.

> There was a turning point. In the Bedford-Stuyvesant section of Brooklyn, I was invited to create an outdoor environment for and with a community. It involved a series of simulated, stained glass panels, with images of people working in their community gardens and the surrounding neighborhood. The neighborhood people helped me build a scaffolding and wrote a text

with all their thoughts of living in the community, working on the project, their hopes and dreams. I designed and painted the 'stained glass' panels. People provided their text in their own handwriting. They participated in the project conceptually and structurally. Though the process was slow, a strong core of community members came to support it.

The project was beautiful and successful. It was never vandalized because community members felt a sense of ownership. In the process, my sense of my self as a professional artist was changed completely. I realized it was not right for me to go into a community and make art for people. Instead, I became the facilitator, the orchestrator. Since then, I've been mounting public art projects which are created by the people for themselves, whole communities of artists. In Bedford Stuyvesant I partnered with a wonderful, neighborhood woman to conduct a 'Public Art and Education' program, which ran for six years. Through this program we secured a second community garden, for which we created a totem gazebo, murals and other artworks. In subsequent public art endeavors I've expanded the involvement of intergenerational community members.

Today, Togut lives in a rural community in New York State. She continues her community revitalization work, along with an expanded interest in the arts and healing. Her nonprofit, grant-based work supports her as she strives to protect her creative time as a practicing artist. Her definition of herself as a public art facilitator, creative artist, educator and healer, has developed, in spiral fashion, informed by this body of experience. She has worked on environmental installations along local waterways and created history mural projects. Additionally, she works with cancer patients and their loved ones, long-term care residents, and others in the creation of healing art, such as mandalas and a permanent 'Healing Circle Arbor.' Whatever she's involved in, Togut sums up, "Above all, I teach people attitudes such as self-esteem, taking risks, awareness of process, and perseverance. Then they can teach themselves to be artists. These individuals become creative microcosms for the community at large."

PART TWO

THE TEN-STEP PROGRAM FOR PRINCIPLED CAREER DEVELOPMENT

Step 1:
Wake Up

"Intelligence is fine, but what really matters is awareness."

— Phil Jackson, basketball coach

Who Are You, and What Do You Think Is Going On Around Here?

The ability to self-reflect is essential to long-term change. But it's one of the hardest skills to cultivate and to integrate into a demanding life. A New York architect I met a few years ago spoke for many people when he said, "Sure, I have time to reflect on my life — sometimes five minutes at a stretch, if I'm alone in a cab." Without this ability, though, people can try on new behavior patterns, but can't fit them into an integrated sense of self and therefore can't keep them going reliably. In transpersonal psychologies and spiritual traditions, there is nearly universal attention paid to the "observer self" or "witness," the part of one's being that watches and integrates the rest. Cultivating this capability is demanding, in the same way that exercise and nutrition are demanding — and equally essential. In *Voluntary Simplicity*, Duane Elgin makes the point:

> *The crucial importance of penetrating behind our continuous stream of thought (as largely unconscious and lightning-fast flows of inner fantasy-dialogue) is stressed by every major consciousness tradition in the world: Buddhist, Taoist, Hindu, Sufi, Zen, etc. Western cultures, however, have fostered the understanding that a state of continual mental distraction is in the natural order of things.*

> *Consequently, by virtue of a largely unconscious social agreement about the nature of our inner thought processes, we live individually and collectively almost totally embedded within our mental constructed reality.*

Self-reflection does not mean self-obsession. In my experience, the people who strike the best balance between introspection and action are those who spend most of their time focusing outward and functioning without undue complexity, but "check in with themselves" with some regularity.

There is a widespread hunger for this level of consciousness. Columnist Colman McCarthy points to the rising popularity of monasteries and other religious retreat centers among people of every conceivable background, who come for weekends and longer spells of quiet, meditation, walking, and reading. McCarthy, who spent some years in a spiritual community himself "to get some traction before lurching into adulthood," has put his ear to the ground to learn more about this phenomenon. He quotes professional golfer Tom Stewart, who checks himself into Gethsemani monastery in Kentucky every fall for a decompression period that is the opposite of a retreat. In Stewart's mind, it's "an advance — because you go forward" more effectively when you stop to get oriented.

Going to a special place for this purpose has the obvious advantage of screening outside stimulation and distraction. But it also segregates the process of reflection from the rest of your life. Many people prefer to identify places and times for quiet that can fit readily into their existing patterns. One useful approach comes from Danaan Parry, a former Atomic Energy Commission scientist who founded the Earthstewards Network and for many years ran workshops internationally on spiritual, earth-centered living. Following the traditions of many Native American nations, Parry recommended identifying your "power spot" in nature, a place "where you can relatively easily tap back into your Aloneness. It's a natural setting that holds for you the qualities of calm, quiet, wild, earthy, grounded, centered. It is for you only." That power spot is close enough for easy access, yet self-contained and far enough away from human settlement to welcome your whole being, not just the civilized parts. A park or rooftop garden, a meadow on the edge of town — any of these will suffice if they ease you out of habitual ways of seeing and into wholeness.

What's important is finding the time to reflect, whatever is going on. This, in turn, requires paying new attention to the balance of life.

What does it take for you to find "down time" for reflection and renewal?

What opportunities for self-reflection exist in your everyday life — morning quiet time, for example?

How could these be expanded or better protected, even in little ways?

From Department of Labor offices to church basements, wherever job search support groups gather, you can see the signs of stress and bad self-care: the gaggles of smokers outside, the coffee and donuts. Don't go there. A life transition is a time to take exquisite care of yourself, and learn low-budget ways to do that. Here is a starter-list for you to build on:

1. take out new kinds of musical records and tapes at the library

2. walk in new neighborhoods

3. go to the museum on "free days"

4. trade massages with a friend

5. stretch and exercise regularly

6. go for a hike or a boat ride

7. hang out with people of many generations

8. call friends on the phone and pay attention to how they're doing

9. dance around your living room ➔

Listen. Question. Listen.

One way to ease into awakeness is through listening: to people, to music, to the sounds of the ocean or the city or the ballpark. Listening is not the same as waiting for another person to finish talking so you can have your turn. Listening means opening up to new experience and ways of knowing, without letting your expectations screen them out.

One of the most powerful illustrations of the potential of listening is a highly effective nonprofit called the Piedmont Peace Project. This multiracial community organization in rural North Carolina has registered over 15,000 black voters since the mid-1980s, and produced a major shift in the voting record of the region's representative in Congress. The project uses teams who make door-to-door visits in low-income neighborhoods, meeting people who are not already jaded by salespeople or pollsters. Without rushing or being required to stick too closely to a script, those teams ask people's opinions about how their tax dollars are being spent and how well their voices have been heard in the Congress. Then activists write campaign materials using the language they've heard directly from their neighbors. Not surprisingly, it works.

Imagine listening, really listening, to people you work with and for, and to people you hope will help you in your job search.

Connected to the art of listening is the art of asking questions. Skillful questioning gets you more than answers. It gets you a relationship of creative exploration with another human being. Career strategists Sam Deep and Lyle Sussman promote the art of questioning as a tool for organizational self-defense in their book, *What to Ask When You Don't Know What to Say: 555 Questions to Help You Get Your Way at Work* (e.g. "How will we determine whether or not my performance merits a raise?"). Seen in this light, questioning is a clear source of wider and clearer options for the questioner. Beyond this, it can help the "question-ee" to focus on an issue and to break out of mental boxes.

Social change consultant Fran Peavey teaches a process called "strategic questioning" — asking questions systematically in order to uncover a higher order of possibilities in a situation. Strategic questions are those that move you beyond obvious information, beyond yes and no and multiple choice. They invite you to imagine new possibilities and explore the ways to remove barriers. "Look for the long-lever question," she advises — that is, the question with the most leverage to get things moving. For instance, "What would it take for this change to be possible?"

When have you really felt listened to, in your private life and on the job?
At work, how often do you listen deeply to other people?
What could you do to promote more attentive, thoughtful communication?
What are you waiting for?

Wake Up to the Story You Tell Yourself and Others

Questioning is a big-time test of awakeness, and a promoter of it. People's answers will only rarely match your assumptions. What comes out of your own mouth may also contain a surprise or two. So the process is a doorway to another valuable awakening: to the story we tell ourselves and the world, about what's happening and what's possible.

→

10. take bubble baths

11. notice sunsets

12. spend time in the natural environment

13. keep a journal

14. read things you don't normally read, and get plenty of fiction and poetry in your literary diet

15. draw or make up stories with your kids

16. sketch, paint, or make collages

17. introduce yourself to neighbors

18. look for free concerts, lectures, and performances

19. plant trees and edible flora, or do local environmental restoration projects, with people you want to spend more time with

20. get interesting cookbooks from the library and make new treats

21. sing

22. meditate ❖

"All the jobs are the same."
"Nobody is going to help me if I take an initiative."
"I'm too old to make a career change."

Interpretations of the past and preconceptions of the future have enormous power in shaping what we think is "realistic" in the present. In the limbo of changing values and tectonic shifts in the global economy, it is dangerous to leave to others the work of interpreting reality. Finding our own words to tell the story of what is happening around us, and in our own lives, is a fundamental act of self-defense. This was theologian Thomas Berry's point when he wrote:

OK, how do you know?
Recall a time when you've felt stuck. How did you explain the situation? Did you make any assumptions that might have limited your sense of possibility?
Recall a time when you've accomplished something exciting, large or small.
Have you made any assumptions about that experience that might limit your ability to build on it?

It's all a question of story. We are in trouble just now because we do not have a good story. We are in between stories. The old story, the account of how the world came to be and how we fit into it, is no longer effective. Yet we have not learned a new story. Our traditional story of the universe sustained us for a long period of time. It shaped our emotional attitudes, provided us with life purposes, and energized action. It consecrated suffering and integrated knowledge. We awoke in the morning and knew where we were. We could answer the questions of our children. We could identify crime, punish transgressors. Everything was taken care of because the story was there. It did not necessarily make people good, nor did it take away the pains and stupidities of life or make for unfailing warmth in human association. It did provide a context in which life could function in a meaningful manner.

To claim our place in this new story, we must each get fully awake to our part in the old, what keeps us attached to it, our potential for contribution, and the environments we need to create to help us fulfill that potential.

What's necessary to rebuild economy and society, to live in harmony with the environment and ourselves, is not just one set of choices. It's a process of making choices with greater self-awareness, a process of learning to learn. The leaps we need to make will only be possible when personal growth is rescued from the puritan ethic and returned to the realm of play and liberation. One of the finest models of this is the town square or tribal council, hillside or coffeehouse where people gather to exchange stories, celebrating their own foibles in the healing laughter and curiosity of kindred spirits.

Start telling stories about your work history. Just do it, whenever the social occasion arises (in small doses, of course, and paying special attention to the interest shown by your listener).

If you're one who finds more structure useful, then write, talk into a tape recorder, or barter "listening-time" with a friend who might find the same process useful. Try a "career autobiography" — but define the range of "career" for yourself.

Or pace yourself with mini-stories — vignettes that have special significance as triumphs, defeats, turning points or revealing episodes.

Celebrate the strength and resourcefulness of the person who lived through all this and is now on the threshold of something exciting.

Wake Up to the Interconnectedness of Everything

A blip on the Tokyo Stock Exchange can disrupt home mortgage lending rates in Kansas City. North Americans' dependence on beef contributes to keeping people in the developing world away from land and water they need for subsistence farming. Whether or not butterfly wings whirring in China can really cause storms in the Gulf of Mexico, as the chaos theorists have suggested, every action we take is part of an intricate web of causes and effects among human communities and the natural environment. Systems thinking is the practice of seeing these connections and appreciating their significance. You are a system of thoughts, feelings, information, unconscious imagery, memory and more, all interwoven and interdependent. You are also part of a complex social and ecological system. You have a choice: to view these dimensions as sources of complexity to be avoided, or as resources to be tapped.

Enlightened self-interest has a lot to do with recognizing opportunities for creative work that are also opportunities to deepen, and benefit from, human connections. This is very different from seeing yourself as a lone, vulnerable contender, competing with droves of others for a limited range of identical spots. When you take interdependence seriously, competition loses its attractiveness, while negotiation and collaboration are revealed as a path of enduring strength.

Interconnectedness Exercise

What's it like to think about all these loyalties? Is it a bit overwhelming? Here's a way to put them into greater perspective. On a piece of paper, start writing brief phrases to describe problems that concern you. They can be personal, community or global, political, economic, or ecological. Whatever pops up, write it down. Instead of doing it in a list, however, scatter them all over the paper as your imagination dictates. If you have a blackboard or big piece of newsprint, that's even better. When you have run out of ideas, filled up the paper, or gotten impatient to consider what's next, draw lines to indicate any connections you see between problems. They may be cause-and-effect connections. They may have a similar source. They may affect similar people. They may trigger the same responses in you.

Who do you work for (or, if you're out of work, who do you imagine yourself working for)?

Did you naturally leap to one answer? How many other ways can you answer it?

Do you work for an organization? A boss? Customers? Shareholders? The people who rely on your paycheck? A social movement? An innovation you dream about? Future generations? All life on Earth? A few cherished people?

What are your agreements, spoken and unspoken, with each of these groups?

When there's a conflict among these loyalties, as there's bound to be, how is it resolved?

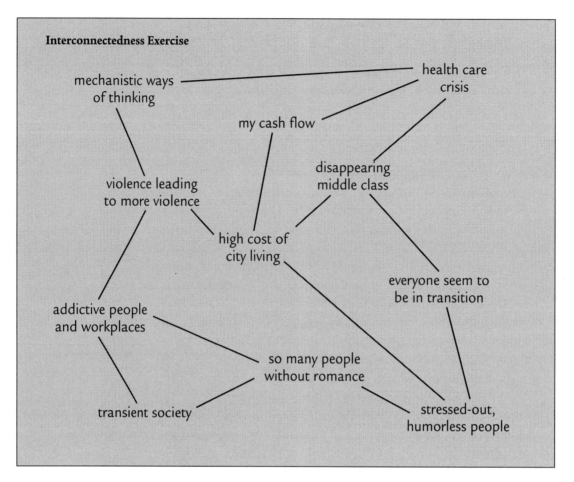

Interconnectedness Exercise

According to psychologist Sarah Conn, who designed this exercise, "Many people have a little 'aha!' moment when they do this; they realize that, wherever they choose to take action or make change, the effects will resonate through the web of connection in ways they never dreamed. What's more, taking action in any area connects you to others in a way that opens up new possibility."

Wake Up to the Beauty and Pain of the World

Waking up to our potential and our opportunities for contribution means taking in the vastness of the disarray and danger around us — not in a spirit of blame, guilt, or victimhood, but as participants capable of focusing our attention in a way that liberates power. Part of this wake-up call is about the present realities of our working lives. In some ways, it's easier to acknowledge the pain of the Albanians in Kosovo or the children of Jonesboro than to face the feelings of compromise, frustration, and failed actualization many of us carry in our own jobs or job searches. A lot of people are on the edge on the job — an observation borne out not only by seething tensions but by overt workplace violence, an epidemic which cost American employers $2.4 billion in 1992. No wonder so many people get so numb. Unfortunately, this adds up to a self-perpetuating cycle.

Psychologist James Hillman has an intriguing theory about the essence of the modern global crisis. In his view, it's the fact that people are anesthetized — literally, cut off from the ability to resonate to beauty in a vigorous enough way to fight for its preservation. To the extent that's true, some of the most potent lines of questioning for uncovering new work opportunities might be these:

When and where have I been moved by beauty lately?
Where can I create beauty? Or preserve it, or make it available more
democratically?
Where can I ease suffering or help to eliminate its root causes?

Seeing, caring, and connecting to the planetary drama in all its forms is also a path to seeing ways out of conflict, stepping out of limiting frames of reference and finding unexpected solutions to problems. It is anything but a soft skill. This attentiveness is what keeps life's tasks and projects on track (and worth doing), a fact recognized by more and more enlightened businesspeople such as James Autry, who writes in *Love and Profit*:

> *Listen.*
> *In every office,*
> *you hear the threads*
> *of love and joy and fear and guilt,*
> *the cries for celebration and reassurance,*
> *and somehow you know that connecting those threads*
> *is what you are supposed to do*
> *and business takes care of itself.*

Waking up, above all, means noticing the richness of life around you, and realizing that you don't have to take care of it all by yourself.

What are your images and feelings about the state of the world?

Do you read the papers or watch the news? When you do, notice how it makes you feel. [This is not as easy as it may sound.]

When you come upon stories that are especially moving — maybe inspiring, maybe wrenching — get in the habit of talking about them with someone. Ask yourself: If I were fearless and had unlimited resources, what action would this story inspire in me?

Step 2:
Stabilize Your Life

"With so much to choose from, no wonder many of us think we can keep doing a little bit of everything, and somehow the important stuff will take care of itself. And small wonder our powers of concentration are so faint we need written instructions to remember to feed the cat."

— Deborah Baldwin

A lawyer I know cut his stress levels and got in shape at the same time with one simple policy. Whenever anyone wanted to meet with him, he suggested that the meeting be held outside — walking briskly. It worked for him. It didn't do his meeting partners any harm either. But it was a good-sized leap out of the box that most people stay in when considering how they might contain the stresses of life. When you are contemplating a major change, those stresses and sources of gridlock do not make it easier. What gets in the way of seeing your next steps clearly? For most of us, a good bit of it is complexity and conflict in our "personal" lives.

One of the strongest reminders of the interconnectedness of the web of life comes when you try to adjust one strand in the web of your own life. Start anywhere. Change anything. And watch everything else shift. Switch jobs, and watch the changes in your social life that result from the new rhythms of your schedule and your new associations. Start or stop a romance, and notice the impact on your motivation to job-hunt. Break out of a limiting self-image, and watch some of your friendships grow stronger while others fizzle or blow apart because your so-called friends had an investment in seeing you as you were.

At this point, it's fair to say the working public can be divided into two categories: those who have taken some steps to simplify their lives, and those who are somewhere in the process of facing (or denying) the challenge. Some of us are seeing how far we can get by taking baby steps. Others of us are considering how radical we can be, in order to go beyond making our chaos more tolerable — to really create lives of coherence.

We all face different circumstances. But virtually all of us can appreciate two underlying themes. The first is shifting our relationship to time and material needs, out of endless cycles of scarcity and excess, into a more steady state: in other words, discovering what "enough" is like. The second is reclaiming a sense of purposefulness in the way we allocate personal resources, including money but also time, good will, emotional energy, and so forth: shifting out of reactive mode and doing whatever we do with deliberateness. Duane Elgin, author of the classic *Voluntary Simplicity*, makes the point that this mode of living isn't just materially simple. It's "voluntary" in the deepest sense — that is, it's about reclaiming control and choice in our lives.

Truly stabilizing your life also includes establishing some kind of right relationship to community and environment. If you live in the Western world, chances are good that you fall into the habit of thinking that you first have to get your "private" self together before you will be capable of being useful "out there" in the world. But if we take seriously the idea of interconnectedness, here's another way the whole picture begins to change. We are highly unlikely to get our lives in balance if they are not integrated into the web of social and ecological community. That's where we get the juice, the beauty, the majesty, the sense of what's important, and the limitations to our own importance. Stabilizing your life is not only about balancing your books: it's also about putting them down and heading for a mountainside.

Everyone I know is wrestling with this. One of the most heartening stories to cross my desk lately is one of the most unsentimental. It's a note from Key Krecker, a college career counselor on the Indian reservation in Arizona, who has evolved his own counseling practice through grappling with the issues of life balancing and priorities. What's distinctive about this story is how much it focuses on visible results, and how much a step-by-step approach actually produced the desired outcomes:

> I'd been attending to spiritual practices for some time and still tried to "manage" a crazified schedule to which I continued to overcommit. Finally, I guess I heard Captain Picard on "Star Trek" say the word "Engage!" enough times that I began to consider what I could actually DO to create space in my life. The list of things that follows seems "simplistic," and I am still engaged with working on them, but I've found that these actions ALONG WITH my attention to spiritual practices, has created more space in my life than I imagined possible:
>
> I committed to a three-year plan to get out of debt.
>
> I got out of debt.
>
> Since I'd gotten out of debt, I no longer needed to take on those "extra" teaching, consulting, and workshop jobs.
>
> I freed up a lot of time.
>
> While getting out of debt, I cultivated practices to scale down my spending, give up recreational shopping, examine my true values and priorities.
>
> I simplified my life.
>
> Living a simpler life opened up time for me to read about and continue developing my commitment to both simplicity and serenity, and deepened my desire for both.
>
> So, a big step in creating more space, for me, was getting out of debt (both financially and metaphorically, as in: no longer mortgaging my time, health and serenity).

> *One of my guides was a line from Ralph Blum's* Book of Runes, *in regard to the rune Eihwaz. It basically says to learn to develop an aversion to the things that cause stress in your life. After "engaging" with the financial stressor of debt, I rewrote my job description (simpler), moved to a smaller home, got rid of tons of clutter (literally and schedule-wise) and found I had more time to be in nature, meditate, and be with family/friends.*

If you are a wild and restless sort, you may be tempted to ignore this chapter and keep thriving on chaos. If that works for you and doesn't drive your loved ones and co-workers mad, fine. But please note that bringing more balance into your life does not mean giving up on all adventure and risk. It just means choosing risks more consciously.

Stabilizing your life simply means creating the conditions for long-term change in the gentlest, most coherent way possible, reducing urgency levels wherever possible and increasing your resilience. It isn't impossible to be resourceful in the midst of a crisis. But it's easier in the calm zones. Don't worry: we're not going to try to solve all the rest of life's problems before proceeding on the work front. We're just going to open up a little space.

You may be in an acute crisis. Maybe you've just lost your job. If so, get your librarian to rush-order Kathleen Riehle's *What Smart People Do When Losing Their Jobs.* This informative and compassionate manual covers everything from financial planning to interim health insurance to unemployment benefits to family coping.

You may be in some kind of acute trouble that keeps you pinned in an undesirable work situation (or keeps you from finding work). You may be stuck in a violent relationship, an addiction, psychological struggles, or even a job situation so dangerous or demeaning that it leaves very little left of you with which to create a future. If this is the case, please do all you can to break free, starting now. Let the attractive force of more interesting work and a saner life give you the courage to draw new boundaries. Consult the resource list at the end of this book for a lifeline or two.

However, if you're in "just" the usual disarray experienced by a person whose work situation is uncertain, read on. The work of stabilizing your life covers a number of categories:

Surveying the terrain — looking at what's working and what needs attention, what personal and material resources you have and what's missing, which struggles are inevitable and which ones are the result of bad planning;

Plugging major leaks in the structure — stemming any uncontrolled flows of time, money, or attention which keep you from effectively making the changes you want to see;

My husband and I fell in love with each other in '61 and got married in 1965. Most of the time we have been each other's best support in holding on to our perspectives about work and life. At this point in our lives we both have work that often occurs on weekends, so we reserve one weekday every week as our "California days," days on which we do nothing practical, just the way we would if we were away on vacation in California! This gets us out in nature together, listening to music together, sharing journaling notes from separate workshops, or whatever we feel like! I highly recommend it!

—Margaret Lobenstine, career counselor and coach from Massachusetts

Removing toxic influences — looking at current relationships (on the job, social, or intimate) that may be holding you back, and at scars from past experiences which may have unconsciously limited your sense of possibility;

Strengthening the foundation — reinforcing your life-support system in every sense, from education to financial self-sufficiency to the availability of tools you need to make your chosen changes.

This is obviously too much to do all at once. But it is a process to begin now and continue with a gentle, steady approach, as if you were untangling a knot of necklaces that have been lying in the dresser drawer for years. That calls for three qualities: finely-focused attention to detail; the ability to look at a situation from many different angles, and to see the parts within the whole; and high levels of frustration tolerance — which can be cultivated through a mindfulness practice, which is why Step 1 of this program is Step 1.

This book is being written in a time of economic expansion and relatively full employment. The instability many of us are experiencing (the "lucky ones") is a result of too many opportunities, flawed though they all seem to be. However, we all know in our bones that this situation is not likely to be permanent. Economic cycles, downsizings, globalization, and other destabilizing forces make it necessary to face how much of the conditions surrounding our working lives will always be outside our control. Social and environmental innovators must think about recession-proofing and disaster-proofing their working lives, by building kinds of security that do not easily vaporize (such as durable goods, strong relationships, and the skill of self-nurturance on relatively little money).

Take it one step at a time. Each step you take toward balance and resilience will make future movement easier. If you are living within the normal chaos range for a working person in an industrial economy, consider what you could do with a three- to six-month Stabilization Plan, starting now. That's not

> **Wisdom from Maine farmer Amy Dacyczyn, publisher of *The Tightwad Gazette*:**
>
> A tightwad tends to be fearless in an uncertain economy. He knows that as long as there is enough money for basic needs, he can live quite happily without luxuries. He knows that there will always be Christmas because he can create it from nothing. He knows he can wring more miles from his old car. He knows he can feed his family well from his extensive repertoire of hamburger recipes. Most importantly, he doesn't feel like a victim of economic circumstances beyond his control. While he might dip into savings for a period of time, his lifestyle need not change. He is in control.

Exercise: A Time Budget

As precisely as possible, estimate the way you spend your time in a typical week.

Consider: employment, formal study, personal development, health, rest and sleep, time in the natural environment, social relationships, play, creativity, citizenship, volunteer activities, business ventures.

Where might you be pouring energy that isn't high-quality or high-priority?

What are your priorities for more attention (or more thoughtful use of available time)?

What is one action you can take to stabilize your life by using these blocks of time more creatively?

Life-Stabilization Worksheet

Aspect of life	Desired results this month	Action steps	Done (For now)?
MATERIAL Where are the toxic dumps? Borrowed items to return? Broken or missing equipment? Unmaintained systems?			
WORKPLACE If you're working, how can you put your house in order? Got sick time for job hunting? Need to activate contacts? How are your references?			
RELATIONSHIPS Do you have time and emotional energy for friends? Are there important relationships that need attention? Do your loved ones understand and support your present changes?			
FINANCE[14] What are your basic expenses? What can you do to generate short-term income? To cut costs? To renegotiate debt? To replace financial transactions with neighborly exchanges?			
BALANCE WITH THE EARTH How earth-friendly is your lifestyle? How much commuting does that dream job require? Is a "paperless office" an oxymoron or a possibility? Been outside lately?			
HEALTH AND STRESS LEVELS[15] Are you clenched? What kinds of food are you putting into your body? Getting enough exercise? Meditation?			

a long time, especially if you are seeing increments of progress every week. This worksheet can be copied and used for each month of the "program" you develop. *(see worksheet on preceding page).*

Stabilizing your life starts with defusing crises that paralyze you. That frees you to create an environment which encourages asking the most interesting possible questions, and following the answers where they lead. The creation of that supportive environment is inseparable from the quest for nourishing work.

Exercise:

Whole Life Values and Visions

For each category in the following "life/work wheel," make notes about your wishes and hopes for a balanced and satisfying life. Consider the relative investments of time and resources into each category, as they are now and as you'd like them to be. This will be the basis for work in future chapters.

creativity   citizenship

play   volunteer activities

social relationships   business ventures
• *intimate friends*
• *colleagues and cocreators*
• *community*   **The
Life/Work
Wheel**

natural environment   employment

rest/sleep/downtime   formal study

health   personal development
• *nutrition*   • *skills*
• *exercise*   • *spirit*
• *de-stressing*

Step 3:
Create a Vibrant Support System

"Build community. It will help you out a whole lot more than money when things start to fall apart." — Fran Peavey, author and activist

In Cartersville, Georgia, there is a halfway house for southern Baptist ministers who have been fired, mostly for opposing racism within their congregations. When it was opened in the early 1990s, the political balance in the church was so delicate and the passions were so high that people of the cloth were being sacked at the rate of one per week in Georgia alone. The house is named for Thomas Holmes, an Atlanta pastor in the early 1960s who welcomed the first black parishioner into his church — a Nigerian exchange student — over the protest of his all-white congregation. Modest but welcoming, Holmes House provides a haven for others who have taken similar risks.

From barnraisings to business incubators to local exchange trading systems, the home-grown principle of voluntary, neighbor-to-neighbor assistance is being rediscovered on a large scale. Everywhere you look, people are figuring out new forms of community. Some of this help is strictly material. But some is on a different plane. It's about mobilizing the power of multiple minds and imaginations to help individuals move through transitions, make decisions, and sustain action.

Co-ops, clusters, and collaboratives are coming to life in all sectors, with a diversity and vitality that suggests this idea is permeating the world's cultures. It's more and more common for cooperation to be seen as a source of business strength. Consider what happened in Los Angeles when Charlie Woo from Hong Kong set about invigorating a run-down section of the city by creating an Asian-style business cluster rivaling New York's garment district and the farmers' markets of many cities. With ten adjacent buildings and a distribution company in the family, Woo reached out through Asian networks to attract complementary businesses including a number of competitors. His gamble created a Toytown that generates more than $1 billion annually and employs 4,000 people.

Not only in business is there a resurgence of cooperative inventiveness. One of the more innovative consumer models is the Eco-Loan co-op, pioneered in Santa Fe, New Mexico. It's a revolving loan fund financed by affordable investments by member households. One at a time, households invest in energy- and water-saving improvements from low-flush toilets to solar collectors. As these devices pay off in terms of resource savings, members repay the co-op and the funds are available for the next borrower. All this happens, of course, with a healthy measure of sociability, show-and-tell, and shared wrestling with the dilemmas of lifestyle change.

Consciously creating a support system helps you navigate through a desired process of change because it brings you several indispensable ingredients:

1. structure — a backup to your internal "enforcement" system, for making sure you follow through with the actions on your plate;
2. focus — pulling you out of yourself and drawing your attention to the significance of your actions in the bigger picture;
3. psychological unsticking — suggesting new ways to view old dilemmas, reminding you of your strengths and resources;
4. normalizing of experience — taking those secret frailties you think are uniquely yours, and showing you — often with a chuckle — just how ordinary they may be;
5. concrete resources — suits, software, childcare, shiatsu — with the convenience and personalized touch of barter;
6. access to new social and vocational networks, which are gold.

In 1979, Barbara Sher published a gem of a career book: *Wishcraft*. In contrast with the common focus on individual introspection, personal effort, private struggle and edging out the competition, Sher talked about cooperation. Reflecting an emerging understanding of the social aspects of career development and personal growth, she raised the heretical notion that we do not have to spend our lives working out the past before we can create a vibrant present and future. She showed that, by consciously creating and utilizing a social support system — relying minimally on professionals and primarily on peers who voluntarily exchange services — you can reengineer your life in keeping with your values, passions, and talents. Sher has taught thousands how to create "Success Teams," one of the many models taking root today as people grapple with the combination of self-reliance and peer support that they need to flourish. This notion has, of course, been picked up and adapted by many; at this point, it is simply "in the air." It breathes new life into the process of creating our livelihoods by shifting the responsibility onto each of us for creating our lives and attracting the resources we need.

Cliff Hakim describes the necessary attitude shift well in his book, *We are All Self-Employed*. It's about independence: taking initiative, taking responsibility, making your own meanings out of what's going on. It's also about interdependence: looking for synergies, attracting support by giving support, and so on. The attitude that's dangerously obsolete, in his view, is one-way dependence.

Ever say to yourself, "I have to solve this by myself. Otherwise it won't be meaningful"? Human beings may be too adaptable for our own good in many respects, and a prime example is our ability to function for extended periods as though we were encased in plexiglass. Consider a new ethic: support

Images of a support system:

tribe
community-supported farm
bridge club
basketball team
faculty meeting
union
chat room
gang
salon
board of directors
mentor
business association
hiking club
choir
singles network
coach (athletic or personal — same idea)
house of worship
café
child care cooperative
business incubator
book club
tango class

equals accountability. This idea comes from my friends Fran Peavey and Tova Green, two San Francisco psychologist/educator/activist wizards. "Support," says Tova, "means getting so close to someone that the only way they can move is forward."

Something powerful happens when people see themselves as part of a healthy, functional community and have a positive experience of that. They learn to value themselves because they feel valued. They learn to trust because they're trusted and because others come through. They are able to see their struggles and complaints as part of a pattern, shared by others, and with causes that the community can address much more effectively than the individual.

Emotional isolation is a great equalizer, affecting people at the top of an organization as much as everyone else. As a (revealingly) anonymous former CEO wrote after sinking into depression and losing his job,

> *Executives and managers, especially those high on the organizational chart, are particularly vulnerable to depression; higher equates with lonelier. Self-protection dictates one can't unburden one's emotional weakness with subordinates or competitive peers — or anyone else for that matter. The ultimate in emotional isolation is the chief executive. He can display no weakness, admit to no doubt or fear, and few, if any, subordinates would dare broach the subject of his mental well-being with him.*

Many readers of this book fall into another prime category of people who are at a special risk for being in isolating situations at work — those who are in flux in terms of values, and may be changing in ways that are frightening to co-workers and managers. The more you struggle with "outsider" feelings, the more attention you need to pay to building a community where you feel at home.

Some of the highest-powered support occurs when a group is part of a social movement — a large subculture of active citizens working to accomplish a desired set of changes that stand to have a wider impact than their private self-interests. When you are part of a living movement, and a fellow participant comes to you for help — with networking or employment or investment or whatever — you want to come through, not only because you care about the individual, but because the work itself is critical and you both recognize that. Many value-driven enterprises have made a discovery similar to Sylvia Blanchet's when she began to recruit employees for ForesTrade in the United States: "We would get 70 or 80 resumes for an ordinary job in our little town in Vermont. We got applications from people across the country, with PhDs in international trade, from multilingual Indonesians, from people making six-figure salaries who hated their jobs. 'Way above and beyond what we are doing directly, our business is succeeding because so many different people want it to."

Fellow activists can be fabulous supporters if your life experience has given you some. If not, the well to drink from is what the social science researchers call your "values

Do you cocoon, to use Faith Popcorn's term for hiding out in the coziest possible domestic nest every moment you can?

When you socialize, do you seek out a diverse crowd or stick with people who think and dress and play the ways you do?

If you tend to isolate, or to hang out with people who don't challenge you, why?

subculture" — that is, that community of human beings who see the world more or less like you do and want to see some of the same outcomes you do. This does NOT mean ghettoizing yourself among people who think alike in every way. It just means making sure you are in regular contact with a core group of people who share enough of a common vision that you don't need to explain the basics, and who see it in their enlightened self-interest to help you out. True kindred spirits are not the only support system you'll ever need. They just give you a very strong foundation for creating the others.

Along the way to clarifying what's essential about the path you hope to follow, it becomes possible to brainstorm about who your "community of concern" really is. This is another way of asking, "Who do I really work for?" and "Who else wants to see the same changes that I do?" When you have a good working definition of this community (or communities), then you can get more concrete by identifying the organizations, social networks, and other specific avenues of entry. These are connections to cultivate or deepen.

With this base, it becomes much easier to accomplish the other kind of community-building that is necessary to make a fulfilling career transition, and to sustain the work ahead. This, of course, involves building webs of relationship that include the people you don't have so much in common with. Research on the use of social networks to facilitate career change indicates that it is most useful when there are several "degrees of separation" within a network. In other words, it gets interesting when you go beyond surrounding yourself with friends who understand and nurture you, and you then use the strength of that network to reach out to their friends and colleagues, and on through several layers. This brings you into contact with people at new levels of influence, in new communities, and with fresh worldviews.

When you have some clarity about "who," the next question is "how" — that is, how to transform a bunch of static relationships into active, reciprocal, resourceful support. As a reminder of what NOT to do, consider the definition of networking offered by one female executive in *Members of the Club*, Dawn-Marie Driscoll and Carol Goldberg's study of high-powered corporate women: "hanging out with people you don't like." Varying this theme, here is a reminder from Jeff Reid[16] about what can happen when networking is not done in a spirit of community:

> You can always use a friend. Unfortunately, some people take this idea a bit
> too literally. Maybe you can blame it on the '80s, when brute commerce
> seemed to muscle into every private sphere. Friendship — a traditional
> value if there ever was one — has increasingly been eroded by that scourge
> of the go-go era: networking

> Networking, of course, derives from the ancient Anglo-Saxon words "netw"
> and "orking," which translate to mean "not working." Indeed, the old
> meaning still rings true: Today's networker most often covets a gig ...

> Who among us, in our search for meaningful human contact and meaning-
> less fun, hasn't been detoured by those craving only business contacts?

There are few things more annoying than thinking you've found a new pal, when you've really just found another amiable hustler on the make, calculating a career move.

This brings us to the difference between utilitarian networking and community-building. The former rises and falls with your needs; the latter is sustained and sustaining. If you are part of a healthy community, it will come through for you when you need to network. In fact, the shared values of your community will greatly contribute to transforming networking from a chore into a pleasure. The best networking occurs not when you are merely looking for a job, but when you are looking for a way to accomplish work that matters to you and your contacts as well.

Leslie Bender is a painter and decorative artist who is self-employed and therefore constantly on the lookout for projects. She exhibits and sells her own paintings, and also does decorative murals, faux finishes, portraits and other projects for clients. Dare Thompson is an arts administrator who confesses she "can't draw beyond third grade level." She just returned to the Hudson Valley community after several years out of state, and was looking for an interesting community arts organization to run. They found each other in a career development group and – completely by intuition – began a committed peer supportive relationship that quickly bore multiple fruits. They attended event after event as a team, introducing each other to everyone they knew and thus opening doors to their complementary networks. They co-hosted parties and exchanged all sorts of day-to-day favors. Within a few months, Dare was hired as Executive Director of the Hudson Valley Writers' Guild and Leslie's plate was filled with projects. Moreover, they had made the entire process big fun.

We are all inventing our own forms here. There are very few firm rules about how to make use of support from your community. There are just a few principles worth noting, based on frequently asked questions and frequently made mistakes:

1. Set about getting what you really need by structuring the process for manageability – for example, breaking down a tall order into a series of modest requests from different people.
2. Make time for the process itself, and the people you meet through it.
3. Give back richly when you receive help.
4. Take stock of the process frequently so you can change course as needed; don't expect it to work without adaptation.
5. Be clear with yourself and with others about what you're asking for.

Five highly effective support systems:

1. Newsletters, 'zines and Web sites uniting people with common interests and/or common values.

2. Personal coaches who provide practical and moral support within a framework of personal resourcefulness and responsibility.

3. Success Teams and similar structures, including Career Change Groups using this very book.

4. Mentoring, which is enjoying a major renaissance in the business world, with fewer rules and more room for inventiveness than ever.

5. Incubators, i.e. a location devoted to startup projects, offering shared resources such as phones, work stations, and computers, and sometimes subsidized overhead. May also incorporate training, technical assistance, and mentoring systems.

Some people prefer to address their support needs intuitively. But there is no harm in orchestrating it more overtly, as long as you are giving back in kind and operating in a spirit of community. Hide Enomoto, who left the Japanese system of lifelong employment to do advanced studies in Organizational Development and Transformation at the California Institute of Integral Studies, then returned to Japan with a vision of planting seeds of a work ethic geared toward "right livelihood" in Japan. Starting out with a Rolodex and a desire to be more conscious in giving and receiving support, he began classifying people according to the kinds of interaction he tended to have with each: emotional depth, playfulness, analytical conversations, concrete assistance, and so on. That part was fun. Then, in his own mind, he

deliberately created different kinds of support groups for different categories. Of course some people are suited for multiple needs. By categorizing people according to their real strengths, I have learned to get the best support of the kind I need at a given time. Even though this sounds like "reductionistic" thinking, it has proved to work for me.

One of the best ways to target a healthy support system is to make it an overt criterion in the workplaces you seek out. Carolyn Shaffer and Kristin Anundsen's *Creating Community Anywhere* reports a number of important experiments in redesigning workplaces in this spirit. For example, at the Quaker Oats plant in Topeka, Kansas, workers having problems of any kind that affect the performance of their jobs can receive peer counseling from co-workers. Initiatives like this have so much power to transform work, and at the same time so much potential for dangerous backfire, that they are a rich topic for discussion in researching any potential employer.

Exercise: Identifying and Activating Your Support System

(as it stands right now — revisit this frequently)

1. Your core personal and professional support system
   Who can you call for emergency help, moral support, and truly honest feedback?

2. Your key mentors
   Who in your orbit is wise, has high credibility and expertise, is clear thinking and takes an interest in your career?

3. Your "access network" into specific sectors
   What doors would you like to see open in the next six months to a year?
   Who do you know who can help you build the bridges?

   How can you get their attention, and how can you help them out in return?

4. The bigger support system:
   Who will benefit if you succeed in your work?
   Who else is engaged in similar efforts or working to create a climate where your work will flourish?
   How would you describe the "community of concern" that you fit in on the basis of your values and the issues that move you?

5. Support-building activities
   Finally, where are the events and projects where you can further your vision and at the same time meet more people who can become part of your support system on all these levels?

In exploring the potential for community in a particular workplace, the juicy discussion comes when you've gotten below the generalities. ("Oh, yes, we have lunchtime speakers and volleyball and we all love it here.") The authors of Creating Community Anywhere point to eight qualities of vibrant workplace community which have been identified in research. The presence or absence of each of these can be investigated by the resourceful job-seeker. They are:

1. Alignment of values (among workers at all levels and the organization as a whole);
2. Employee-based structure, reflected in ownership or open-ended responsibility;
3. Teamwork whenever possible;
4. Open communication (for example, face-to-face dealing, two-way performance reviews, open financial books);
5. Mutual support;
6. Respect for individuality, reflected in diversity of people and flexibility of policies;
7. Permeable boundaries — for example, between union and management roles, between work and social life, and between the organization and the outside world;
8. Group renewal.

Certainly, finding a workplace which reflects those principles is one of the premier strategies for keeping your overall support system healthy. If that's not the reality for you right now, look for the handful of kindred spirits on the job. Even one makes a difference. For example:

- A group of seven Harvard employees meets monthly for coffee and brainstorming help toward their shared goal of becoming former Harvard employees.
- Two women, who are employed by different branches of the same workaholic nonprofit organization, stay in touch by phone for support in their shared goal of maintaining balance in their lives and refusing work that goes beyond their negotiated schedule.

To me, the move toward reinventing community and making use of social support is one of the most encouraging social trends out there. And once we give ourselves permission and pay attention to what's possible, it's amazing how natural these processes are.

I first witnessed the power of a support system in the hardest class of my college years, Physical Chemistry. Known as "the bone-crusher course" for chemistry majors, it required a tough problem set each Monday morning. After struggling in isolation with the homework for many weeks, I took myself for a walk one frustrating Sunday night and saw a light on in the Chemistry building. This was a surprise, since the building was theoretically open only on weekdays. In the library, 85 percent of my classmates were assembled around tables. Several who had part-time jobs in the lab had opened the building with their keys. Pizza crusts and a guitar were strewn around, and a dog slept in the corner. The group was hard at work on the homework — collaboratively. Each table of students had taken on a cluster of problems.

This gathering was a weekly ritual, I learned. It had arisen almost spontaneously in the first weeks of the semester. By dawn, the problems would be done and the answers would be shared. Everyone in the room would have a decent understanding of where those answers

The Kitchen Cabinet

From native tribal councils to corporations, groups of nearly every description have used the ceremonial council as a place to ripen ideas, examine scenarios, engage in serious deliberations, and give voice to commitments in the presence of witnesses. But few individuals have realized how well this model can be applied in their own career development. I have experimented successfully with a slightly formalized version of the "kitchen cabinet" for clients in transition, and I encourage you to adapt this idea to suit your needs.

The basic ingredients are these:

1. A "brain trust" of reliable friends and colleagues, chosen for varied expertise, diverse perspectives, and having their own lives well enough together to be credible as sources of wisdom.

2. A conference table, which could well be a dining room table, with refreshments, note pads, and enough space for resource materials.

3. A facilitator, who basically moves the agenda along, makes sure everyone is heard, feeds back major discoveries, helps dissolve confusion — taking responsibility for process, but not for the outcome.

4. A note-taker or high quality tape recorder, if desired.

5. An open but on-purpose attitude.

6. A focusing question or questions you'd like the group to help you with, and the background information that's needed for them to put the situation in context. This can be written and shared in advance, or spoken in the opening section of the group, with time for clarifying questions before the group launches into problem-solving mode.

I know I want to use my communication and design skills, but how?

Why have I been unemployed so long? What can I do differently?

How will I research the viability of my idea to open a nutrition counseling center and natural foods restaurant? What do I really need to know?

The brain trust can clarify what's been happening and what may be missing; share from their knowledge about the fields you're interested in; spot limiting assumptions or blind spots in your presentation; point out avenues of opportunity that haven't occurred to you. They can also, if desired, serve as an ongoing support system. In several cases, groups of half a dozen or so have divided up the role of "phone buddy" for the friend-in-need, each making a call or two during a designated week to check progress and offer encouragement. The first time I tried this, it was with a friend who had been abruptly fired from a job as Director of Communications for a small nonprofit organization. A seasoned writer and editor, she was sabotaging herself by sending out résumés full of typos, putting on an optimistic face in public, and spending her days watching television. By the end of her evening "kitchen cabinet," her friends had sent her back to the computer until the résumé was flawless. Then they each thought up a few networking contacts, and divvied up the support calls to keep her on track in the weeks that followed. She was reemployed, in a better situation, before the six weeks of her scheduled support had run out.

It may seem like a stretch to ask people to devote a few hours to helping you think clearly about your future, but consider how much more effective this is than the hours they would otherwise spend hearing you whine. When you extend the invitation, have a clear description of the process and your expectations. Give them an opportunity to bow out gracefully, so that the group you convene is wholeheartedly present.

came from. Those who found the subject easy stayed awake until dawn with those who were having a harder time. That's the part that has remained in my memory all these years. Rebelling against the rules, this group of students did not fall into an exploitive mentality, but a collaborative one. True, these secret sessions played hell with the grading. But they unblocked us all enough that we were able to learn something.

It is outrageous that so many of us have lost the ability to give and receive help, exuberantly and with pride. This is a skill that is eminently worth relearning. The more exuberant, irreverent, resourceful and focused we can be in giving and receiving support with people who share our values and goals for changing a bit of the world, the more we will be able to weave together a fabric of meaningful work that will make a difference.

Step 4:
Turn on the Light of
Connection with Your World

Self-employment, in the highest sense, means finding or creating work that stretches you as well as satisfying you, and yields maximum benefits and minimum harm in the world. This step is about the "you" part of the picture: what moves you, attracts you, concerns you, inspires you in your world. Here we will cover some of the territory that conventional career counseling calls self-assessment. Borrowing a term from cybernetics, I prefer to call it exploring the self-world connection. It's about you as a social being, and as a life form sharing the Earth with many others — and the wise, curious, generous, strong, compassionate Self that comes to light when you remember all you're part of. This includes your own life story; the struggles that have formed you and the values they reflect; and which of the many concerns about your world have the most emotional significance for you, and the most power as motivators in your work.

Each of the exercises in this section will take a modest block of time, half an hour to two hours for most people. I recommend structuring those times in, and working with this material steadily over a few weeks. Obviously, go where the attractive force is highest, but give each exercise a try. At the end, be sure to devote enough time and attention to evaluating what you've generated and how the elements fit together. This is not as obvious as it may sound.

This step contains a good deal of work. Do what you can. Use what you learn. And stay with it. As Joseph Campbell once said to a student who complained about the workload, "You have your whole life to finish it, you know."

Uncovering Your Values: Icebreaker Questions

When we begin to talk about values and visions, it's hugely tempting to come up with low-risk, socially desirable responses. If all your friends work in the nonprofit sector and are ambivalent about business, it's a little loaded to put down "entrepreneurial attitude" on your list of values. If a lot of your colleagues are athletes, admitting that you value noncompetitiveness might feel a little awkward. One way to get past those expectations and into the truth of your experience is to review critical incidents in your history and consider what has motivated you in the thick of them. Try these questions as points of entry.

1. *Your dream job:* Do you ever daydream about an ideal job? It doesn't have to be related at all to what you've done or rationally consider possible. Spend some time imagining your dream job in detail.
2. *The job from hell:* Now for the opposite: what, in your mind (or your experience) is a "job from hell"?

3. List the accomplishments in your career history that you are honestly most proud of. What motivated you to take them on? What values were reflected in the ways you handled these challenges?

4. What have you fought for in your work? Elsewhere in your life?

5. Who are your heroes and role models? How have they moved through their working lives?

6. What have been the roughest times in your working life? What values were behind your responses and survival strategies?

7. How are you different from when you started to work for a living (assuming that's more than a month ago)? What values have become clearer/stronger? More ambiguous? How might you answer the question "Who am I becoming?"[17]

8. Consider people you've been meeting lately, especially those with whom you've "clicked." What do they seem to have in common? Do you notice any differences between new people in your life and the more long-standing relationships you keep up? What does this suggest about your emerging values and sensibilities?

9. If you won an all-expense-paid educational experience — from a field trip to a degree program — anywhere on the planet, what would you study, and in what ways? What would you be attracted to in that experience?

10. What volunteer activities have meant the most to you in recent years — from service projects to citizen activism, anything you've been involved in? What volunteer activities have looked attractive, but haven't quite drawn you in?

What does each of these answers reveal about your values? What are its implications for the kinds of work in which you'll thrive and contribute?

Naming and Prioritizing Your Values

Consider the values listed below. Add any others that occur to you. Reflecting on your history and checking in with your intuition, which of these values do you consider very important without compromise (VI); fairly important, depending on the situation (FI); and generally less important (LI)?

When you've prioritized these values, let the list sit for a day or so, and then review it. Pay special attention to the balance among the categories. For example, if you indicated that just about everything is very important without compromise, consider the ways in which you would and wouldn't be flexible. If you see just about everything as situation-dependent, ask yourself what your core values are. And if most of these values seem unimportant, try to find some better language for your real values. Or ask whether you've been feeling cynical or burned out lately.

If you're so inclined, you might consider ways to keep this statement of values in your consciousness by making a drawing or symbol, chart, collage, a poem, a musical composition, a mandala — or a few phone calls to talk it over with friends.

accountability	excitement	pace and rhythm of work
achievement	flexible policies such as	physical challenge
advancement opportunities	scheduling	power
approval & recognition	helping others	security
autonomy	high ethical standards	social contacts
caution	holistic ways of thinking	spiritual development
contribution to general	honesty	spontanaeity
knowledge	intellectual challenge	stature (social/professional)
contribution to organization	keeping a low profile	time for life outside work
contribution to people in need	leadership opportunities	variety
contribution to social change	leaving work at work	vigorous competition
cultural opportunities	living where I want to live	Other values not on that list
democratic workplaces	meticulousness	
diversity	money	
educational opportunities	multiculturalism	
emotional expression	nonviolence	
environmental sustainability	organization's health	

Open Your Heart to the World
(Adapted from "Spiritual Exercises for Social Activists," in Joanna Macy's *World as Lover, World as Self*)[18]

Many of us go through life transitions in a bit of a trance. This visualization will assist you in stepping out of "ordinary mind" to focus on how your values may translate into direct engagement with the world. Do this in a quiet, calming setting and give it plenty of time.

> *Get comfortable, breathe deeply and slowly, and empty your mind of thoughts and images.*
>
> *Now call to mind someone you love deeply. Anyone. Gaze at them, see their face, notice their strength, be aware of how much you want their lives to be free of suffering. Let another image of a loved one arise, and another. Hold them in your caring gaze, and feel the particular love you have for them.*
>
> *Let the circle expand, to include those you see regularly, at work and in the community. See all their differences and quirks, and feel the particular quality of love you have for them.*
>
> *Expand the circle further to include people you see less often, long-distance friends and family, those who are lost but missed.*
>
> *Include people you have some conflict or difficulty with. From the safe base of this visualization, see them in their full humanity, and hold them in a gaze of simple compassion.*

Let the circle of empathy widen to include nonhuman life, all the winged ones, the furry ones, the leafy ones, the single cells. Let into your awareness the wonder of all this life. Hold it in your mind's eye. Feel the particular love you have for all the life forms we share this Earth with.

Now imagine yourself leaping out beyond the Earth, and watching this beautiful blue-green orb from a million miles away. See the teeming life, the vibrant communities, the suffering and the stagnant and the happy, healthy ones. See the humans, interacting in a thousand ways with all the other life forms we share this Earth with. Notice where your gaze is most attracted. Stay with it as long as the process is alive. Notice where there is work to be done, to preserve life on this planet and quality of life in human communities. Notice the work that most attracts you.

Finally, when you feel ready, bring your awareness back to Earth, to one of those places you have chosen, and feel the center of your awareness returning to the body you have been given in this lifetime. Come back slowly, and, when you feel ready, open your eyes.

Take some time to write down your impressions. What aspects of the exercise were most vibrant? Which areas seemed "flat" or hard to visualize? The blanks we draw can be as instructive as the images that arise. How would your "career development" be different if you did it in this state of awareness?

Lifelines

On the six timelines *(opposite page)*, note major phases and changes during your working life. Along each axis, note major themes and milestones. In that inviting blank space after "today," note ways in which you think you're growing and changing. Be aware of how far in the future you're able to visualize.

A related approach that's widely recommended is the "spiritual autobiography." It's nothing more than a heartfelt narrative of the way you've moved through life: the work you've been attracted to, the civic work and community projects you've participated in, the vision that animates you. What's distinctive about the way you have moved through life and the gifts you are most interested in giving? What experiences have been most formative, in your personal life? What major social and political events have had a lasting impression on you? What major events in the natural world caught your attention or influenced your path? What messages have you gotten from the world around you about the work that's needed? That's rewarded? That's off limits? How has the particular evolution of your life — in social and environmental context — shaped the vocational quest you're now on?

Values in context

At this point, you have named some values that are primary for you. Now, how do they translate into practice? Suppose you value "healthy living." Does this mean you want to eat

When you started	today	chosen future

values

skills & strengths

accomplishments

characteristics of a favorable work environment

desired environmental contribution through work

desired social contribution through work

In each area, how do you describe your "growing edge"?

right and get to the gym every other day, or that you want to work in an office built with state-of-the-art nontoxic materials, or that you want to make sure that the projects you manage are nonpolluting throughout their life cycle, or ...? Choose a small cluster of values you consider important to you in your working life. Now explore, by talking or writing, how you want each value to guide your action. As much as possible, consider what that value suggests for your relationships with all the different stakeholders your choices will sooner or later affect. For example, these include:

1. You — your overall career development
2. Your family and other close relationships
3. Your community
4. Cultural and ethnic groups you're a part of
5. Cultural and ethnic groups you're not a part of
6. Co-workers
7. Competitors
8. Bosses
9. Customers
10. Investors/funders
11. Other species
12. The ecology of your bioregion
13. The planet as a whole
14. Future generations

As you digest these answers, take them one step further. How will you recognize a workplace where these values are taken seriously? [If you want more direction on this question, see Step 5.]

Making a Life

What we pay attention to is often what we build up, while other areas of life can wither for lack of attention. Working lives encompass everything that feeds our work and everything that is fed by it, from family relationships, to education and training, to the civic action that protects our career options. The Life/Work Wheel is a visual approach to looking at these dimensions in relationship to each other. The separate schematics are offered to address the clusters of related questions below each one (you may want to photocopy the page and then write your notes alongside the various categories, as in Step 2).

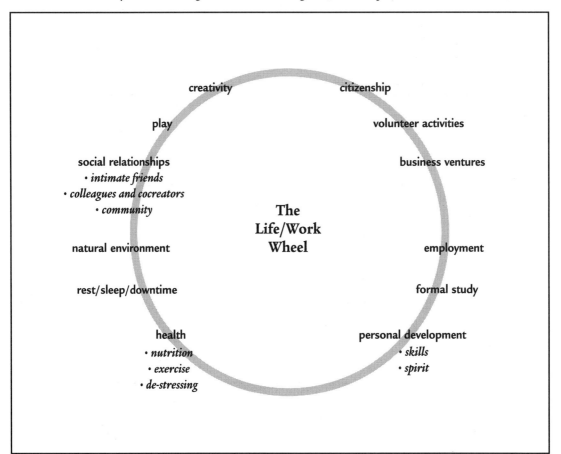

For each category

1. What are some visual images, feelings, and words that arise in your mind when you consider this aspect of your life?
2. How is this category "working" for you?
3. What's strongest about this aspect of your life?
4. What's most shaky about it?
5. What would it take to make this area of your life really satisfying?
6. In this area, what is one step (however modest) that you could take right away to bring the reality more in line with your vision and goals?

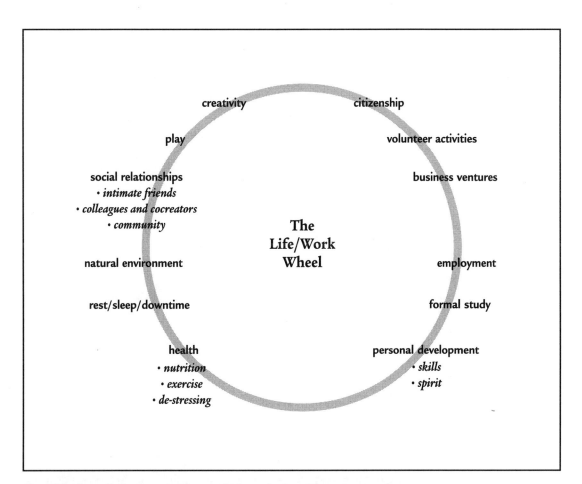

Considering all the categories and the relationships among them:

7. To which of these aspects do you pay the most conscious attention?
8. Which of these aspects of your life are most in need of some more attention from you?
   How could you simplify or adapt your life in order to make this attention available:
   > *By letting go of activities (at least for now)*
   > *By combining or reorganizing activities*
9. Which areas are working best? What strengths that you exercise in those areas could be transferred into the areas that need attention?
10. How could the elements of the wheel be better integrated into your life?

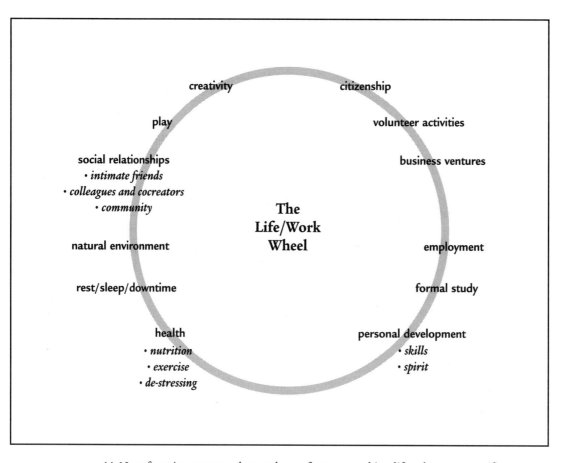

11. Now, focusing on your plans or hopes for your working life — however specific or general they may be at this point — in what ways can your awareness and choices in each of these areas of your life make a difference in the process of career change?

12. Based on this assessment, how would you sum up the changes you hope to see in your life as a whole and the role of work in it?

Listening to the Headlines

This exercise and the next two provide some ways to think about the work to be done in the world. This exercise lets you look from many angles, taking events in the real world as your starting point. *(See collage of headlines on opposite page).*

Let any headline catch your eye. Visualize the picture it paints. What does that picture tell you about work that's important? Consider work that's been done, to achieve something of value; work that's been neglected or done unwisely, to achieve an unfortunate outcome; work that's emerging as necessary based on events of right now. For example:

"Frank racial dialogue thrives on Web" may lead one person to focus on new media content development, another on legal advocacy to oppose censorship on the Web, another on intercultural communication, another on mediation.

"No-mow lawns aren't too far off" can be asserted because of the experiments of

botanists and landscapers, the receptivity of seed companies, the pressure of consumers and their advocates, and the pressure for alternative lawn care generated by advocates for clean air, fuel efficiency, water conservation and other environmental benefits.

"New prosperity brings new conflict to Indian country" draws attention to the work of tribal entrepreneurs, bankers, and economic development strategists; community organizers, political and spiritual leaders focusing on tribal unity; attorneys and advocates defending tribal economic rights; and the lawyers and mediators whose work is cut out in responding to the conflicts of the new era.

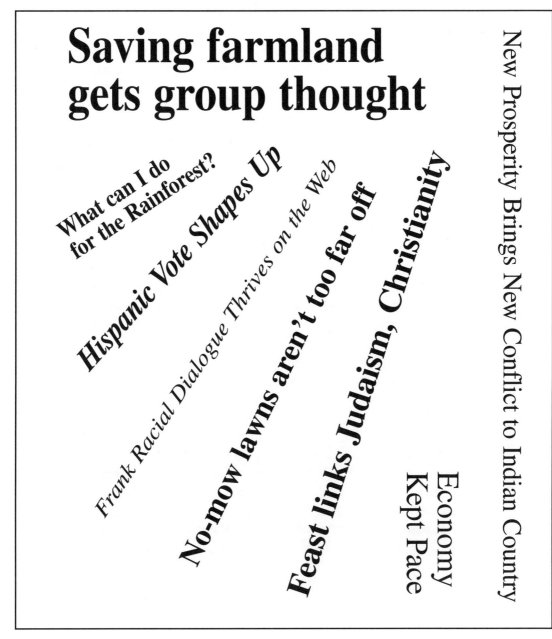

Walkabout

Take a walk in your neighborhood, or another neighborhood that interests you. Better, meditate and then take a walk. You may want to carry a notebook, but do not lose yourself in it. The idea of this walk is to pull your attention out into the world. Where does your gaze naturally move? What's overlooked? Do you feel drawn to explore a new direction, or to follow a path that's safe and known? What does this reflect about the state of your being?

Simply pay attention to whatever your eye catches. Look at the storefronts, the gardens, the homes with TV lights in their windows, the kids on corners. Look at the downtowns and the malls, and the movements of people and commerce. Look at the gardens, and the vacant lots, and the traffic patterns, and the land use. How clear is the air? What vistas are attractive? Where are people thriving? What's growing, and how healthy does it look? What enterprises are at risk? What lives are at risk?

How do you feel about this state of affairs? Does anything make you angry? Sad? Fearful? Bitter? Amused? Excited? Impressed?

Now, step back into thought-mode, and speculate. What's the work that led to this state of affairs? *(Visualize. Write. Take time. This is juicy.)*

What's the work that could make this picture more attractive and hospitable for humans and the web of life?

Letter to Future Generations
(Adapted from exercise designed by Joanna Macy.)[19]

You actually have an opportunity to send a message to the future, and specifically to young people. How far ahead can you imagine with some concreteness? Ten years, or 200? Whatever era it might be, focus there and let a picture of that world arise in your imagination. Wherever your attention is drawn, let it rest so that details can come into focus. Imagine the dwellings, the streets, the countryside, commerce, how people move from place to place. Watch the adults as they work. Watch the children, wherever you see them.

Let one or more young people draw your attention. In your imagination, turn to them and invite them to listen to you. When you feel ready, begin to tell them what's going on around here today and what kind of impact you would like to have on it through your work. Tell them about the state of the planet today as you see it: what's beautiful and valuable, what's threatened and threatening. Describe your life and the choices about work that you are grappling with. What's the experience of living with these concerns? Finally, tell them how you hope your life will make a difference in the quality of the natural and social environment their generation will inherit. What patterns do you want to change? Who are your allies in this? What forces and individuals get in the way? How would the changes you hope for actually happen? What are you willing to do to have an impact?

Impact Analysis

At the end of your career, what long-term trends of social or environmental change would you most like to be part of? Would you like to be able to say "I protected these five acres and this riverbank" or "I helped replace a seriously toxic chemical with something safer" or "I turned graduating seniors loose on the world with an ability to find their way"?

How do you think those changes occur — e.g. by what mix of education, legal advocacy, political pressure, creative inspiration, models that can be imitated, etc. etc.? Take some time to write about the change processes you think are most important in achieving the results you want to see in the world. Now reread what you've written with an eye on the actors: who has done the work to make it happen? And where might you fit?

How would you characterize the patterns in the ways you typically exercise impact? For instance: by intervening in problem situations as they arise, by mentoring and supporting people when the need arises, by orchestrating educational experiences for people, by creating policies that stretch people, by trying to be a role model ... There are probably many. How do they relate to your answers to the previous question, about how changes you want to see in the world are likely to occur?

Of the ways you generally try to have an impact, which ones have historically worked well for you? How can you create more opportunities for these kinds of influence? Which ones have historically backfired? How can you let go of these patterns (or be more selective in their use) and find opportunities for new ways of influencing situations?

Aptitudes and Skills

Let me begin by confessing a bias. Based on work with clients and my own experience, I believe that what you care about is more important than what you're good at. If you are guided by attraction and commitment to something you value highly, you can learn enough of what you need to know.

Still, what you're good at, and what you're most comfortable doing, is certainly a factor in deciding among multiple paths of action.

Aptitudes are natural tendencies, as opposed to cultivated skills. In most areas, formal testing services can be found for establishing with high statistical reliability what your aptitudes are. Alternatively, the test of play and experimentation can work quite well.

The skills you have to market and apply are the ones expressed in your work history and the rest of your life. The standard way to get a handle on them is to list accomplishments, both those that were honored by external rewards and others you personally value. Pay attention to the verbs. What impact did your actions have on all the bottom lines

Much more important than specific skills, which are learnable, are the more general functional capabilities that apply to any situation. Business writer Steve Bennett proposes the following list of basic survival qualities for the "ecopreneur" (meaning all of us):

1. ability and willingness to keep highly informed on changing regulations, competitive factors, and emerging markets

2. "foresight and pioneering courage" due to the innovative nature of many businesses

3. especially high ethical standards, due to the sensitivity of consumers and cohorts in the field, and the public's wariness of "eco-scams" and "eco-marketing campaigns"

4. ability to deal with very knowledgeable, vocal, activist consumers, requiring an unusually high degree of skill in customer service: "Ecopreneurs must go beyond the traditional rules of customer service and view customers as partners who can help them shape better businesses."

5. "Finally, true ecopreneurs are driven by a special passion — to heal the planet. That commitment often gives them an extra edge when it comes to weathering the psychological and fiscal storms they will inevitably encounter as they grow their fledgling enterprises."

you care about, from profits and market share to acres of forest saved and infant mortality reduced? There is no shortcut to choosing your own indicators of success.

Besides specialized skills of one trade or another — and often more critical for open-ended transitions — are the transferable skills that keep you functioning and effective in any situation. Once they were called "soft skills." Nobody thinks that anymore. A good laundry list of these basic skills is the US Department of Labor's SCANS.[20] Here is a very simple framework for self-evaluating on these skills. You can also ask a friend or colleague who knows your work to offer feedback:

Skill	When have you exercised this most effectively?	How would you rate yourself on this skill?
effective participation leadership interpersonal relations negotiation teamwork self-esteem goal-setting & motivation career development creative thinking problem-solving listening oral communication learning to learn		

Personality, Interests, and Preferences

How much importance you place on the personality you have today depends to a great extent on how much you expect it to evolve, which in turn may depend on how well developed your skills of adaptation are. But it's useful to have enough self-knowledge to avoid raging mismatches. The introverted among us probably shouldn't rush into a sales career. The psychological testing industry offers a cornucopia of instruments to shed light on different dimensions of your temperament, interests, aptitudes, and the conditions in which you are most at home.

When you are at one of life's Square One points — either starting out or in deep transition — and you want to look beyond the known universe of possibilities, a good organizing tool is a standard test called the Strong (and its variant, the Strong-Campbell) Interest Inventory. This very simple multiple-choice test invites you to reflect on what you've already done, and consider how much you enjoy working with your hands, with language, with concepts, and so forth. Most career centers on campuses or in the private sector can administer this test or guide you as to where to go.

Somewhere between personality theory and depth psychology is the notion of "career anchors," first articulated by organizational psychologist Edgar Schein. Career anchors are the deep motives that underlie major patterns in your choices. He identifies three: power, achievement, and affiliation. This framework has been the basis for many typing systems. Psychology and sociology have given us archetypes like the "organization man" in the 1950s and 1960s (declared dead by *Business Week Magazine* in the early 1990s) and Michael Maccoby's "gamesman" in the 1970s — the person who is motivated by the pure challenge of organizational maneuvering.

More recently, there has been a proliferation in the use of typing systems drawn from depth psychology, including:

1. the Enneagram, a nine-point system drawn on Sufi mystical teachings and western developmental theory, focusing on the psychological agendas we all bring from our experience with trauma and healing;

2. archetypal systems such as the Heroic Myth Indicator developed by Carol Pearson and Sharon Sievert, including such archetypes as the Warrior, Caregiver, Magician, and Wise Ruler;

3. the seven energy centers or chakras, used as a basis for self-discovery by popular authors including Rick Jarow and Carolyn Myss.

Tools like these can be valuable in holding up a mirror, but can also short-circuit the process of understanding yourself on your own terms. I urge you to be a smart and critical consumer, try a variety of these if you try any, and reject anything that does not absolutely ring true as a reflection of your Self. As Jarow writes in his valuable book, *Creating the Work You Love*, "It is up to us to find our own voice, to choose from our own place of clarity and power."

Generating Options

Get yourself a good-sized piece of paper. Like newsprint. Start thinking up all the options you're entertaining for your work, and put them down on the paper any way *except* in a list. You might represent them as a sky full of stars, some of them in constellations together; a tree with branches and twigs; a fanciful collage; or simply related clusters. Stay with the process until you can look at the paper and say, "This completely represents the options I'm interested in exploring."

Review the options you generated. Which ones look like a possible fit based on your exploration so far? Are there any others that don't seem to fit the criteria you've identified, but that still glow mysteriously in your mind and need to be checked out?

You might want to copy this picture, keep the original intact, and cut up the copy so that clusters of similar options are kept together, but major categories are separated. This makes it possible to paste each section onto a notebook page, leaving enough blank area to start notes for brainstorming ideas and questions.

Self-Assessment Summary:

This structure may help you to gather together and summarize the results of this chapter's exercises.

Because I:	I would thrive in workplaces that:
_____	_____
_____	_____
_____	_____
_____	_____
_____	_____
_____	_____
_____	_____

Identify which ones are possible now, which ones are longer-term, and which current possibilities might be stepping stones to the longer-term interests.

For each option or cluster of related options:

1. What do you already know about these areas of work?
2. What do you need to know about these areas of opportunity?
3. What sources do you already know about for gathering this information?

Just make notes for now. Step 5 will help you learn more about these.

Three Unorthodox Queries

We have now covered most of the questions that are conventionally considered in a career exploration, and a few others. Now we are going to address a cluster of concerns that mostly come up on people's radar after they've made choices they regret.

1. *How do you understand your sense of place and comfort zone with respect to geographic mobility?*

It is often assumed that we are infinitely adaptable in choosing where we will live and how. Or, if we aren't, there's something wrong with us. Migrant workers, language teachers, corporate trainers or eco-tour guides — many of us are becoming what a friend calls "global nomads." Understandably so. It is enticing to follow the seasons, rack up cross-cultural experience, and follow the kind of customized track — be it fast or slow — that mobility allows. But the costs of this flexibility are becoming clear, even for the moderately mobile, ranging from disrupted families and neglected friendships to a sense of incoherence in working relationships themselves. In March of 1998, the *New York Times* magazine devoted

Self-Assessment Implications — Characteristics of an Attractive Workplace			
Characteristics of the workplace with regard to:	your comfort zone	stretch zone	no way!
size			
structure			
culture			
tools and technologies			
compensation			
travel and overtime			
location			
flexibility			
ways of enforcing policies and performance			
physical appearance, layout, esthetics			
mix of people in workforce			
possible career paths			
other considerations			

a special issue to "business class as a way of life," proclaiming that "The borderless economy has created a new elite of glazed nomads with all their needs catered to — except those that really matter." Part of the countertrend toward "downshifting" is being more discriminating about the choice to pack up and move, or accept a travel-intensive career. Ever so slowly, employers and working people are remembering that we do have a choice about this, and there's much at stake. Roots shape and hone the individual, in the words of poet Wendell Berry, allowing us to grow "whole in the world, at peace and in place." If a more rooted lifestyle were adopted by a significant number of people, even the planet could benefit through reduced fuel use and road building, and because it would be harder for any of us to stay one step ahead of our own bad decisions.

> *In what ways has geographic mobility enhanced the quality of your working life?*
>
> *In what ways has it detracted?*
>
> *What parts of the world do you feel a particular affinity for? Is there a simple answer, or do you live with conflicts?*
>
> *If you are conflicted about where home is, what steps could you take in the next phase of your career to get closer to resolution?*
>
> *What kinds of emotional or expressive needs do you sometimes meet through job mobility or frequent travel? What would it take to meet those needs closer to home?*

2. *What kinds of tools and technologies would you like to see in use where you work, and what kinds would you prefer to stay away from?*

To question something isn't necessarily to reject it. But tens of thousands of people are now living with injuries — from infertility caused by IUDs to carpal tunnel syndrome — because we did not claim the right to ask tough enough questions about technologies that we interact with intimately and regularly.

> *In what ways have technologies been a help to you in creating work that reflects your highest values?*
>
> *In what ways have technologies created barriers in that effort?*
>
> *How have technologies affected the balance of power between you and various stakeholders you deal with, such as customers, suppliers, management, and the public?*
>
> *Have you ever been in a situation in which a technology "saved" you from labor you wanted to do or skills you wanted to exercise? How did you reconcile that situation? How has the experience shaped your attitudes about technologies and your power to make wise choices in their use?*

*Have you ever been in a situation in which you were uncomfortable using
a technology, but everyone else around you seemed to accept it, so you
went along? Looking back, how do you feel about that experience?
 Is there any other approach you could take if a similar situation arises
in the future?*

One powerful, provocative, and richly documented source of counterbalancing wisdom to offset the easy acceptance of technologies is Jerry Mander's *In the Absence of the Sacred*. In it, the author of *Four Arguments for the Elimination of Television* proposes a list of "Ten Recommended Attitudes About Technology":

1. Since most of what we are told about technology comes from its proponents, be deeply skeptical of all claims.

2. Assume all technology is 'guilty until proven innocent.'

3. Eschew the idea that technology is neutral or 'value free.' Every technology has inherent and identifiable social, political, and environmental consequences.

4. The fact that technology has a natural flash and appeal is meaningless. Negative attributes are slow to emerge.

5. Never judge a technology by the way it benefits you personally. Seek a holistic view of the impacts. The operative question is not whether it benefits you, but who benefits most? And to what end?

6. Keep in mind that individual technology is only one piece of a larger web of technologies, "megatechnology." The operative question here is how the individual technology fits the larger one.

7. Make distinctions between the technologies that primarily serve the individual or the small community (e.g. solar energy) and those that operate on a large scale outside community control (e.g. nuclear energy). The latter kind is the major problem today.

8. When it is argued that the benefits of the technological lifeway are worthwhile despite harmful outcomes, recall that Lewis Mumford referred to these alleged benefits as "bribery." Cite the figures about crime, suicide, alienation, drug abuse, as well as environmental and cultural degradation.

9. Do not accept the homily that 'once the genie is out of the bottle you cannot put it back.' Such attitudes induce passivity and confirm victimization.

10. In thinking about technology within the present climate of technological worship, emphasize the negative. This brings balance.

3. *What are your requirements for joy and beauty, and how will you satisfy them in your working life?*
 Visiting a colleague some years ago, I was reminded about the lovely moments
that can find their way into a workday. We were driving from lunch to her office when she
made a sudden multilane change, hooked a left, and pulled into a parking lot. "Back in a

flash," she said with a smile. "This is my boyfriend's office, and I just want to stop for a quick kiss." Two minutes later we were back on course, with attitudes nicely adjusted.

Walking in beauty does not require a fancy office or other material resources. It's an inside job and a matter of resourcefulness with the materials at hand. One flower in a

---

Before You Travel:

Questions to Ask About Any Opportunity to Relocate Or Work "On the Road"

1. Where am I going, literally and symbolically?

2. What am I leaving behind?

3. Who will be affected by the work that I do in this situation?

4. Will the outcome of my work involve winners and losers?

5. Are there actions or attitudes I could take on the job that would make it more of a win/win situation?

6. What do I know about the people, cultures, and ecology of the place where I'm considering working?

7. How have I chosen my sources of information about them?

8. What technologies and tools will I use in my work?

9. How will they affect the quality of life and the balance of power my co-workers and I have with the local population?

10. What do I most want to believe about this place?

11. What attracts me most?

12. What scares me?

13. What can I do while there, to help protect or restore a healthy ecology, including taking responsibility for the impact of my style of living?

14. Who has held this place sacred?

15. How will my actions affect their lives, communities, and cultures?

16. What can I do to learn about the communities that live here and bring their message back to my home community?

17. Will I displace or compete with local people who could be doing "my" job?

18. What local social or political groups will I be most closely allied with in doing my work?

19. Could that put me into conflict with others?

20. Are there ways I might realistically serve as a peacemaker in the community where I'll be functioning?

21. Are there ways I could do all the good things I've imagined so far, in a "virtual" relationship with this new place, while staying in my current home base?

22. What kinds of power will I bring to the situation?

23. How will it compare to the power of the people I'll be working with, supervising, and reporting to?

24. Are there ways I can make this power balance fairer, or more fluid?

25. Is this trip or move a rite of passage for me in any way?

26. Are there ways I could achieve the same symbolic goal with accomplishments or adventures closer to home?

27. How do I define my commitment to my home community?

28. Whatever choice I make, how can I maximize the positive impact of my international work and minimize the negative?

---

glass on the desk, or a few fragments of poetry on the wall, can establish a tone. Some employers recognize the value of these "small" amenities, like a full employee refrigerator, and provide them as an investment to keep people happy and effective. Mitch Teplitsky, Director of Marketing for the Film Society of New York, has infused his workplace with humanizing touches in this job and others. He has brought in a yoga teacher for lunchtime sessions, which over a season became such a magnet that they had to be expanded. He has helped co-workers lobby for bicycle racks to make cycling to work easier — and watched with delight as people got the picture that they could organize and ask for something without fomenting a revolution.

One of the driving forces in the resurgence of interest in "right livelihood" is a craving for a juicier quality of worklife. This can be a criterion for screening workplaces — or the basis for creating one.

When and where have you been moved by beauty lately?

If you could design a fantasy workplace, furnished and decorated to make you glow whenever you walk in, how would it look?

What are your assumptions about how much beauty and joy are "realistic" on the job? Where do they come from?

In your choice of vocation and niche, where and how could you create beauty, or preserve it, or make it more democratically available?

Finally ...

Some of these lines of exploration will come alive for you more than others. Please take what's useful and let go of the rest. For the findings that really resonate for you, take time to ask, "So what does this mean for my working life?" The answers may not be obvious.

Eventually, though, the moment will come when self-exploration reaches a natural conclusion for the time being. You will know when this happens. You may feel stale, or restless, or frustrated, or simply done. Go forward. When it's time for more self-examination, you will know.

Step 5:
Cultivate Critical Research Skills

Information is only power if you can deal with it. When you begin to consider all you'd like to know about the work opportunities out there — and all the legwork, mindwork, eyework, 'Network, and phonework it will take to gather this information — it is easy to get crazy. But, if you want to make choices you can live with long-term, you must become a synthesizer and interpreter of information, in order to stand clear of other people's assumptions and value judgments.

Becoming a bit of an information-warrior, willing and able to track down data and wrestle the meanings out of it, is also wonderfully empowering. Your mind engages in the quest for new options, in a fresh and sometimes delightfully warriorlike way. It's more than a baby step toward being subject rather than object in life. You may even experience a distinctive sense of creativity and personal power known to reporters, researchers, private investigators, and others who make sense of complicated stories. You rapidly learn that there is no formula to follow — you have to trust your intuition and judgment, and so you do.

In the process, you recognize how big a difference there is between data and information. Data is piles of unprocessed facts and assertions. Information is data interpreted and organized according to some kind of meaning. Meaning is what you draw out, and what you have to rely on in deciding your direction — not just in choosing the next step, but in moving effectively along the path from there. As Fred Friedman, a research librarian for the US Environmental Protection Agency, observes, "The key step in getting a grip on almost any research process is framing your questions in ordinary, simple English that is meaningful to you."

"If we knew what we were doing, we wouldn't be calling it research, now would we?"

— Albert Einstein

A good first step in gaining control over information is to think critically about the forms it comes in, and the sources it comes from. Who wants to know the same information you want to know? Who has collected it, or is investigating it right now? In broad brush strokes, people and organizations gather information for several reasons:

1. for its civic or commercial value, if they're libraries, publishers, or other neutral sources;
2. for the purpose of advocacy, if they're trade or professional associations or other interest groups;
3. for the purpose of vigilance, if they're investigative reporters, watchdog organizations and the like.

This is to say two things: there is lots of information out there on fields of work and specific workplaces; and very little of it is free of bias. You can counter some of this bias by considering the probable viewpoint of each source, and by consulting multiple sources, and by stepping back to ask at intervals, "What have I really learned here, and how solid are my facts?"

There are at least five major traps to avoid as you get knowledgeable about the prospects out there:

1. outright propaganda
2. honest bias
3. missing information
4. out-of-date information
5. content without meaning

Has Company X reduced its toxic emissions by means of a thorough pollution prevention campaign? Or has Company X reduced its reported data on the US EPA's *Toxics Release Inventory* by moving a couple of factories to Poland? Did Nonprofit Q just have a major shakeup because it's mounting a visionary new initiative and the old staff couldn't stand the heat, or because its CEO was worse than useless and everyone finally jumped ship? Or are there other factors going on that you may not have considered?

It is also worth noting early that every workplace has its strengths and limitations, sometimes adding up to breathtaking contradictions and trade-offs. Deborah Leipziger, international program director for the Council on Economic Priorities, notes that "the very same enterprise can be wonderful in Singapore and terrible in Taiwan." Consider the trade-offs represented by some exemplary organizations.

For instance, would you like to work for Stride-Rite Shoe Corporation, one of Boston's most respected charitable givers, a civic-minded company which has lobbied state and federal officials for enlightened family leave policies? But it's the same Stride-Rite which recently closed down its inner-city plant in the shell-shocked neighborhood of Roxbury, laying off 160 employees who could least afford it?

Or McDonald's, which has made leaps with lower-bulk packaging, recycling and smoke-free restaurants, but which would not exist without the car culture and helps keep that culture alive?

Or the Commonwealth of Massachusetts Department of Environmental Protection, which in the mid-1990s released research findings indicating that the state's worst environmental violator was the state itself?

For that matter, what about working for Greenpeace, protector of forests and dolphins, whose young canvassing staff a few years ago saw no choice but to start a union drive in response to low pay and lack of job security?

In terms of getting accurate information, fact-check everything you rely on. Excesses of "shallow green" marketing and greenwashing have flown back in the faces of many companies, creating a climate of somewhat greater conscientiousness in communication than a decade ago. But it is still important to have one's antennae out for green marketing hype. As Greenpeace's Bill Walker fumed at a "green marketing" conference in the early 1990s:

Green garbage bags. Green gasoline. Computers, hamburgers, compact discs; all here, all green, already. In California, where I live, supermarket chains that refuse to stop selling pesticide-dusted grapes are trying to promote themselves as environmentally correct because their pickle jars are reusable (you know, you can stick flowers in them). They're getting away with it. The chairman of DuPont has the New York Times *practically comparing him to John Muir. An oil company is forced by federal regulations to put a few bucks into preserving wildlife habitat, so it spends 10 times that much to buy newspaper ads patting itself on the back for obeying the law. Do people buy it? People do.*

If that credulity is a handicap for consumers, it is many times worse for the job seeker. Overcoming it requires literacy on the issues, as well as skill in asking questions and integrating the answers. This skill can only be cultivated through lots of conversations: with employees of a company you're considering; with people, representing a range of views, who have reason to pay attention to the company's practices (for example, union representatives, community activists, colleagues in professional and trade associations, local government and Better Business Bureau people).

There are many useful approaches to questioning. You may want to write down specific questions, or more general lines of questioning; you may want to think in advance about your goal and then wing it on the details. Edwin Nevis, an organizational consultant, points to two completely opposite styles that can each produce breakthroughs: Sherlock Holmes — deliberate, systematic, deductive and smooth; and the TV detective Columbo, who intuitively muddles and mumbles his way into solutions for baffling crimes. Whatever style works for you, and whatever questions arise in your mind, the important thing is to ask them and listen thoroughly to the answers. Where's the information? What are the assumptions underneath? Who says it's true? How recently? What did they have to gain or lose?

A few questions to ask frequently when evaluating information:

1. Is there a precise definition for terms being used? "Natural," "earth friendly," and "green" are in the eyes of the beholder, whereas "Certified Organic" is based on a precise definition mandated by state (and, one of these days, federal) law.

2. If an achievement is being touted by an organization, is that achievement required by law or by the settlement of a legal claim, as many waste-cleanup and pollution-reduction measures are? Does it amount to compliance with regulations, or is it an out-front initiative?

3. Is the issue being brought to your attention a priority topic, or did you just let your local chemical company distract you from its toxic emissions by sponsoring a TV special on the rainforest?

4. If an employer expresses commitment to a social or environmental principle, how is that commitment reflected in formal programs and budgeting?

On a more concrete level, how you make use of the information resources out there is partly a matter of style and skill. Some people actually enjoy making cold calls but break into a sweat at the thought of going to the library. For others, it's the reverse. Still, there are inherent strengths and limitations to every information source. For example, consider these differences between hard-copy (print and on-line) sources and direct human interaction.

Hard-copy sources offer a wider scope, but may give you fewer of the subtle signals that are available in face-to-face conversation.

Hard-copy sources are updated at intervals, which may or may not be known. Human sources are updated continuously. That is, people keep learning (some more than others).

You can use hard-copy sources for hours and hours, and nobody gets tired except you. The most valuable human sources tend to be the busiest people.

Therefore do as much information gathering as you can by consulting nonhuman sources (and people paid to help, such as reference librarians, including those at specialty libraries who can often be wellsprings of info). Use meetings with people when they have the most distinctive benefit. Often this is at the beginning, to get an overview and recommendations on resources; and in the final stages of research, to answer questions that you haven't been able to address and to test out your conclusions. Other useful guidelines are to:

1. Focus on questions that the interviewee is uniquely qualified to answer and that will make a major difference in the decision you are facing (for example, be very careful of expecting individuals to generalize on "what it's like to work in this industry" based on their own experience);
2. Offer information in return when you can (from your research using publicly available sources, being very careful not to breach any confidential conversations);
3. Plan lines of questioning ahead; if that's difficult, second best is stating your ultimate goal or quandary and asking, "What do you know that could help me with this decision?"
4. Take no longer than half an hour, unless the conversation is taking off like wildfire and your source begs you to stay.

In terms of prospecting for opportunities, keep in mind the vastness of the "hidden job market." Only a small number of jobs make it into general interest publications like newspapers. To track opportunities in a given field, consider the factors behind the creation of a job. A market. A regulation. A grant or contract. Look for these, and the jobs will pop up.

For example, many emerging job fields, from pollution prevention to transportation planning, tend to be mainstreamed largely as a result of government regulation and incentives. And so, going upstream to follow the changes in policy will tell you the direction of the emerging work opportunities. That same "upstream" strategy also means tracking the flow of foundation funding, and private sector investment, in order to know where the work is about to occur. This requires an understanding of the field, which takes some time. But it's more empowering and typically generates more leads than waiting for the actual jobs to materialize. The trick is to identify a small number of key information sources to monitor for your specific interest, including trade publications, association newsletters, databases on grants, and even the good old *Wall Street Journal*.

More than 20 Questions

Take a look at the "Options Map" you created in the previous chapter. Now study the categories as you've defined them. For each one, play a game of More than Twenty Questions. Ask what *you* would like to know about this cluster of opportunities in order to evaluate where you might fit, and find your way in there. For starters, here are some questions ...

About a particular job

1. What's the fit between the job description and your goals/hopes?
2. How will your performance be evaluated?
3. What's the pace? Are people around you considered hyper? Is it typical to work nights and/or weekends?
4. How about the attractiveness and comfort of physical setting? (Consider lights, noise, cleanliness, smoke, organization of workstation or office and your freedom to adapt it to your needs, occupational/environmental hazards including potential for injury from computers and other equipment.)
5. Will you have access to tools you need?
6. What's your budget and support system?
7. Where does this position stand on the organizational chart (and what can you determine about the informal power available to you)?
8. Why did the last person in the position leave it?

About the work environment:

1. How much mobility is available — up and/or around the organization? Does the culture encourage lateral moves? What training and development opportunities are there to help you expand responsibility if you want to? Are there multiple career tracks with increased recognition (e.g. scientific/technical, managerial)? Do educational benefits such as tuition reimbursement apply to all employees, or just selected classifications?
2. How are decisions typically made by your potential colleagues and supervisors?
3. What's the culture like?
4. How much flexibility is there in scheduling? (Consider formal programs such as flextime, job-sharing, telecommuting, and family care leaves of absence. Consider also the informal attitudes toward them: How much are they used? Are the patterns of use fairly democratic? Are they associated with lack of ambition or commitment?)
5. What is the ratio of salaries allowed in the organization — from the highest paid executive to the lowest paid go-fer? Are there formal guidelines to promote pay equity?
6. Is there an Employee Assistance Program or similar source of support for people with personal problems?
7. Is there support for childcare and other kinds of dependent care? How does the degree of support compare with other employers of similar size in the same field?
8. Are there programs for quality management, skill sharing, teambuilding, etc.? Are they loved, hated, ignored, or some of each?
9. Are there opportunities for community service with co-workers, whether it's a little bit on a regular basis or a sabbaticals program for long-time employees?

10. What's the organization's record on occupational health and safety? This is important not only in factory situations but for professionals who use many kinds of lab or office technology. Consult regional offices of the federal Occupational Safety and Health Administration, and the Coalitions on Occupational Safety and Health which exist in many states.

About the workplace's social performance:

1. What's the mission? What does this enterprise aim to do in the world?
2. Who are the "stakeholders" affected by the success of the enterprise? How is each stakeholder affected (ideally and in actual practice)?
3. How have decisions been made about physical siting of the offices, plants, etc.? Before the organization was here, what was here? What's the story behind their departure?
4. What specific programs does the organization have to contribute to the well-being of the surrounding community, financially or with service? What kinds of reviews do they get in the communities affected?
5. What local and federal taxes has the organization paid in the last few years? How does this compare to revenues?
6. Does this organization publish a social audit (as, for example, member companies of the Social Venture Network are committed to do)?
7. Would you give the product or service of this organization to someone you love as a gift?

About environmental performance:

1. Are endangered species or resources affected by the company's practices?
2. What is the organization's record on resource use and waste handling? If it's a manufacturing company, does it tend to rely more on pollution prevention or control?
3. How are products packaged? What efforts have been made to minimize solid waste, use recycled packaging materials, etc? Is there an office recycling program in effect, and is it taken seriously?
4. How are environmental policies different in the organization's US and foreign operations?
5. Are products or processes tested on animals? If so, are alternatives being developed?
6. What efforts has the organization made to improve its environmental performance? For example:

   — Have performance goals been set?

   — Does the organization subscribe to formal environmental management systems such as ISO 14000 or 14001, and/or to a code of conduct such as the CERES Principles?

   — Are there incentive systems for environmental excellence for individual workers (e.g. awards, bonuses)? How about for the organization (e.g. a "green tax" on pollution, resource use, etc.)?

— Is there a commitment to regular eco-auditing, with public reporting of the results?

Potential Employer Datasheet

Name of organization _____

Address _____

Phone/fax/email _____

Position(s) of interest_____

Contact person, address, phone & title _____

What does the organization do?
(What's the mission? And what are
the methods for accomplishing
that mission?)_____

Form of organization (e.g. nonprofit,
family business, government agency) _____

Number of employees _____

Location(s) _____

How big is the organization's impact? _____

sales volume (if business)_____

budget (if government agency or
nonprofit) _____

number of clients served _____

Who owns the organization?
[If a business, who are shareholders?
If nonprofit, who is on the board
of directors?] _____

Stock trends (if business) and other
indications of health _____

Strategic plans _____

Significant historic events
(e.g. changes in products/services;
reorganizations; controversies)_____

Potential Employer Evaluation Sheet:

Use this form to list positive aspects of a potential job (**+**); aspects about which you're neutral or need more information (**?**), and drawbacks (**–**).

1. Job satisfaction factors

+	**?**	**–**

2. Work environment factors

+	**?**	**–**

3. Social performance factors

+	**?**	**–**

4. Environmental performance factors

+	**?**	**–**

The Socially Responsible Job Interview

Joanie, an educational psychologist applying for a high-powered job in a school system, got completely disoriented in her home city on the way to the interview. She knew where she was going, but drifted into that peculiar brain-fog that takes over in the presence of strong emotions. She knew it was a sign of her mixed feelings about the job. On arrival, she put on the Interview Mask and impressed the superintendent's staff with her qualifications. But something about the conversation just felt too unreal. "I want to discuss one other thing," she blurted at the end. "On the way here, I had some really strong feelings about whether or not I'm a fit for this job, and they were so overpowering that I drove in circles. And I was embarrassed to tell you that. But I can't walk out of here pretending I want to work for people I don't feel safe enough with to share something like that. And I like you, so I'm opening my mouth." The interviewers laughed, prolonged the conversation for another half hour to discuss the ways the school system had been struggling with staff communication issues, and hired Joanie because they thought her directness and bravery might help the situation.

Think about your next job interview, whether or not you know when and where it will be. Who are you becoming, and what selling points do you want to get people excited about? Where do you want to use these talents to do some good? And what makes you think you can tell in advance that a particular workplace will welcome your values?

The rituals that formalize working relationships — from interviews to performance reviews to company outings — are exquisite reflections about what a society really believes. So it fits that norms of interviewing and hiring are in tremendous flux. On one end of a spectrum, there is the increasing use of psychological testing, group interviews, computerized scanning of résumés, and other tools designed to get quantitative — which is at least one way of getting clear, or clearer, about measuring what matters. At the other extreme, there are stories out there about interviews in which the conversation jumped out of the box — as if interviewer and candidate forged a nonverbal agreement to test out each other's risk levels — and people got hired explicitly for the virtues of self-knowledge, self-respect, and communication skill.

At the very least, this means the game is not as narrow as the rulebook, and the interview is an opportunity to test what's possible in doing the actual work. Whether you are a job-seeker or potential contractor exploring a match, or a person with an idea doing the mating dance with financial backers, remember: an interview isn't just where you try to get a "yes." It's where you try to get a "yes" that doesn't launch a disastrous mismatch — for example, by discussing your honest hopes, strengths and struggles concretely with your manager-to-be; by looking at how tough dilemmas have been handled and letting those "organizational integrity" levels inform your decision about whether to take the job.

For the purposes of this discussion, there are two kinds of work situations: those where you think you're a good fit in terms of values, and really want to bring your whole being to work; and those where that isn't the case, but for some reason you want to be there. Situations of the second kind obviously require circumspection. But situations of the first kind invite a more expansive approach. Advance research will help you to set your trust meter accordingly.

When you make a conscious decision to bring these additional levels of dialogue into an interview, here are some guidelines for preparing and helping to set the agenda:

1. First, establish good rapport and let the interviewers' agendas get taken care of.
2. Use open-ended questions to draw others out and get information that's relatively free of the bias of your expectations.
3. When raising a difficult question, try hard to show how your concerns are compatible with the enterprise's mission and can contribute positively to the organization's success.
4. Draw on your knowledge of industry standards and best practices.
5. If you open up a discussion topic, be prepared to follow it up in a way that shows your knowledge and mature judgment. Be prepared for success as well as barriers. For example, what if the interviewer says "So, how would you go about reducing the carbon emissions in this plant?"
6. Continually test the waters and have a safe change of subject ready.

In-Depth Investigation: When and How to Dig Deeper

This final section contains information you will only need in a tiny minority of situations. But when you need it, you often need it fast. In doing your job or in looking for one, a question may pop up that is not answered in print or electronic media. That question may matter to you quite a bit, especially if it applies to an organization where you are already working. Is this company as lacking in cultural diversity as it looks? Why was this policy on chemical waste handling just changed? What is that bland-sounding political action committee the company has been supporting? Why have these lawyers been coming around? Critical research skills are not just important in identifying suitable kinds of jobs and getting hired in them; they're strong assets in doing your job with integrity.

Especially if the enterprise you're concerned about is privately owned, and therefore does a minimum of reporting to public agencies about its doings, you might be faced with the need to dig personally for large amounts of the information you need. Independent investigation might also be called for if the enterprise you're concerned with is a major employer whose practices have a wide impact; if the misdeeds you're concerned about are actually abusive to people or the planet; or if the truth or falsehood of your worst fears would make a major difference in your own choices about where to work and why.

Digging deeper is always an option — although it's one to be used judiciously. It's a matter of balancing investment and impact. On one hand, many secrets are poorly kept, and the act of unearthing them can be exhilarating. On the other hand, after you've done so, you have to live with the knowledge and so do other people.

In scoping out what's going on in a situation of concern, starter-questions include:

1. Who's in charge? What's that person's background? Strengths and limitations? Ideology? Possible conflicts of interest? What's that person's primary (probably unwritten) agenda on the job?

Exercise: Talking Back to Telemarketers

Since this exercise was first published, I have begun to rent counseling space in an office building with two telemarketing firms. In the elevator and the coffee line, I have been frequently reminded that the people who work for these enterprises are interesting, fully-dimensioned human beings who may have their share of trouble with the premises under which they are operating. Some are actors, artists, and graduate students. All are human, and this exercise should be done in a spirit of tweaking the premise but respecting the person.

Here's a truly wicked way to develop your critical questioning skills. It's an exercise called "Talking Back to Telemarketers." I'm embarrassed to admit that I have actually done this.

When Brad from Opinion Dynamics Corporation calls you at dinnertime, sounding like he's reading from a script designed by highly paid psychologists, instead of hanging up or answering the questions with businesslike numbness, pretend that Brad is a long-lost friend and is actually interested in meaningful dialogue. Take your time in answering the questions. Add juicy tidbits. When you're given multiple choices, consider options that aren't on the menu. Toss some questions back and ask Brad how he feels about them. Probe the assumptions underlying other questions.

Give the poor guy some usable answers, but make him work for them. The game here is twofold: to face down a totally scripted conversation and get comfortable setting your own agenda, and to become aware of your "hot buttons" which may be pushed in your mind when you are confronting confusing or distorted information.

2. What's the organization's mission, as expressed in its corporate charter or other founding documents? What have been the major controversies when continued authorization and funding have been debated?

3. Who are the organization's major critics (individuals and watchdog groups)? What pressures do they exert?

Charles Nicodemus, an award-winning investigative reporter for the Chicago *Sun-Times*, offers the following advice to people who are thinking of launching an investigation into the practices of an employer:

> *First, find out how the system is supposed to work, when it works. This applies to a company, a government agency, or a process within an organization. When you see a specific disparity between the way things are supposed to function and the way they do, start asking why.*

> *It's usually the 'little people' — who keep the files, do the typing, transcribe the memos and keep the calendars and appointment books — who know what's going on. Cultivate people who have direct access to documents and may be able to share them for a good cause. But be very, very careful to protect these people.*

> *Finally, successful investigations often hinge on the temperament of the investigator. Be imaginative, resourceful, judicious, determined, skeptical.*

In dealing with important information, always get a second opinion. Be careful whom you trust, if you trust anyone at all. Don't let your wishes influence your judgment.

Some of your rights to information held by government agencies or private companies are spelled out in the law, including the federal Freedom of Information Act, the national security classification system, trade secrets laws, the federal Right-to-Know law and many state counterparts. Your reference to them can sometimes help convince a source to cooperate with you. Court rulings have set strict limits on the situations in which companies can withhold information that is relevant to public health and safety by calling it a trade secret. For example, many questions about chemical hazards are covered by the federal Right-to-Know law, which provides that no information covered by the law can be considered a trade secret if:

- it has been disclosed to any person without binding them through a confidentiality agreement;
- it would be required to be disclosed under another law or requirement;
- disclosure of the information would not hurt the firm's competitive position; or
- the identity of the chemical could be readily discovered by an engineer working in reverse from the product ('reverse engineering').

Finally, if your investigation uncovers serious abuses, you will be faced with a bigger quandary than whether to accept or keep a job: whether or not to go public with the information you have gleaned. This can be a life-changing decision. If you are considering going public about a major abuse you have discovered through investigation, refer to Step 10 for a discussion of the realities of whistle-blowing and some sources of support for doing it wisely.

Charles Nicodemus adds this encouragement: "It is becoming increasingly fashionable to be ethical, and that's a change in substance as well as appearance. Someone has to stand up first, but that act makes it easier for others to stand up in the future. One person can make a difference. If you find problems with an organization, tell somebody. Your disclosure will make it much easier for others. It does work that way."

Step 6:
Identify the Essence
of Your Work in the World

If your workplace burned to the ground and you had to start over, what would you do? If you distilled all the ingredients of your values and guiding images and cares for the world into a single drop, how would it taste? If you listed all the attributes and impacts of your desired work, then one-by-one crossed off all you could live without, what are the exact words that would still live on the page? What have been the underlying characteristics or themes of your working life regardless of the jobs you were doing? What have been the primary roles you have gravitated toward and loved most? What have you found a way to do in almost any situation? Somewhere in these answers, there is an essential impulse to action that guides your choices — a gestalt or organizing principle. It may be well-developed or embryonic, but it will come to life when you begin to name it and take action on its behalf. As you do this, you take charge of your working life.

Here's an example. One friend of mine started her adult life as a music major and choir director. Then she married and spent some years as a mother and homemaker. As her kids grew, she became more and more active in the community, hosting a TV talk show and getting involved in the civil rights movement. Moving back into paid employment, she joined the field staff for a national nonprofit organization concerned with peacemaking. Then she became a fundraiser for another grassroots organization. Through all these shifts, people who have known her for years say she has always done essentially the same work: gathering people together for sociability and celebration, for learning about each other and working together to solve common problems. Issues of widespread concern, from nuclear arms control to family planning, have been focal at times. In every job, she has used superb social skills and a sensitivity to group dynamics. In every job, she has learned a new set of technical skills to do her work in a new way. Whether her overt role is "fundraiser" or "community organizer" or "teacher" or "mother," the essence of her work is building community in a way that gets people participating in social movements.

I've been listening lately to people's simple statements about their work, and hearing powerful messages about who they think they are and can be. Craftsperson, communicator, organizer, healer, advocate, technical innovator, marketer, and builder are one-word descriptions that speak volumes, not only about the specific job but about the values and priorities that animate it. Many career counselors advise a slightly more detailed, but still simple, descriptive statement, not only for self-definition but for self-promotion as well:

— "I'm a teacher with international experience who really wants to see a new kind of intercultural program in our school system."

— "I'm an engineer with ten years experience in transportation systems, and I want to help
small-to-medium-sized cities design mass transit systems that work for communities."

— And this from the manager of the computer department for a small nonprofit organization: "I'm the guy who does everything around here that doesn't require social skills."

Fundraising expert Laurie Blum draws attention to her books and consulting services with the title "Free Money." Author and seminar leader Barbara Winter supports self-
employed people she calls the "Joyfully Jobless." A tailoring service near my house caught my
eye with the name, "Clothes Clinic." Attorney Kimm Walton syndicates her well-researched
column on legal careers in more than 300 outlets by proclaiming herself, "The Job Goddess."
My neighbor Gene Fischer calls his consulting business on nontoxic homes and lifestyles
"House Doctor."

Naming focuses the nature of your work and its market. Maria DuBois was only
sure that her role involved some kind of information exchange in the realm of health services until the term "health care broker" crystallized in her mind; what she does is help people navigate through the maze of specialties and the dilemmas regarding alternative care,
make wise choices, identify providers, evaluate costs, and line up regimens of care without
making themselves sicker in the process. Entrepreneurs get to choose what to call themselves. Some companies conspire with employees to create interesting and informative job
titles — like the Endangered Species Chocolate Company, where the webmaster and designer
is called Director of Intelligence and the Director of Finance doubles as Director of Defense.

Beyond its focusing and marketing value, the ritual of naming can have an enormous mythic impact on the person who accepts it and internalizes its meaning. John Cronin
grew up on the Hudson River near New York City and tried on many identities for protecting the waters, including several years as an aide in the New York State Assembly. Eventually,
in the 1970s, he let himself be persuaded to work for a minimal salary patrolling the river in
a small boat, representing an embryonic nonprofit organization with a bold name, "The
Riverkeeper." In his 1998 memoir co-authored with partner Robert Kennedy Jr., *The
Riverkeepers*, he vividly remembers the moment his resolve was first tested. He encountered a
huge barge discharging a large quantity of something unknown into the river. "Who goes
there?" he demanded with megaphone in hand. The Exxon Corporation identified itself.
"And who goes there?" came the counter-question. From somewhere in Cronin's being came
the authority to shout out, "The Riverkeeper." His documentation of this discharge, and
many more, contributed to the successful prosecution of the polluters. The Riverkeeper
became a legal advocacy project of some sophistication, and quickly sent a message that the
Hudson River was no longer a place to take illegal wastes "away."

This individual step — taking full responsibility for naming what you have to offer
and why it matters — fits interestingly with the evolution of business into a more knowl-
edge-intensive realm. Many of the best employers are recognizing that one of the primary
factors that can distinguish them in the marketplace is the knowledge and human talents

they hold uniquely. Intellectual capital is valued as never before. As Matthew Arnold and Rob Day of the World Resources Institute note in their study, "The Next Bottom Line: Making Sustainable Development Tangible,"

> *The key to resource productivity lies in making creative use of knowledge to drive resource use down and the value to a customer up. Knowledge can increase the efficiency of an operation, and also the value of a product. We agree with business writer Thomas Stewart: "Knowledge is more valuable and powerful than natural resources, big factories, or fat payrolls. In industry after industry, success comes to the companies that have the best information or wield it most effectively."*

> *Information is so important because it differentiates a company from its competitors. As professor Michael Porter points out, "A company can outperform rivals only if it can establish a difference that it can preserve. Competitive strategy is about being different. It means deliberately choosing a different set of activities to deliver a unique mix of value." The link between Porter's competitiveness argument and Stewart's intellectual capital concept is clear — firms should invest in information over material use because anyone can have access to materials, but each company has a unique set of information at its disposal.*

Simply put, cookie-cutter workplaces need cookie-cutter people, but distinctive workplaces are recognizing the need for distinctive people.

Some people find it helpful to think about these capsule descriptions in terms of personal "mission." This seems to work best when it comes from within, authentically and easily, and when it's held lightly. If romanticized or taken up uncritically, a sense of mission can also provide an escape hatch from the mundane but necessary day-to-day questions about how to live. It can lead to fanaticism, inflexibility, and unrealistic expectations for staying on a single track. As Rick Jarow observes, "Many people who are absolutely sure of what they want to do with their lives are clinically crazy."

Lots of people think there is an automatic fit between qualities they see in themselves and kinds of work they could do. They think that self-assessment and investigation of the options, by themselves, will force a choice to pop out. Choosing work is not a logical activity; it's an informed gamble as to which of the available possibilities will really draw the most from you. This process of discrimination comes to life when you identify two aspects of your work:

- the essence or core ("What's necessary if I'm going to be myself with integrity in my work?") *and*
- the limits you need to set to work with integrity ("What's not okay for me — what's an unacceptable compromise or a violation of my values — in my choice and performance of work?").

These are two complementary ways of asking, "What conditions do I need to hold out for in my work if I want to be able to look at myself in the mirror in the morning?" You may not always be able to meet those conditions. But you can keep them in mind, put your antenna out for new approaches to the search, and give yourself permission to keep asking whether a particular compromise position is still necessary. That questioning process often uncovers assumptions that are unnecessarily restrictive. A client of mine with fabulous administrative and financial management skills struggled, for a time, about whether or not to admit to prospective employers that she had gained these skills by living on a large ashram. Eventually, her attention was drawn to the discomfort she felt in the interviews when glossing over this most important part of her history, which still shaped her spiritual life. She wondered how comfortable it would be to go to work every day and be apprehensive about disclosing this part of her history to co-workers. Exploring the options for talking about it, she got clear that:

1. Those years had been a rich time of professional development because they had involved so much collaborative decision-making, cross-training with co-workers, and implementing the techniques of stress management and conflict management they were teaching others, years before these tools gained common currency.

2. Potential employers who had no experience with ashrams might have legitimate questions about her experience — for example, how she would fit into the workplace culture — and she could demonstrate her communication skills and proactive stance by shifting her role in the interview subtly from "applicant" to "educator" in addressing these concerns

3. She could transform the situation with warmth, humor, and fearlessness.

Even if your sense of personal purpose is quite general, you are still operating within an ethical framework and can still benefit from making it explicit, first and foremost to yourself. One approach to this is illustrated by my friend Steve Kropper, the CEO of a Boston information business called Inpho which helps prospective homebuyers find out about neighborhood property values and other factors that might influence their buying decisions. Having more than paid his dues in the world of high-risk — running innovative energy conservation businesses in the 1980s and surfing several turbulent waves of governmental funding — Steve rediscovered the value of having time for a marriage and family, and decided that the content of his next business was less important than its ability to create a platform for viable lives for his workforce, and a climate where people could learn to value themselves. He entered a stage of life where what mattered most was the immediate: the ability to give excellent training and mentoring to quality employees, to create a nondiscriminatory environment, and to have time on the side to take his Cub Scouts out on environmental projects. Steve created a matrix for evaluating job opportunities when he was working for other people; it can also guide him in business opportunities today. It has two dimensions: a company's growth and its impact.

HIGH GROWTH/ POSITIVE IMPACT	HIGH GROWTH/ NEGATIVE IMPACT
LOW GROWTH/ POSITIVE IMPACT	LOW GROWTH/ NEGATIVE IMPACT

He explains: "I figure that a growing enterprise will be best able to afford to be generous, both with opportunities for me and in letting me use my position to do good for other people. So I look for businesses that are growing. They also have to be at least neutral and preferably positive in their impact, as I see it. I won't work in a company I think is doing harm, no matter how much it's growing. I'll work in a place where the impact is lukewarm, if the business is expanding and the culture allows me, personally, to have a positive effect through my work. That formula is simple enough that I can put it into practice and still find work. And it generally keeps me out of big trouble."

When you are interested in more than minimizing harm — in accomplishing a particular purpose, it becomes all the more important to sift through your options and images of playing them out, until a sense of honest purpose crystallizes. Consider what different paths can be traveled by people using a superficially similar set of skills in service of similar values — and why the particulars of a situation make all the difference. Here are two stories of people with similar skillsets. Both would call themselves designers. But they have each evolved quite different and distinctive bodies of work. For each of them, the distinctive aspect is not the skills being used, but the organizing vision and strategy that guides the use of the skills. Both illustrate the kind of evolutionary process that comes into play as people hone their definition of their own work through practice. Wendy Brawer helps cities and other large groups of people develop "green maps" of environmental assets and damages. Brawer graduated from art school in Seattle in the 1970s, with a major interest in design. She gravitated to the field of industrial design — that is, designing things that are mass-produced, "one of the most flexible of design fields." Although resource-efficiency naturally attracted her, she did not consider herself an environmentalist beyond that. But she couldn't help but take notice of the turbulence throughout the community as Seattle's major industry, Boeing, was coming apart. The common slogan was "Last one to leave Seattle turn out the lights." Brawer left, for Tokyo, with the aim of making money by teaching English and making sure her life didn't grow dull.

Two experiences, together, got her attention: getting involved in an artistic collaboration on a "countdown to the millenium" clock, and taking a vacation in Bali. "Here you are in this absolutely gorgeous place," she reflects, "and you come out of your cabin one morning and find a swath of landscape just razed and another guest cabin put on it. People who always walked or rode a bike are suddenly on a scooter. These were things I could see in two weeks." The combination forced the question, "What am I doing wasting my time?" and she resolved to redirect her life to do as much as possible to protect the environment.

Back in the US, Brawer's design focus led her to think hard about materials use — not only substitution and reduction, but the size of the stream of manufactured goods she saw. "People are drowning in stuff and here I am helping to produce more stuff for them," she lamented. Professionally, she learned all she could about alternative materials and more streamlined approaches to design. On the side, she got involved in an ambitious campaign, "Stamp Out Junk Mail," ultimately sending free information to hundreds of agencies, from state attorney generals' offices to the grassroots. This was satisfying, but not income-producing. She got funding and did several high-visibility educational projects in waste reduction, including a major display to encourage recycling in Times Square and a waste-reduction project in a housing complex that helped 1,700 apartments each cut water use by 65 gallons a day. This was moving in the right direction, but still felt reactive.

Seeing Your Impact

Imagine yourself working in the field of your choice. Let your imagination expand to include your colleagues, mentors, young ones coming in, other enterprises you interact with — the social ecosystem of your work. Your mind can't know in advance where you'll go, but your imagination can bring forth possibilities to try on for size.

What do you imagine this collective enterprise might accomplish? What might they try and fail? In what ways are they (and you) brave and encouraging? In what ways might the collective effort be disappointing?

Just sit with the possibilities your imagination brings up; pay attention to what's concrete and rings true for you as a possibility, but don't think too much about what's socially defined as realistic.

Homing in on your personal role:
Where did you end up? What did you contribute — through the direct impact of your work and its ripple effects? Finally, how did this phase of your working life come to fruition?

Now, if you want to maximize the positive outcomes you imagined, what kinds of actions will you need to take? What dilemmas will you have to resolve to do these things? What kinds of support will help to make this possible?

Brawer also began teaching at Cooper Union, blending regular industrial design with "Design for the Environment." While she knew that New York was "a tough city to capture people's imagination," it captured hers. By 1992, when large numbers of delegates to the United Nations Earth Summit were descending on the city, Brawer had figured out that they would want to find the health food stores and parks. That led her to propose and spearhead the production of the first Green Apple Map, giving birth to a Green Map system that now involves 70 municipalities in 20 countries. The New York City map uses a simple system of icons to represent 700 sites including community gardens, coastal wetlands, nature trails, green businesses and recycling centers. Still supplementing her income by teaching, she lives and works in a Soho loft that is the nerve center of Modern World Design, the nonprofit that helps communities from Adelaide to Berkeley in conceiving and carrying out their green mapping projects. Like many good designs, the idea was evolutionary rather than preconceived. But it's ecological and educational on many levels, she explains: "Maps are very resource-efficient, they're universally understood, and they encourage discovery."

Another design professional, Ken Geiser is Executive Director of the Massachusetts Toxics Use Reduction Institute, which helps industrial companies in planning and implementing pollution prevention systems. Geiser was trained as an architect and came of age in the extended community orbiting around Frank Lloyd Wright. He has this to say about the path into his current work, which on the surface is far from architecture:

> I didn't intend to do anything like what I'm doing. However, I've always had a huge commitment to social justice and community rights. As I became more involved in civil rights and antiwar work in the 1960s, my commitment to architecture became very complicated, and I left it after two years.
>
> I went to MIT to study urban planning, and did a lot of grassroots organizing there. I helped stop a highway. I helped set up a home-based school. I had a growing interest in the environment and working-class life. That drew me into working with trade unions, and into a kind of working-class environmentalism — a notion which, in those days, made no sense at all.
>
> By my early 30s, I had begun, seriously, to find out what my work was. I realized that jobs and projects were ancillary to the work. They were a means of getting the work done. For me, "the work" meant saving us from annihilating ourselves, whether that meant focusing on urban rats or on racial injustices in exposure to environmental hazards — whatever the specifics. Toxic chemicals became my primary vehicle, because that was the most ripe area for organizing.

Geiser spent years integrating an awareness of the condition of human society into his life and identifying different approaches for doing something useful. He had a strong, but general, commitment to the greater good, but was able to entertain many different ideas about how to serve that good. Over the years, through action on his commitment and a whole lot of paying attention, he fine-tuned his views about how to do the work. An unorthodox but powerful organizing principle came to him after a few years in the fray:

> I realized that I needed to code this thing in a new way, so to speak. Jokingly at first, and then more seriously, I said I needed a metric for measuring what I was achieving, so that I would be able to take stock at the end of my life.

I chose one that seemed rather silly, but that I've actually taken to heart. I've developed a list of toxic chemicals that are generally agreed to be environmental health hazards of a very significant magnitude. I've decided that the world isn't big enough for them and me. So they have to go. I have dedicated myself to the removal of this series of chemicals from commerce. That way, I can mark my success not only in terms of this passion, but also in very clear behavioral terms.

In the short run, this journey took him out of the profession he loved. But lately, he has come around, full-circle, to new possibilities in using his design training and sensibilities. Now they are directed toward finding new, nontoxic materials for building and industry, and understanding how industrial decision-makers choose their materials in the first place, in order to "tap the most creative forces in the society for building a much better house in the future," metaphorically and literally.

This illustrates a common experience among people who allow themselves to be led by an unfolding sense of purpose, and who — within the limits of real-world alternatives at any given time — do their best to choose jobs that help them do "their work." New ideas and images come, and are integrated sooner or later. Obsolete understandings are shed. It is not a process any of us can control. We can only pay attention and use what we know about ourselves to shape our strategies, holding onto as many elements as we can and letting go when we have to. Somehow, doing that can lead us back to new ways to make use of the experiences and commitments with which we started out.

A healthy sense of purpose comes from the land of the living. That is, it arises through engagement with people, communities, and nature, in the course of trying to do even a little something useful. You learn that you are a nurturer by working for a community agency teaching handicapped people how to garden. The garden is threatened by a highway right-of-way, and you discover overnight that you're also a fighter. You learn about the untapped reservoirs of community support when people come out and get involved. You learn about betrayal, during the court battle, when your agency becomes factionalized. Over the years, your sense of professional identity and direction grows a lot like the garden. It gets less idealized and more personalized. You are challenged to make peace with overlapping and conflicting loyalties in terms of who you really work for: the clients who benefit from the garden directly, the agency that oversees it, and helps many others, the vision of urban gardening ... or hands-on education ... or land preservation. You know the kind of soil you need to work productively, and the kinds of fruits your labor can produce. You refine this understanding as you move

Your Distinct Gifts

"There is a vitality, a life force, an energy, a quickening that is translated through you into action. And because there is only one of you in all time, this expression is unique, and if you block it, it will never exist through any other medium. It will be lost. The world will not have it. It is not your business to determine how good it is, nor how valuable, nor how it compares to other expressions. It is your business to keep the channel open. You do not even have to believe in yourself or your work. You have to keep aware and open directly to the urges that activate you. Keep the channel open."

— Martha Graham

forward, through small choices and larger ones, identifying the essence right now, and then further refining it through each action you take.

Step 7:
Commit Yourself to Doing Your Work in Some Form, Whether or Not Anyone is Paying You for it Right Now

"Sentiment without action is the ruin of the soul."

— Edward Abbey

Listen to Lisa Conte, CEO of Shaman Pharmaceuticals, which successfully reinvented itself when costly federal requirements made its primary product line impossible to bring to market:

> *It's a matter of simple endurance, which for me is fueled by the belief that what we're doing is the right thing for the planet. The possibilities we're working to realize will never have another chance to be achieved by any other company. Our niche is that distinctive. And there has never been a time like this in healthcare, what with all the rising interest in self-medication, changes in access to information, not to mention branding opportunities via the Internet. I grew up in a rural setting, where you had to see every change as opportunity and keep a flexible mind. That, plus love for what we're doing, keeps me going.*

Listen to George Bliss, who is working to commercialize bicycle-powered "pedi-cabs" as a transportation alternative in New York City.

> *New York is the hardest place in the world for getting this idea to work. New Yorkers are very prone to lawsuits, very jumpy about insurance issues. Storage space is at a premium. And there are no institutions that have a stake in seeing locally produced alternative vehicles. So I figure that if I can get it to work here, it can work anywhere.*

Listen to Paula Gutlove, director of the Balkans Peace Project, a team of mediators and trainers who visited areas outside the war zones of the former Yugoslavia to train community leaders in conflict resolution methods, hoping to prevent new explosions of violence like the 1999 war in Kosovo.

> *I'll get into the taxi to go to the airport for these mammoth journeys, with one of my kids clinging to each leg saying "Don't leave." I'll get into the taxi asking "Why am I doing this? This is insane. I don't want to go." I meet up*

> *with my colleagues, who are saying the same things. Then, after the work-*
> *shop, we know why we're doing it. Seeing the people there and participating*
> *in the process — it feels like what we're doing could make some change.*
> *Bringing together a group of people from different ethnic backgrounds, and*
> *having them hear each other — that's success for me.*

In these cases and many more, the source of commitment is decidedly larger than the individual's narrow self-interest. Difficult paths are accepted and even embraced because they are
connected to a large enough purpose — sometimes larger than the individual can figure out
in the moment. Those of us who are metaphysically inclined might say that we're being
acted-through, or that transpersonal will is kicking in. Sharon Welch, theologian and
women's studies professor, reminds us that in many cultures this is an ordinary mode of
operation. It is a fairly rare luxury to be able to hold change at arm's length and choose only
those risks that have clear payoffs. People holding a large measure of social power can do
this; most of us, most of the time, need to unlearn the expectation, especially if we are working on behalf of projects or interests that are part of a new order rather than the entrenched
one. In *A Feminist Ethic of Risk*, Welch tells the stories of African-American women in positions of leadership in the civil rights movement. Consistently, they took action, not when the
risk was necessarily low or the payoff clear, but when the need was pronounced.
Paradoxically, as they let go of controlling the results, their actions had impacts that rever-
berated far beyond their conscious vision. The letting-go occurred in the context of commitment to a vision larger than personal hopes or outcomes.

Psychologist Laura Sewall, who created a pioneering ecopsychology program at
Prescott College in Arizona, expresses a similar view:

> *When I get hung up in making a commitment, it's always the same old*
> *thing in the way: ego. Wanting to wait and see. Wanting to keep those*
> *options open. It's such an old, stale game. And the only thing that gets me*
> *out of it is remembering that I'm not doing this just for me, for my tenure*
> *or my reviews or even just my students. I'm doing it for the Earth. When I*
> *get a grip on that fact, my ego is able to rest and the commitment flows.*

Many effective people who find ways to integrate personal and planetary concerns in their
work show a distinctive kind of purposefulness which is worth a closer look. Healthy commitment comes from within. It offers a path for self-expression and actualization. It may
require deferring gratification in significant ways, but it doesn't require stuffing down your
essential self. It is not about self-sacrifice, but about Self-expression, about uncovering a
personal vision and steadily directing inner and outer resources toward bringing that vision
alive. Naturally enough, when that vision is capable of touching other lives, leaving a legacy,
or changing the conditions around you, its attractive force can be especially strong.

One of my lifelong heroes is the character played by Dustin Hoffman in the 1984
film, *Tootsie*. He's a struggling actor so committed to his craft that he takes on a female identity and auditions for a soap opera role. He is chosen, and becomes dangerously successful.
In mythic terms, there's something there about being willing to suspend even your most

Exercise: Balancing Risks and Opportunities

If you still react to the possibility of life changes by obsessing on the possible downside, you're not alone. The following exercise helps put the risks of any contemplated change into perspective by considering also the benefits of making the change — and the risks and benefits of staying put. A simple grid helps you organize these four elements and then look at them all together.

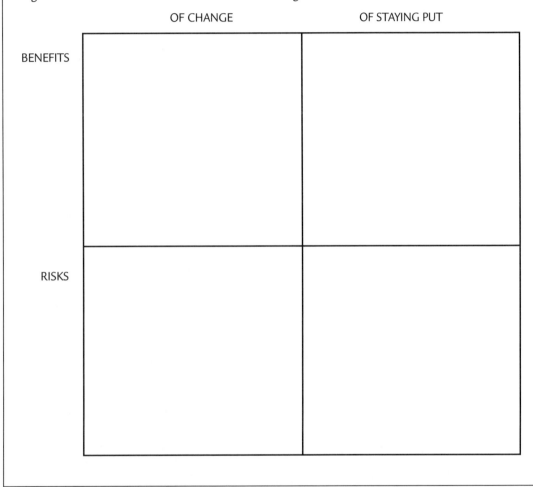

	OF CHANGE	OF STAYING PUT
BENEFITS		
RISKS		

cherished assumptions as to who you are and how you can live, in order to create something magical that expresses your deepest core. This story is also a reminder that one of the most frightening aspects of commitment is the specter of success. But my attraction to the movie is actually more mundane. It has to do with one critical scene, just before the famous gender switch. Hoffman is teaching an actors' workshop in New York. He's skinny and intense. Stalking the room, he says to a mesmerized group:

> *Look. You're in the most competitive industry in the world. You're in the*
> *toughest city for that industry. We have 95 percent unemployment. But*
> *none of that matters. Find a way to work.*

Find a way to work. That is what we're all up against: a situation that doesn't let us get away with being our ordinary selves, but calls forth the extraordinary resources we all suspect we have down deep but haven't quite found a way to tap. Find a way to do your work, however you understand it at any given time, whether or not anybody else in the world is willing to pay for it or even understands it. This may seem like the ultimate unfair proposition. You can't play the oboe part of a symphony alone onstage. You can't be a literacy teacher if there's nobody there to learn from you. But you can offer demonstrations, attract collaborators, write proposals and business plans, give talks, volunteer a little time to assist people who are noted in the field, and otherwise take action that will strengthen your connections and credibility — all while waiting and watching for a more formal opportunity. Doing so will rarely hurt in attracting that opportunity.

"I told my writing students that practice is something done under all circumstances, whether you're happy or sad. You don't become tossed away by a high weekend or a blue Monday. It is something close to you, not dependent on high-tech gyrations or smooth workshop-leader talk. Writing is something you do quietly, regularly, and in doing it, you face your life; everything comes up to fight, resist, deny, cajole you. Practice is old-fashioned, not hip or glamorous, but it gets you through Monday, and it lets you see the ungroundedness of hyped-up New Age workshops or quick ways to write a best-selling novel that you end up never writing."

— Natalie Goldberg, *Long Quiet Highway*

Unconditional commitment is not the same as addictive attachment. You can be totally committed to your work while continuing to exercise critical judgment about acceptable means for doing it. No matter how much you want to gain experience in corporate communications, for instance, you may decide against volunteering your labor for a profitable company that has just laid off several hundred of your neighbors. But you might design an internship with them, and seek out a scholarship fund that would pay you a stipend. On the other hand, you might prefer to learn the same skills by proposing an internship with the outplacement firm that's helping those laid-off workers find other jobs, or with an agency concerned with economic development, or with a community group fighting to save jobs. In most situations, there are multiple paths to the same goal.

Another caveat: commitment to doing your work, whether or not you're being paid, does not mean giving up on making a living at your chosen work eventually. This is an especially important point for people who have been giving it away for too long. The spirit of healthy, Self-affirming commitment means discovering the kinds of actions that let you move toward a goal with satisfaction and even joy, so that commitment to work and commitment to personal well-being coincide as often as possible.

Commitment means opening up to possibility and removing barriers. It is also a matter of intent, which focuses and disciplines actions even in modest amounts. When Susan Belgard of San Francisco thought up the Safety Net Project to help people with life-threatening diseases create support systems for independent living and customized care, the idea started out totally abstract. Belgard, whose lines of work include personal coaching to guide other people in making their dreams a reality, had to come up with a project vision for a coach's training. This was it. She presented it to her training group and picked up their excitement at the idea's potential. But she was visibly ambivalent herself. The trainer picked up on it. "Tell us about it like you mean it," she challenged Belgard, who rose to the challenge and came home with a commitment that soon gave rise to a training workbook and business plan.

"OK," you say, "I'm committed ... but to what?" It might be to a long-range vision, whether or not many details of getting there are clear. Your commitment might be to working with a population or region or species or issue, although your roles and specific interests may evolve greatly. Your commitment might be to finding a way to participate in an election or campaign by the time it is launched: you might use this as a challenge and try out everything from phone banking to speech writing as a possible mode for carrying out the commitment. Of course, you might find that the most important thing to be committed to is a healthy process of moving forward, in the spirit of a client of mine who responded to the exercise above with the pledge: "Every week, I commit myself to spending at least one hour NOT obsessing on finding work."

Exercise: From Essence into Action

Start with your definition of "what's essential." What actions that are within your power, could you commit yourself to, that would place you in the stream of "your work" for real? What kinds of support would you need to pull them off? How would you need to "grow yourself" as a human being to sustain these commitments? Of the choices of commitments before you, which one(s) would be the most powerful?

Two Models

The approaches to the challenge of coherent, life-sustaining commitment are infinite. But they all build on two basic economic modes: the volunteer and the entrepreneur.

A volunteer works without pay — but not necessarily without a role, respect, and other forms of compensation. Volunteers are not all envelope-stuffers. Some serve on boards of directors. Others are strategic advisors, speechwriters, computer helpers, canvass directors, project managers and more.

Entrepreneurs are not all lean-and-hungry marketeers. They may be piano teachers or acupuncturists. Some build up their practices through word of mouth in a single community, while others work by mail order or computer network on a national or even international scale.

Barbara Winter, a trainer and chronicler of the "joyfully jobless," sees this trend as stemming from the reassertion of personal values: "People are becoming self-employed because their self-esteem is in good order and they want to learn more about what they can be as human beings. For a lot of them, that's connected to a vision of a different kind of world they'd like to build. I see this as the most powerful force in entrepreneurship and a tremendous source of commitment. It makes things like driving an eight-year-old car or working on weekends seem really unimportant."

By accepting full responsibility for launching your work in this spirit, you are reclaiming the initiative, powerfully. You're shifting the focus away from the apparent barriers, onto the emerging possibilities, cultivating will and focus. You are also presenting yourself to the world as a do-er, not a "want-to-be," and this shift can be mirrored in your self-image. This is a guaranteed way to stand out, to learn fast, and to attract all kinds of support that can help move you toward your goal. There is no better way to get to know leaders, innovators, and other allies in the field, increasing your access to information about ways to do your work for pay.

Getting yourself out there — as a volunteer, entrepreneur, or some of both — helps you develop your knowledge and skills for doing a job and for job-hunting. It strengthens your commitment in the same way that exercise strengthens your muscles. It identifies you publicly as an initiative-taker. Finally, especially in the case of major innovations and the fragile new organizations that often come into being to support them, your efforts may help to bring a movement or a profession into being. That effort, in turn, may radically alter the picture in terms of jobs five or ten years from now.

In fact, at the risk of sounding crass, I know of no better network for cultivating job and project opportunities than a movement for social change. Movements unite people and provide great networks of individuals who share your values and may well want to support you by sharing resources and contacts. Veteran activists often relate to each other with high levels of trust, a common ethical culture, and a history of cooperating in the name of a larger goal. Needless to say, this works only if you are authentically involved in a movement and have shown your commitment in tangible ways, not if you are cruising it for contacts.

"When we are pursuing our Right Livelihood, even the most difficult and demanding aspects of our work will not sway us from our course. When others say, 'Don't work so hard' or 'Don't you ever take a break?' we will respond in bewilderment. What others may see as duty, pressure, or tedium we perceive as a kind of pleasure. Commitment is easy when our work is Right Livelihood."

— Marsha Sinetar, *Do What You Love, The Money Will Follow*

People who become truly caught up in making something happen often work as a volunteer and an entrepreneur at the same time. They do whatever is needed to keep the work going. In more everyday situations, you have the luxury of thinking ahead about which image, the volunteer or the entrepreneur, will be your best organizing principle. Both orientations require high levels of initiative and commitment. But both can feed your spirit richly. Each of these paths has strong advantages and disadvantages.

Volunteer situations often carry considerable freedom to experiment. Because it lacks the perceived high stakes of a paid position, volunteer status allows you some room to try on new personalities and styles, and to test out new skills in a relatively safe environment. In fact, there are fields in which it is difficult to be hired without significant volunteer experience. Fair or not, there are reasons why this is true.

- In the arts, you simply have to cultivate and free up your talent before you're employable.
- In many service fields, such as human rights and crisis counseling, many people come in through a volunteer path; that is because there is no shortcut for the experience necessary to tap into the inner resources that make you effective. This path lets candidates show potential employers (and themselves) that they can not only perform but cope.
- In many startups, whether of businesses or nonprofit organizations, months if not years of time can be invested in defining, testing, and articulating a concept in a way that will attract financial backing.
- Similarly, researchers often invest unpaid time in developing proposals for funding. And

even the most experienced journalists may reluctantly spend some time putting together article proposals on speculation.

Be warned: in some of these situations, the fields are structured in ways that quite unfairly demand freebies from the novice practitioner. Still, the challenge of breaking in remains — without feeding these trends and without letting oneself be exploited.

Jonathan Hickman graduated from Vassar College with a degree in English and a passion for video. Like most people, he felt he was a little more than his formal education reflected. He had a history of environmental activism, but had never thought it could turn into a job. Hickman worked in publishing for a year, but "that was definitely not IT" as a career path. He regrouped.

To keep peanut butter on the shelf while regrouping, he worked as a temp, and found himself in the offices of the prestigious Council on Economic Priorities in New York City. This twenty-five-year-old nonprofit has carved out a major role for itself in documenting corporate social and environmental responsibility, awarding the brave and shining a light on the laggards. The Council's campaigns have led a number of major corporate polluters to begin cleanup. Its consumer guidebook, *Shopping for a Better World*, is a widely used tool, and its investor research has been invaluable to the social investment movement. Not since Vassar had Hickman felt so close to heaven.

When the temp job ended, Hickman was determined to stay connected to CEP. He kept on temping part-time for income, and proposed a part-time volunteer position that would facilitate a professional courtship. "They wanted to be very accommodating," he

---

GPA doesn't just mean "grade point average"

One growing support system for commitment to work that makes the world a better place is the Graduation Pledge Alliance, based at Manchester College in Indiana. Pledge campaigns, now on over 30 campuses, are opportunities for graduates to affirm to their peers that they will thoroughly investigate the social and environmental responsibility of any employment they consider. Campaigns, initiated by students or faculty, generally start with programming to familiarize students with the issues and promote exploration.

Graduates report a variety of impacts as their careers evolve. Chemist Christine Miller found her first job in a company whose name contained the word "environmental." But before long she chanced to be part of a water-cooler conversation in which her boss asked her opinion about a potential contract involving something too toxic to meet her approval. She expressed her opinion. Her boss approached her later and said, "We've decided not to go for that contract." Heartened, Miller nevertheless found herself more and more attentive to the health, safety, and environmental issues around her. She grew less and less comfortable with her job, and finally sought out another. Thanks to the Pledge, she is now happier, working as a chemist for Abbott Laboratories, developing infant formulas and nutritional products.

Find out more about the Pledge at: www.manchester.edu.

---

recalls, "and to make sure the experience would be valuable to me as well as to them." He wrote research reports on the environmental performance of large corporations. After "only" a year, he ended up with a full-time job that's the envy of many: as a researcher on a major new project, documenting the best companies for ethnic minorities to work in, published annually by *Fortune* magazine. Not bad exposure for someone two years out of college.

Some volunteer situations lead this directly to employment opportunities. Many others simply pull you into the "values subculture" you want to inhabit, and the connections carry you along from there. This was the case for Bonnie Wells, now director of the volunteer program for the International Center in New York, who launched her career as a Peace Corps volunteer in Ghana in the 1970s. Wells grew up in a service-oriented family and started out as a secretary in a business school. She found her way into the training department of American Airlines, but reached a career plateau. The Peace Corps was an option she knew little about, when she was notified of an opportunity to teach business in Ghana. "It challenged me to the max. It changed my life. That experience became the benchmark for the rest of my life, defining the standards I can aspire to."

> "This is not work for the timid of heart. The benefits of it are immeasurable. Yet it requires personal struggle. Only when you change internally will you see those benefits reflected in the outside world. You have to go through a process, and it's painful. You have to show up fearlessly."
>
> — Richard Barrett, interviewed in *Fast Company* on spirituality at work

On her return, Wells held various management jobs, and steadily volunteered as well as serving on the board of the Peace Corps Association, the network of former volunteers. She was hired by the Peace Corps as a recruiter, and found her way as a volunteer into the International Center, whose mission is helping foreign students learn English and adjust to US culture. When her five-year Peace Corps staff contract ended, she was able to "take full advantage of being in career transition and explore the options. Managing other volunteers in a high quality program is a way to weave together an incredible number of the threads of my life."

While Jonathan Hickman was clear in his goal and used volunteering to target something like a dream job, Bonnie Wells uses volunteering to keep her networks vibrant and her challenge levels high. For her, the organizing principle is not purposefulness as much as openness. "It drives me crazy when people ask me what my five-year plan is," she admits. "For me, it's all circumstantial decision-making and keeping an open mind."

Depending on the organization where you choose to volunteer, you may or may not receive quality supervision and leadership. Similarly, you may or may not be regarded as an equal member of the team. In many organizations, it is up to the volunteer to define the relationship, not to mention setting limits on it. Finally, it is always important to examine the consequences of volunteering in an organization where one wants to work for income in the future. Depending on the circumstances, the volunteer experience could be seen as a strong plus, or it could lead you to be identified as "different" from the paid staff.

In many business settings, the entrepreneurial approach gives you higher status and credibility than volunteering. In many nonprofit settings, the reverse is true. But these boundaries are blurring rapidly. Businesses are realizing the feats accomplished by low-resourced, high-stakes nonprofit work. Many nonprofits are eager to attract entrepreneurial juice.

You can learn a lot, and fast, by dealing with the practical questions an entrepreneur must face: how to price a service or product, and how to market it in a systematic fashion. However, you can also get sidetracked into building a business for its own sake, to the detriment of your original goals.

Support and commitment go hand in hand. Commitment in isolation may be unthinkable; commitment in community doesn't guarantee success, but allows an idea to bear whatever fruits it contains, and allows the idea-holder to move through the development process with some grace.

The way this works is highly individualized. But a typical example is the life-changing experience of David Griswold, who worked in the office of an innovative nonprofit called Ashoka, which matches social innovators with financial and strategic supporters around the world. When his wife got a year's job in Mexico, Griswold talked his way into accompanying Ashoka Fellow Arturo Garcia to work in Mexico's coffee country. "I thought I might pick coffee or something," he recalls. "But soon the coffee farmers — who were organized into small cooperatives — started opening up to us and saying, 'What we really need is some help in marketing our crops in the US.' " Griswold and Garcia made an initial foray, visiting nearly a hundred coffee wholesalers and being rejected by them all.

"Before the revolution, I never realized how much more difficult it is to create than to destroy. Our task as dissidents was to question authority, to disturb the peace, to attack the basis of totality's existing structures. Now that they're gone, though, it's suddenly on our shoulders to create something workable in their place."

— Ivan Havel, on the rebuilding of eastern Europe, quoted in Mark Sommer's *Living in Freedom*

Amid the rejections, though, were seeds of future projects. A visit to Ben & Jerry's led eventually to a coffee ice cream partnership. The pair's first success, however, came when they knocked on the door of Paul Katzeff's northern California business, Thanksgiving Coffees. "Not just a cup, but a just cup," is the slogan of Katzeff's mail order business, fueled by the former social worker and job trainer's visits to Nicaragua in the mid-1980s.

Exercise:

Attitudes Toward Commitment

What positive memories do you associate with commitment and self-discipline?

What negative memories? You might do some journal writing on each set of memories.

What commitments, related to your working life directly or to your personal development, have you had trouble with?

How would your life change if you were able to keep any one of these commitments?

Is there anything scary about moving into that new life?

What barriers to these commitments could you set about dismantling?

What kinds of help would you need to do that?

Thanksgiving is committed to buying from farming cooperatives, and to supporting organic farming methods, in the interest of safety for both consumers and workers.

Griswold and Garcia formed Aztec Coffees, a two-person shop in the US which buys the top-of-the-line beans from nine Mexican cooperatives, supporting some 15,000 farmers. These are sold to Ben & Jerry's for a new flavor, Aztec Coffee; and to Thanksgiving for its new Aztec Harvest blend. So serious were they about empowering the coffee growers that they issued stock to the cooperative owners and made themselves salaried employees. At times in the first few years, even those salaries were deferred.

For Griswold, the gamble was manageable because his family — with Peace Corps and Presbyterian missionary ties — backed him from the start. But he has been drawn into a much deeper commitment than he ever expected from his original year Mexican jaunt. He reflects, "I thought I would set up this little business and then move on, maybe go to law school or business school. But in the process, I developed a relationship with a lot of people in Mexico who had stuck their necks out to work with us. One collaborator in Oaxaca, Arturo Zavaleta, drew me aside once during a very difficult period. He said, 'Down here, in the rainy season, when the rivers swell, the campesinos know that you can't turn back if the

---

Exercises:

Strategies for Commitment

Make a list of all the activities that could be part of doing your work without waiting to be paid. Include ideas that are big and small, wild and cautious. Identify the ones that are possible in light of your current situation. Now, among those possible actions, identify the ones that seem to have the most potential for moving you along in a sustainable fashion. Do any of these seem exciting?

Choose items from this short list — possible actions that have greatest potential for moving you along your path. One at a time, consider what might happen if you took this action. You might write a little story about what you did and what resulted.

Which of these scenarios provide a basis for realistic action?

What steps could you take to expand the options for realistic commitment?

What steps could you take as a volunteer?

Where could you find out more about those possibilities?

How would you support yourself financially if you followed this path?

What steps could you take as an entrepreneur?

Where could you find out more about those possibilities?

How would you price your services if you followed this path?

Now place the actions you've chosen on a timeline. What's missing to turn these steps into a clear path that could plausibly bring your work to fruition? Can you scope out those additional steps and write them down?

What kinds of support would be necessary for you to follow this path? Referring back to Step 3, where and how could you line it up?

---

water is too rough. You have to keep going and get across.' He drove home the point that there were a lot of people down there counting on me. Every time I would feel ready to bag it and go to business school, they would take me by the lapels and say, 'Hold on, gringo.' "

Griswold's commitment, in turn, has made him able to attract other high-powered resources at very little cost. "I have friends who are consultants, lawyers, graphic designers, and so on who have a great interest in what I'm doing. And they're always willing to pitch in, whether it's to design a logo or stay up late to ponder problems."

The bravest aspect of a commitment is often the initial decision to let it into your life. After you say yes, opportunities for action have a way of presenting themselves. Rob Yeager, a record producer who spent 20 years too busy with other people's music to write his own, felt a stronger and stronger desire to express more of himself through music. But his responsibilities to his job and three children did not vanish. For months, Rob felt drawn to songwriting, but was too overwhelmed to take any action — except, in a moment of inspiration, to move his three guitars out of storage and arrange them in his office. Committing himself only to face them every day, he soon responded to their silent presence. Rob began to write songs.

Step 8:
Let Go of Assumptions
About How You Will Do Your Work

"There are at least two kinds of games. One could be called finite, the other infinite. A finite game is played for the purpose of winning, an infinite game for the purpose of continuing the play ...

> *Finite players play within boundaries; infinite players play with boundaries.*
> *Finite players are serious; infinite games are playful.*
> *A finite player plays to be powerful; an infinite player plays with strength.*
> *A finite player consumes time; an infinite player generates time.*
> *The finite player aims for eternal life; the infinite player aims for eternal birth."*

— James Carse, *Finite and Infinite Games*

"Dr. Martin Luther King did not say 'I have a strategic plan.' "

— Eric Britton[21]

The anarchy of these times has at least one positive consequence. New ideas are being adopted, and new rules written, by thousands of people without conventionally-defined status or successful track records. Originality has never been more of an advantage. Shift your line of sight even one degree away from the obvious, and you will almost certainly notice unexpected possibilities for new careers, clientele, styles of working and ways to contribute.

Denise Caywood, a newly certified massage therapist, was running dry in her job hunt until she had a dream about trucks and set up a muscular therapy practice in the Triple T Truck Stop outside Tucson.

Jim Malloy, a business professor at Northeastern University, designed a popular course in business development, specifically for athletes on the major sports teams who are getting ready to retire.

These stories show the power of approaching your work as an infinite game. No finite attitude, no matter how generous or how right it may be in some circumstances, is adequate to deal with the degree of flux and complexity out there. What's more, no finite attitude can match the complexity in you, and open you up to the inner resources you need in order to respond to the shifting context.

The career paths and strategies that used to go unquestioned are not just question-able today; in many cases they're discredited. Try to outcompete others in the wrong setting, and you can end up offending co-workers and even bosses who are discovering how far they can get by cooperation. Tell a job interviewer that you want to stay with a company for the rest of your life, and prepare to see a furrowed brow.

These times call for four particular kinds of assumption-busting:

1. Don't assume that the organizations, sectors, and job fields that have been your home in the past will continue to be hospitable.
2. Don't assume that the organizations, sectors, and fields you have ruled out in the past will continue to be off limits.
3. Don't assume that the outward manifestations of a job — the forms and formalities — are a major indicator of security or satisfaction. There is much more going on, and some of it is positive.
4. Don't assume that there's a single right next step or even a single right path for you. You get to choose.

Assumption-busting helps us to be attentive to the opportunities that are right here, right now. Jan, a social worker, realized this a few months after she was laid off by a service agency that had employed her for many years. She spent part of every week playing the role of an unemployed person: collecting her check, answering job ads, having weighty conversations about the future. Another part of her life was devoted to activities she loved: a small private practice, and a satisfying volunteer role in her community, producing cultural activities such as cabarets and storytelling festivals. But the enjoyment didn't feel right. "I have to stop all these free-floating projects and figure out my career!" a voice in her mind kept screaming. Then, in a workshop, she had an opportunity to list her strengths and skills and examine the possibilities they presented. Scanning them, she realized: "These projects aren't a distraction from my work. They *are* my work! I can make a living by marketing these ideas."

Can you think of any aspects of your career that have "always been this way" and seem unchangeable?

How about industries, professions, trades, or parts of the world you've always been in? Roles you've always played? Definitions of success that have always attracted you?

Where and how did you decide that these were necessary?

Is there anyone you're trying to please, or rebel against, by hanging onto these assumptions?

When you have been in the most open, "assumptionless" states in your life, what conditions have helped you function that way?

What has it been like to work, and make choices about work, in that state?

Fewer Assumptions, More Choices

To be anchored in a sense of personal purpose and a community of shared values is a necessary replacement for other kinds of anchors which are no longer reliable, such as structured career paths, generous organizations, and reliable information about where security lies. Nobody really knows whether this will be enough. Nobody really knows the impact, on coherent decision-making and planning, of the climate of constant flux in which so many people live and work. But it is clear that the art form of this era is living with a combination of clear identity and flexible strategy.

It is necessary to let go of assumptions because so many of them become obsolete so fast. But there's a corollary: the value of an open, "assumptionless" attitude in seeing the essence of a situation and doing what's needed with grace. This is nothing new, but its survival value grows in turbulent times.

Most of us are redefining and renegotiating the conditions of our work, most of the time. We are also dealing with a constant stream of new working relationships. This has radical implications for our ability to figure out whom to trust, and thus for the nature of working relationships. This does not mean that there is any higher percentage of untrustworthy people than at any other time in history. It just means that we are all, continuously, "checking each other out." Even people we've counted on in the past can be transformed by circumstances — for the better, sometimes, and other times for the worse. In *Leadership is an Art*, furniture executive Max DePree reflects on a conversation with a well-to-do executive who deeply regretted the frequency of mergers, acquisitions, breakups, and other turbulence going on around him. "All this uncertainty means I can no longer feel comfortable giving my word," he explained. "Without being able to do that, I don't know who I am anymore."

In many cases, these changing circumstances are outpacing people's ability to grieve their losses, adjust their images of themselves in the world, and interpret events in the ways that are needed to move forward coherently. Nobody really knows the effect of this kind of continuing radical uncertainty on human development — on our institutions, ethics, community relationships, perceptions, and cultures. We certainly do not know enough to decide that it's a healthy way of living.

On one level, the decision-making that shapes a life's work can be reduced to a series of resolutions to dilemmas:

> *Shall I work as an employee or entrepreneur right now?*

> *Shall I take this weekend workshop or go to the mountains?*

> *Shall I gamble on my future in this organization by committing to another extra project, or update my résumé and spend my free time networking?*

> *Shall I stick my neck out on these administrative battles now, or save my energy for the environmental initiative we're planning next month?*

Behind every "either-or" decision, there is a less polarized way of asking what's real and important about values, needs, priorities, and strategies. While rising to the daily dilemmas, we are challenged to go deeper and find a synthesis that lets us be increasingly clear on our core values and increasingly true to them. All this requires a flexibility of response and a deeper flexibility of mind, anchored by a set of core values and loyalties which are continuously clarified. You can't fathom the resources that will come into your life. You can't predict the time frame for change. You can't guess the kindred spirits you'll meet, or the complementary organizations and projects you'll bump into at conferences or even in the course of doing your work. You can only keep on carrying the ball, using your best skills, and pay attention to changes around you — including those that result from your actions. But doing "only" this can have a near-miraculous impact on learning and creativity. Here's Natalie Goldberg again, discussing the way discipline and openness intersect in meditation or any other practice (such as the practice of lifelong clarification of one's work):

I've watched meditation students come and go. They use anything as an excuse — "My knee hurt," "The teacher said 'he' instead of 'she,'" "The schedule just wasn't good for me." There is no excuse: If you want it, go for it. Don't let anything toss you away. The other extreme is to accept blindly everything a teacher does: He's sleeping indiscriminately with the women in the community and you think, 'Well, it's part of the teachings.' It is best to stay alive, alert, trust yourself, but not give up, no matter what the situation. Get in there, stay in there, figure it out. If we want the teachings, we have to let ourselves be hungry. If a green pepper is offered, eat it. If it's a steak, devour it. If it's something indigestible — a turd, a cement block, a shoe — figure out what to do with it, but don't back away.

Obviously, then, this kind of flexibility is not a passive or indecisive stance. It's about showing up and "waiting for instructions" in a very alert, disciplined, responsive and playful spirit — paying attention to the subtleties of every decision, doing your best to be well prepared for the right opportunities and even taking initiative to test out the wrong ones. It means treating each situation as unique, and making the fullest possible use of all the faculties you have developed in response to it.

Listen to the testimony of one woman who tried to analyze her way into a new line of work, but only moved off dead center when she let go. Virginia Kellogg now has a successful practice as a personal coach, based in rural Pennsylvania and working with clients around the world to help them achieve their goals, and she reflects:

About four years ago, I was pretty lost. I had been teaching my kids, doing lots of outside work on leading personal empowerment workshops and just knew some change was needed. I did not have a clue. I spent a year working hard to "figure out" the best thing to do, exploring possibilities, and still I was no closer to an answer.

One day I was sitting by the pond writing. This is something I do lots, and I have been for years open to the messages that the natural world sends my way. This day the pines on the hillsides just seemed to be telling me to "ask and listen and act." So I did. I simply told whatever the power is that listens (spirit) that I needed to be told what to do. That I would commit to do whatever it was, no second guessing, no asking questions. I knew this commitment to myself and spirit was crucial. I totally accepted whatever came my way and committed to DO IT.

My whole being relaxed. I knew that this was right. It was several days later, while walking down the road, that I felt literally "hit in the face" with a thought that I needed to help people pull their lives together, in balance. I had no clue how to do this (and I took several paths for the first months that were in the general vicinity but off), but I dove in that day. Immediately doors opened (money, training, clarification of the path) and it has not stopped.

What made the difference was daring to notice that the answers were speaking to me all around me. Someone told me later: "the intuitive mind will instruct the thinking mind where to look next."

That is, use all you have, and give all you can, without depleting yourself in a way that makes it impossible to bounce back. When you have fewer assumptions to fall back on as a source of structure, the arts of limit-setting and dynamic decision-making become much more crucial to living through times of uncertainty. Saying yes and no appropriately are both acts of self-affirmation. Hyper-adventurousness — trying new things in a way that's out of proportion with your ability to assimilate them — is just as damaging as hyper-protectiveness. To get a fix on whether I'm being open to a given opportunity in a spirit of relaxed faith or of compulsiveness, I rely on a handful of questions:

1. Am I looking at my options from the standpoint of what's needed, right now, to meet my goals or to address a specific problem — or am I driven by old business such as proving something to someone?

2 If I don't do this, will it be picked up by somebody else who is in a better position to accomplish it in a sustainable and healthy way? If nobody takes the action or initiative in question, will harm result?

3. Is there a simpler, less risky or labor-intensive means to the same end?

Part of healthy limit-setting is realizing that all you have to give will not be enough to bring to life the great visions you're capable of seeing. Not enough by itself, that is. But tiny, isolated acts of unpredictable significance can often be a key element in helping major changes to take place. Think of the campaigns that have been won and lost by a handful of votes, and the number of businesses that have stayed open or folded based on the choices of a handful of customers or a critical investor. As Gandhi captured the paradox, "What you can do may be too small to matter, but it is very important that you do it."

Life and Work Beyond the Rule Book

Whenever you meet people who seem to understand this process, ply them with pastries and get them to talk about their lives. It is these stories, rich and unpredictable, that provide the best antidote to that arid, fearful quality that invades too many career discussions. Be warned: this life can seem (and be!) very scary. That is because it involves letting yourself feel more of your responses to the choices and limits in your life, and using those feelings as a homing device, whereas a more structured and less individualized approach makes it more possible to stuff down those feelings. Be warned, also: one of the scariest feelings known to humanity is fear of success. Letting go of assumptions includes letting go of self-imposed limits.

On stepping over the line, whatever it may be:

Howard Newman, a Los Angeles engineer and pacifist, did not feel comfortable working on weapons projects. He took a direct approach, typing at the bottom of his résumé "no war work." As a result, he has had a satisfying career in industries from toys to health care. Newman has never been out of work as a result of his position. But he did struggle, in the beginning, wondering what the path would be like.

During that struggle, Newman did a little interview project. He tells this story: "I figured that the real experts on life's trade-offs would be people who had lived a long time and could look back, so I started talking to all the old people I could find. I asked them what they were happy about and what they regretted in their lives. I had conversations with 50 or 60 people. And with one exception — just one — they all said what they regretted were the risks they had not taken. Mistakes, failures, struggles — all those they had made peace with. Their lasting regrets were the risks, and the opportunities, they had missed."

My first exposure to the art of assumptionless evolution was a meeting in Managua, Nicaragua, with a Seattle woman on her way to Alaska. I am going to tell you this story in some detail, because it runs counter to every form of "rational" career planning and yet has a logic which I believe is characteristic of a growing number of people's paths today.

In Central America for a conference, I happened to be sitting on the front porch of a small guest house when someone I'd interviewed years before pulled up to the curb. Not knowing I was in town, she was looking for a fellow guest I hadn't met yet. That is the coincidence that introduced me to Janet Levin, a teacher and writer with a "useless degree" in educational psychology.

In the final years of the contra war, Levin was a shoestring traveler working with children, parents and teachers in communities touched by the war. Her project was simple but psychologically sophisticated: getting kids to draw pictures about their lives, and talking with parents and teachers about the meaning of those drawings for the children's development. Levin knew that, when people experience trauma, their ability to heal and reclaim their lives is increased a great deal if they are able to give some voice to their emotions soon after the fact. By helping adults to recognize and support the children's need for catharsis, she was also creating a structure for communities to find their voices.

Levin's leap of faith — or, as she called it, "the kid pictures project" — resulted in a manuscript, *Guatemalan Guernica*; a traveling exhibition; media appearances; and expressions of gratitude wherever she went. It led her on to demonstrate the same idea in a Russian village of resettled refugees from Chernobyl; and in Alaskan fishing villages with high levels of domestic violence. Finally, Levin found her way into a tailor-made job in Alaska, directing a statewide counseling program to combat community violence. Here is how she tells the story:

> My work and life have been a spiral. Now that I'm 45, I can see from this vantage point how I've chosen each step. Each successive five year period beginning with twenty, I was involved with work and place I didn't know existed five years earlier. A five year plan? I don't think so.
>
> It's taken years of groping in the darkness to realize that I actually had a system, even when I thought I was just groping. I often describe my process as 'organic,' which means that at times it stinks. I don't recommend my process to everyone.

She started out teaching kindergarten, and without trying to do anything unusual she evolved an innovative open classroom model good enough to attract the attention of the administration and be videotaped. That classroom contained the major elements that Levin would carry with her in the years to come: "comfort and curiosity in a culture not my own, children, families, community, poverty, innovation." And the tendency to take very thorough

Love and surrender

"We must scrutinize all our assumptions about how we earn our livelihood ... Only you can establish new priorities for what you do with your energy, especially as it relates to what you receive in exchange."

— Michael and Justine Toms,
   True Work: Doing What You Love and Loving What You Do

"breaks" from work every five years or so. Levin's first break was a trip southward, with Mexico as the carefully planned destination and Guatemala as the real end point.

> *Traveling taught me to follow my feet. Yes, have a good map. Be knowl-edgeable about the surroundings, ask about safe places and restaurants. Talk to the locals, and to the travelers. And then be still. Feel where you're drawn, and move in that direction. When the street curves or dead-ends, look around; pay attention; go toward your curiosity. Consistently a place or person of interest is there.*

> *My experience in Guatemala affected my senses, but my mind didn't understand. That taught me the power of my own sensate experience. I did-n't have to understand. My attention was firmly grabbed. I felt at home. At first, I thought it had to do with the geography and the Mayan culture. Now I'd say it's a state of being I learned.*

On her return, Levin had the predictable reverse culture shock and waves of insight about her place on the planet. She settled in the Pacific Northwest and took a series of jobs in early childhood education:

> *I mourned having to conform to a nonorganic life. I couldn't follow my senses. I had to show up. But I didn't have to work full time, so half my awake time was passed strengthening "traveler's senses." I didn't really know what to do in this new situation, so the traveler in me went with the organic approach and the evaluations were much like those in Philadelphia.*

> *The ending of a grant coincided with a birthday visit to Eastern Oregon, an introduction at a party, and by the end of the weekend, a job. A temporary one for five months which would leave me eligible to collect unemployment and my thoughts. I wanted out of the classroom. I wanted to work with ter-minally ill children. But it didn't happen on my timeline.*

> *I spent five years as director of a university daycare co-op in Seattle, loving the people but not the work, all the while learning budget management and staff supervision. On my own time, I volunteered with the hospice, drawing with the kids and talking about their feelings. What was desire for change at 30, was a fever pitch by 35.*

Note that all the "organic" approach in the world did not get Levin off the hook for learning budget management and staff supervision, and being fully present to the left-brained aspects of her job. Nor does it take the place of planning and active prospecting for opportunities when it's time for a change. As Levin testifies:

> *I have a Native drawing on my wall. It's a straight line, with a spiral, like DNA, going around it. The straight line stands for the planned actions I took to hunt for a job. I read the paper every day. I wrote letters, wonderful*

fictions, for jobs I didn't really want. I went to the employment service. I networked. As I was doing all these things, I had the distinct feeling that they were baby steps, but very necessary. Then there was another, simultaneous process: the spiral. It accounts for what I would call the outside influences: what's bigger than my ego or my perception. All the surprises. They're part of me, too, but they're bigger than my conscious mind could handle.

These two processes converged to lead Levin to Central America. She only knew she was deeply restless, and suspected it would be a good idea to be in an unfamiliar place, "in order to pull the newness out of me."

I thought, "Somebody should do a book of kid drawings in Central America, and let the kids speak for what's happening down there." Then I met somebody who knew somebody who knew the bishop in southern Mexico, who was visiting in the US. I was introduced, and the bishop invited me to come with him and meet people who could get me into the refugee camps. All this I did. I ended up with 300 drawings and a changed life.

Several aspects of Levin's lifestyle have made it much easier for her to follow her feet. She lives a life of material simplicity. When she is employed, she saves money fiercely. She barters, borrows, and thrift-shops. And she has built a large supportive network. These are things that can expand anyone's flexibility; you only have to do them.

Try this. Go around and ask people you respect, whose work you find fascinating, how they ended up in their present jobs. You will find all manner of non-linear stories. You may even notice people straining to put their experiences into logical sequences, when the real plot line was anything but straight. For that matter, how have you found work? What has been the mix of rational planning and unexpected magic?

One of the biggest assumptions in need of busting is the idea that we don't matter and our influence will inevitably be small. At the root of so many battles people face in taking charge of their work is the struggle to value themselves, their intuitions, their sensibilities, and their desires to be useful, in the face of a barrage of "be realistic" messages. It's common to assume that, if what we're doing isn't working, the proper response is to think smaller. But increased self-esteem is a root of both creativity and responsibility, and that self-esteem often comes from living in greater connection with the wider world. Only when we learn to hold onto the awareness of our own value and vocation, can we free ourselves from the devaluing messages of the workplaces where we have been considered expendable. Only with that freedom can we set about finding or creating more worthy alternatives. Letting go of assumptions means waking up to our own role in creating the next possibility.

John Cleese, ex-Monty-Python comic, has achieved success in a new career, using high-voltage humor in the workplace through his corporate training company. Interviewed by the *New York Times* in 1999, Cleese reported that he is in another career transition. Says the newspaper:

Mr. Cleese is intent on remaining among those who do enjoy themselves, but he is taking some tortoise time to decide precisely what his next steps will be.

"The truth is, I don't know where I go now," he said. "If you try to plan with your hare brain, you'll think along the lines of what you've done before. The only way that you find a slightly new direction at this kind of juncture is to create a space and see what flows into it."

Many spiritual traditions — Christian, Buddhist, and Native American, for example — recognize the notion of letting oneself be "acted through," serving as a conduit for developments more significant than you could be expected to know. Intermixed with commitment-to-act, and commitment-to-results, is another, more mysterious form of commitment, which might more accurately be called surrender. Thomas Merton said it this way, in 1966, in a letter to peace activist Jim Forrest:

Do not depend on the hope of results. When you are doing the sort of work you have taken on, essentially an apostolic work, you may have to face the fact that your work will be apparently worthless and even achieve no result at all, if not perhaps results opposite to what you expect. As you get used to this idea, you start more and more to concentrate not on the results, but on the value, the rightness, the truth of the work itself. And there too a great deal has to be gone through, as gradually you struggle less and less for an idea and more and more for specific people. The range tends to narrow down, but it gets much more real. In the end it is the reality of personal relationships that saves everything.

Step 9:
Mine Your Experience for Gems

Often I am asked, who taught me how to write? Everything, I want to say. Everything taught me, everything became my teacher, though at the time I was not aware of all the tender shoots that helped me along, that came up in Mr. Clemente's class, in Mr. Cates's, with all the teachers I can't remember anymore, with all the blank times, the daydreaming, the boredom, the American legacy of loneliness and alienation, my Jewish background, the sky, the desk, a pen, the pavement, small towns I've driven through. The list could go on and on until I named every moment I was alive ... And we can't avoid an inch of our own experience; if we do it causes a blur, a bleep, a puffy unreality. Our job is to wake up to everything, because if we slow down enough, we see we are everything.

— Natalie Goldberg, *Long Quiet Highway*

A moral center

Here is why résumé writing is so annoying and so rewarding. Your story doesn't want to be constricted. And when your working life is on track, you feel present to it in a way that makes use of more dimensions of you than you can possibly fit on a page. The wizardry of crafting a worthwhile working life starts with using all the resources available to you, including your history, rough spots and all. So there's a benefit to continuously reinterpreting your experience to bring new facets of your connection, commitment, and competence to light.

Margaret Burnham, a co-founder of the first African-American women's law firm in Boston, has had a rich and varied career as a lawyer, judge, mother, teacher, and community activist. Through it all, her choices have revolved around the moral center established in the moment when her life first turned toward the law.

> *I was a teenager in Mississippi in 1964, passing out leaflets in Jackson.*
> *A police officer took a leaflet and rounded me up as an illegal demonstra-*
> *tor. I was sitting in jail, contemplating my existence, when a woman*
> *showed up. She was my lawyer. I had never seen a lawyer, much less a*
> *black woman lawyer. I said to myself, "This has got to be magic."*

Certain experiences become guiding metaphors for our lives and work. In Burnham's case, it has been about "living as part of the freedom movement," whatever form that takes. Her early trials connected her to her inner power and helped her to define herself through its symbolism. As Burnham puts it, "That time set up the canvas on which I have painted my life."

The Ten-Step Program is a structure covering preparation, focusing, and active creation of opportunities. Its essence is the continuous interplay between self-understanding and action, which is most sharply focused in the four principles of Steps 6 – 9: articulating a core definition of "your work" in terms that are as clear and personally meaningful as possible without being oversimplified (Step 6); a focused commitment to action on that path (Step 7); release of assumptions in order to maximize options and resourcefulness (Step 8); and, finally (Step 9), a serious respect for life's experiences as sources of understanding and direction. This step is about digging deep, learning continuously, seeing your life in its social and ecological context, and continuously reweaving this biographical narrative into the tapestry you want your life to be.

Some of those crystallizing moments are the "aha" experiences of life, sources of the insight and healing so memorable that you want others to know them firsthand. Many of the moments that help crystallize career directions have to do with our own healing and development. People or experiences that throw us a lifeline have a special way of capturing our attention with a sense of new possibility. This is true when we're starting out, and no less true later when we're mired in a set of circumstances that aren't quite working. Will Fudeman, a social worker and musician, recalls what happened when all the more or less reasonable parts of his life did not add up to a satisfying whole:

> *I had three great jobs. I was a therapist part-time. I worked in an educational nonprofit part-time. I was a Sunday School program director. On top of that, I played in a Klezmer band. And I was saying to myself, "What do I want to be when I grow up?"*
>
> *In fact, I said this to myself at great length at two in the morning, when I should have been sleeping. Now, you can give me the obvious response, that I was doing too much and my body was out of balance. But I've been over-committed before, and this restlessness was new.*
>
> *I've studied a lot about the immune system and the energies of the body. I took myself to my acupuncturist, who told me I've got a yin deficiency — too much fire in the head. Whatever else that may mean, it meant I got to lie there with needles in me for half an hour, which made me feel a lot more grounded. The worries of my life didn't go away, but I'm better able to deal with them.*

Four years later, Fudeman had graduated from New England School of Acupuncture and was combining counseling, music, and teaching with a practice in oriental medicine in Ithaca and Syracuse, New York. Bringing a perspective on mental health and community issues to his work, he soon developed a specialty consulting with mental health professionals, helping people cut their dependency on prescription drugs for managing pain.

Some "aha!" moments are connected with healing and insight. Other gems to be mined are the ambiguous moments and dark times whose memories can put up barriers to forward movement until they are faced. Some of the finest gems may come directly from darker times in your history. The most uncomfortable situations in your work history are often the ones in which you are forced to face yourself and take stock of your values. The catalyst may have been pressures, ethical dilemmas, or obvious mismatches between you and the work situation. Times of difficulty on the job are often times of major learning about the conditions we need in order to work sanely and productively, and about the ways we fail ourselves by accepting unacceptable conditions. Ken Geiser, whose evolution from architecture into a different kind of ecological design we followed in Step 6, reflects:

> The losses that I've suffered have tended to be some of the best material I've gotten to work with. It took me a long time to realize that the things I was losing were really kicking me along in a way that was very, very powerful. It's all in the perception you have of yourself, and your ability to hold some things steady even as others change. If you start thinking there's a grand plan — and then you discover that architecture is not going to satisfy you, and the wife that you have is going to leave you, and suddenly you have this collapsed image of yourself — you have to say, "I guess I was wrong. I'm going to have to start over."

If it weren't for those external pushes, it might have been much harder for Geiser to let go of comforts at times, in order to say yes to challenges. Like many people who feel they have found their life's work, he is continually coming to terms with its high demands. "I never intended to have this kind of life," he admits. "For years, I constantly looked for it to flatten out and become normalized." That hasn't happened, but he has learned a lot about self-preservation and the sanctity of the weekend.

Unless he is forced to do so, Geiser does not abandon one set of self-images or goals when others come into focus. He thinks the way a designer does in his work to promote the use of less toxic materials. When necessary, though, he can draw on talents cultivated over the decades, from administration to lobbying to community organizing. He explains:

> I've always brought themes forward from each era in my life. I think that's really critical. We're like books, and the first chapter shouldn't be forgotten. There are metaphors and reasons that come from those early experiences that help make sense of what comes later. One of my models early on was Nat Owings, founder of one of the biggest architectural firms in the country. In his late 40s, he and four other guys walked away from an office in Chicago that they were in trouble over. They all uprooted themselves and went to San Francisco to start over. I always thought, "Well, that's very romantic — but foolish." In my mind, you don't throw out what you've learned. You are one person. You might as well bring the lessons forward. Actually, it has a lot to do with one's respect for oneself, belief in oneself, and, quite frankly, love for oneself.

This is not to suggest that every personal breakthrough is material for a career reassessment, or that it's necessary to have made complete peace with your history before moving on the work front. In fact, the opposite can be true. Moving forward with career choices, especially challenging ones, can be a source of rich revelation about who you are and what you need. For many people, a handful of crystallizing experiences like the ones we've been discussing provide enough material for a life's worth of career development. Looking at insights from personal work history in some depth can sometimes bring obvious connections to light between insults and struggles in the past, and perceived limitations in the present. At times, too, dipping into those painful memories can bring unexpected reassurance. Experiences that seemed like pure failure can take on a very different meaning with time.

For example, in the early '80s, Rose Diamond was a secretary, mother of three, and part-time college student in North Carolina. She could not have predicted the sequence of events that would lead her, by the middle of the 1990s, to be training as an art educator in Boston. Diamond had only a faint sense of what was ahead — a fascination with the arts, a drive for more education, and an exploring nature. Her memory of that era illustrates the way many of us really move our lives forward — by leaping into opportunities that are somehow compelling, even if we are not always being able to make full use of them right away:

> I had always wanted to work in radio, and they were just starting up a National Public Radio station in Charlotte. I went in and volunteered. I had an idea for a huge project: a storytelling show for children. Storytelling was just starting to come back into the culture, and there were wonderful mountain stories. My son's friend's father was a great storyteller. I got the go-ahead to get a pilot show together and apply for funding from IBM.

> I had never done anything like this before. I was scared to death. But I went ahead. I developed the proposal. I got the story recorded. And then I went to do an interview with a local literature professor whose backing we needed. I took my tape recorder but pushed the wrong buttons. We did an hour-long interview. But when I went to play it back, there was nothing there. I got so scared. I thought, "There's no way I'm going to make this happen." I backed out, and I was so embarrassed that I didn't follow through for years.

During those years, Diamond put one foot in front of the other to keep her children fed and uncover more of her skills and strengths. She finished college with a major in art history and museum studies. Her marriage ended. She worked for a time in a museum. Then, disabled by a car accident, she was forced into an entirely different rhythm of living for many months: resting, physical therapy, and days that were wide open for writing or drawing or working with clay. During her convalescence, she was showered with attention by co-workers in a way that profoundly increased her own self-esteem. Eventually she was able to say, "I guess I'm an artist," and, some time later, "I suppose I could be a good teacher." No single event led to either of those acknowledgments; they grew organically out of the life she was leading and her openness to new images of herself.

Curiosity drew her to a more urban setting. Moving to Boston, she found her way into a small graduate school whose programs integrate the arts and education. By coincidence, the college was home to a national center for oral history and storytelling, bringing her around full circle to that earlier interest. Viewing the potential and unknowns at the beginning of the program, she was able to say,

> *I'm finally going to find out where Rose's creativity is. For the first time in my life I'm able to take the risk and not worry, just take one hurdle at a time. Since I've stopped to pay attention to my inner life, I don't have the need to be an overachiever anymore, so I'm much more free to act. I know now that I wasn't ready, back in 1980, to do that public radio show. My self-esteem wasn't high enough. That's why I quit.*

Only by making peace with that earlier "defeat" could she see herself rising to the present challenge. These cycles of incubation and expression are essential to the process for many people. Often a shift from one phase to another is triggered by a crystallizing moment that pulls diverse puzzle pieces together. Consultant Judy Otto describes a slow evolution of her professional focus, from industry to health care, during a period when friends of hers were facing life-threatening illnesses and the health care crisis was becoming national news. Those events brought numerous possibilities into her mind, but at first they did not easily translate into a course of action. She was able to coast. One day, though, she was struck by a line of poetry by Antonio Machado: "What will you do with this garden that has been entrusted you?" She knew it was time to act, simply by directing her marketing efforts toward the clients she most wanted to help rather than waiting for business to come in the door.

In finding the gems in your experience that will help you to value your work fully and accurately, one of the most important processes is learning to see yourself in an evolutionary sense — that is, to assimilate actual changes into your subjective image of yourself, rather than hanging onto outdated aspects of your self-image. If you take this for granted, consider yourself lucky. Without the skill of continuous reassessment, new experiences don't become part of your evolving self-image; you may test and prove yourself endlessly because you've never paused to notice real accomplishments; you may find yourself stuck, at midlife, in the self-image of a beginner.

One of the most important kinds of experience to assess, when you are in the midst of a transition, is how and where you've moved in the most recent phase of life, just in case your self-image hasn't completely kept up with events. For example, here are some questions for taking stock of where you stand in a time of job transition:

1. How have you grown in your present or last work situation?
2. What did you set out to accomplish, personally and professionally, in this role?
3. In what ways did you accomplish these things?
4. What were you most appreciated for on the job, and by whom?
5. What strengths of yours were not given the acknowledgment they deserved, and how has that fact shaped your ability to move into the next phase with confidence?
6. What were your characteristic struggles on the job?

7. In what ways were these a reflection of the work environment, and in what ways were they a reflection of your style and psychological needs in the situation?

8. What did you learn from those struggles that could help you to achieve the same goals with less suffering?

9. What accomplishments in this job are you most proud of?

10. How do these suggest new areas of responsibility, and new sources of marketability, for you in the future?

Integrity as Creative Force

One of the powerful driving forces in adult development, including career development, is the quest for internal consistency, or at least coherence, between what we profess to believe and what we live out. We differ vastly in our comfort zones regarding consistency, and in the options handed to us to work with. But leaps forward tend to take place when we can ask challenging questions about the contradictions in our working lives, and the resources we have to work with in transcending them.

Until 1990, Abhay Bhushan was living two lives which were morally and logically consistent, but quite different. For his livelihood, he was a successful strategic planner for Xerox Corporation in Palo Alto. In his leisure time, he pursued an interest in sustainable development in his native India, raising money and doing educational work in support of village economic projects. That commitment had been steady ever since 1978, when Bhushan took a paid social service leave from the company and went with his family to visit the area in northern India where his grandfather, a follower of Gandhi, had worked to start cooperatives. But somehow it had never occurred to him that his two lives could, or should, have much to do with each other.

Are you leading multiple lives?

If so, what are the benefits and costs of this?

What areas of overlap do you see between your career and other "lives" you lead?

What tensions?

What might you want to do to more fully integrate your "lives" and expand your choices?

The line between them began to blur around the time of Earth Day in 1990, a celebration which attracted sponsorship and public statements from many major corporations. Preparation was also in high gear for the 1992 UN Earth Summit. "Corporate environmentalism" seemed more necessary than ever, and more possible.

That entire season could be described as one big crystallizing moment for Bhushan as his two worlds began to blend. Bhushan knew people at Xerox who biked to work, brought in coffee mugs rather than using disposable cups, or conferred on e-mail about environmental issues. But there were no company-wide initiatives to deal with the paper, chemicals, and packaging that were at the heart of the company's business. The idea just hadn't come to life yet.

Bhushan decided it was time for someone to remedy that situation. He developed a proposal to devote a part of his time to launching internal environmental programs such as recycling and minimizing waste. He got enthusiastic approval from top management, and in a few months was asked to take the responsibility full-time. Bhushan remembers the incredulous responses of colleagues who saw the job as a professional backwater. In fact, it has been just the opposite. What's more, his 20 years of extracurricular interest and commitment made him the ideal person for a job whose creation, sooner or later, was inevitable.

He could see this because he did what corporate strategists are supposed to do. He looked dynamically at the changes underway in markets and regulations and product possibilities and public sentiments, as they affected both the company's potential and his own. He thought through the alternatives until he came up with an intelligent synthesis that would let him meet a recognized company need while bringing more of his values and interests into his work. He made a rational proposal, and was fortunate enough to get a rational response — an invitation to help create an operation with considerable potential to change the entire company.

Self-knowledge is worth the pain, and not just for idealistic reasons. Crass though this sounds, it will help you out a whole lot in marketing. Mining your history for gems,

---

A Time to Let Go?

Now it is time to talk about the situation facing a special working population: those who have cast their lot with organizations, or with entire industries or professions, that are now, for various reasons, not the sources of opportunity they once were. You may be recovering from a layoff or anticipating one. Either way, you are entitled to feelings of vulnerability, confusion, grief, and rage. The reasons may be primarily economic. Or they may have to do with changing views among consumers, regulators, or investors about the value of a product or service. To use an obvious example, there are a host of reasons why tobacco marketing is no longer an uncomplicated career choice. As one salesman for a large cigarette company said after being laid off and finding a new job in a different industry, "I wasn't really motivated to make a move on my own. But it does feel better to be out of there. I was getting tired of being kicked by little old ladies in the supermarket."

Suppose you find yourself in a field whose outlook has changed dramatically, in terms of financial success or public popularity or ecological sustainability or all of the above. Suppose you went into this field with solid reasons for believing you would make a positive contribution. Suppose further

that, over the years, you sensibly enough paid primary attention to doing your job, not to the broader trends. But now you may be feeling less certain that the strategic minds at the head of the industry have a full grip on the situation. It may be time to assess whether you're still meeting the needs that drew you into this work, and are still being true to the values that matter to you.

1. What do you wish you had been told, or had asked, about the industry before you joined it?

2. How will you use this awareness to ask more useful questions from now on?

3. Suppose you stay in your present position or make a conservative move elsewhere in the industry. What will your working life be like in five years?

4. Suppose you take a leap into a new field. What kinds of work might let you serve the values that matter to you now?

5. What would it take for you to feel "finished" with this phase of your life?

6. What historic themes in your working life seem most powerful and affirmative of the ways you want to work now, and most important to carry forward? What aspects of your history seem most stale and ready to be shed?

---

including the unpolished ones of failure and struggle, is a powerful antidote to the feelings of vulnerability that stick to many job-changers. The "knockout" questions that blow your confidence in an interview often have such deadly impact because they direct attention toward your real vulnerabilities. Every step you take to make peace with those nagging memories and reclaim self-esteem will make a difference in your ability to respond to hard questions with candid, mature, specific, relaxed answers which set you apart. Standard job interview guides advise you to respond to questions about your vulnerabilities in some standard ways: by describing weaknesses that will be perceived as strengths, or by deflecting the questions entirely. These are sometimes necessary strategies to fall back on. However, answers to tough questions that show courage, creativity, individuality or growth will be appreciated by some employers — including, perhaps, those you most want to work for. Especially in the entrepreneurial world, there are many hiring managers smart enough to value an applicant who has learned and grown through failures much more than one who minimizes their importance by acting impervious.

Think of a rocky time in your history. Write the story out, or tell it to a friend or a tape recorder. You can do this any way that seems authentic, with one rule. You have to talk about yourself in an active voice. That is, do not focus on what happened to you or why you were so powerless, but on the choices you made, the actions you took and the perfectly legitimate reasons you had for responding as you did.

Once you've made some peace with the difficult times in your history, you will have much more access to recollections of satisfaction and self-valuation. Memory does work that way. Mining your experience for gems, including the rough-cut variety, expands your ability to move through life with confidence.

Step 10:
Be a Co-Creator of
the Workplace You Want

"It is natural for any system, whether it be human or chemical, to attempt to quell a distur-bance when it first appears. But if the disturbance survives those first attempts at suppression and remains lodged within the system, an iterative process begins. The disturbance increases as different parts of the system get hold of it. Finally, it becomes so amplified that it cannot be ignored. This dynamic supports some current ideas that organizational change, even in large systems, can be created by a small group of committed individuals or champions. "

— Margaret Wheatley, *Leadership and the New Science*

"Be gentle as doves and wise as serpents."

— Jesus of Nazareth

So far, we have been talking about choosing your next steps. Whatever you choose, though, you can count on its being imperfect. And so this chapter is about promoting healthy change and expanding your maneuvering room, moment by moment, in the course of doing your work. There are a thousand ways to do this, all of them difficult as well as rewarding. You can be an idea person, an ethics watchdog, a teambuilder, a supporter of the underdog, a redesigner of systems for getting things done, a prospector for new products or services. The term "co-creation" is used here to indicate that whatever you do is collaborative and evolutionary. Making significant changes at work is almost never a solo act.

There is an intimate connection between strategies to promote change in a work-place and strategies to protect and advance your own position. Both require a measure of clarity about personal power, both in a psychological sense and organizationally. Starting to think about change-agentry means thinking about how much we really believe in win/win, how we assess the trustworthiness of co-workers, how resilient we believe humans and orga-nizations to be, and where the leverage is in a given situation. This discussion will assume that every workplace has its own mix of communicators and backstabbers, and its own set of organizational forces operating both for and against cooperative change. Yes, it's a jungle out there. But a jungle holds thousands of peaceable creatures as well as predators. It's home to stable communities. It thrives on diversity. Its relationships are characterized by massive interdependence. Survival requires a wider set of skills than competition alone.

The first step in co-creating the workplace you want is sinking roots in a job, being known as a credible and valued team member, and learning the basics well enough that you're able to devote some attention to the bigger picture. As Lawrence Otis Graham points out in his book, *The Best Companies for Minorities*, "Organizations want to be understood before they are changed. They welcome change from someone who seems like an insider more than from someone who is totally different." Therefore, any efforts to spearhead change in a workplace have to be grounded in a solid understanding of the organization's mission; the agendas of those you work for; and the degree of maneuvering room you have (both officially and unofficially).

Just as all politics is local, all career strategy boils down to the interpersonal. It's about how you handle each assignment, meeting, memo, task list, or chance encounter in the hallway. Career self-defense and self-promotion are as necessary as ever. At the same time, they're an arena for putting forth the image of yourself for which you want to be known: your preferred balance of working solo and collaborating; cooperation and competition; directed-ness and acceptance; flexibility and limit-setting. These are the dilemmas in which strategy and values intersect. Where do you want to go? How do you want to get there? What is your position on Gandhi's famous principle that ends and means must harmonize? What factors do you pay attention to when you're assessing the potential for change, and the barriers?

The complexity of organizational dynamics is outside the scope of this book, other than to say that having a conscious, halfway sophisticated perspective on how an organiza-tion works is a marvelous advantage for surviving in one, to say nothing of making it a vehi-cle for the expression of your own values. Gareth Morgan's classic *Images of Organization* reminds us that workplaces can be understood on many levels. Politics and cultural forces, financial and performance incentive structures, information flows and unconscious dynam-ics — experience tells us they are all in there helping to determine where the stepping stones lie on our paths. And so, "If one truly wishes to understand an organization it is much wiser to start from the premise that organizations are complex, ambiguous, and paradoxical."

For those with a reasonable tolerance for this type of complexity, one of the most welcomed forms of innovation and culture change is to help others navigate through it. You can do this as a mentor. You can do this as an information resource. You can do this as a resolver of conflicts and a problem-solving helper. Rick Sparks, a technical program manager for the software firm Dialogic in California, became an informal but recognized internal mediator after longstanding interest and self-education. The message he put out to co-work-ers was simply, "If you feel like you're in a Dilbert cartoon, come see me."

One of the most powerful kinds of workplace innovation is expanding the defini-tion of the job you presently hold, whatever its level. For example, Nashville judge Penny Harrington presides over the nation's first county-wide environmental court, a role for which she volunteered after her colleagues had gone out of their way to distance themselves from the idea. This began a pattern Harrington has repeated successfully several times since: "taking on something everyone else hated, and realizing I knew what to do to make it work."

The season Harrington ran for the bench, a community groundswell was building for a special civil court that could address the backlog of building code violations in the city and surrounding countryside. A county "environmental" court, modeled on a successful citywide one in Memphis, would hear cases ranging from landlord-tenant disputes to illegal disposal of motor oil to Harrington's favorite, that of a man who could not seem to keep his 20 roosters properly caged. But Harrington understands the link between local and global, as well as the need for real judicial wisdom in these cases: "When you have an elderly lady who fails to remove the trash and debris from her yard, and her yard is in the watershed of the Cumberland River, and you don't know what kinds of medical wastes could end up in that trash, it's not a simple issue."

In her first three years of running the court just a few days a month, Harrington saw tangible changes. Lawyers are more willing to take on local environmental cases. Building inspectors say they get more cooperation from landlords. This feedback encouraged her to launch a second special docket, this time on domestic violence, with similar success. Largely due to the publicity, Harrington feels, "Women are saying for the first time, 'I don't have to take this. The courts will protect me.' "

"It's mostly a matter of being creative and noticing what the needs are," she advises. Of course, it doesn't hurt that Harrington has worked extensively on political campaigns and has been a lobbyist for a statewide environmental coalition. She readily admits: "I am no political neophyte."

At times, what starts out as a routine step to improve performance can lead to an entirely new emphasis or line of work. Richard Paradis and his fellow engineers in the US Navy found this out after a meeting in which they were inspired to wrestle with a question: Why is it that we have such good regulations on paper for environmentally sound building construction, but we're not really doing it at its full potential? Out of that discussion came a Green Buildings program which began with a model renovation in the Navy's Virginia headquarters. Other projects followed. Guidelines, specifications, and training materials arose from these. Soon the Navy was serving as a resource on greener buildings for the other military services and the federal government as a whole, and Paradis found himself representing the program in venues like the National Town Meeting for a Sustainable America. As his national program gained recognition, ironically, what captured Paradis' imagination most was bringing the same vision home to his own neighborhood, as a co-founder of the Hampton Roads Sustainable Communities initiative.

The potential for this kind of initiative varies from workplace to workplace. But it is not just an option for those in the inner circles. In fact, often it's the new people who have the greatest chance at redefining their jobs. This is illustrated by the story of Annette Szumaski, who joined a large Washington law firm as a paralegal. Within a year, she had her superiors' blessing to create a new position as the firm's first environmental site inspector.

Her proposal filled a troublesome gap for her employer, whose business concentrated in environmental insurance litigation. Many of its cases involved long-standing, poorly documented claims of illegal practices, some with serious health effects. Private investigators hired from outside didn't always understand the environmental issues or the firm's needs. With a varied background that included technical writing and a period as a Pentagon analyst, Szumaski provided an intriguing combination of technical and political sensitivity.

For years, the fantasy of law school had danced before her eyes — but not with quite enough life to inspire commitment. She trained as a legal assistant to get her feet wet, and intuitively looked for "an opportunity a little out of the ordinary." Szumaski was hired into the support staff to travel, conduct research, organize information, write reports, and juggle all these demands. Her workload soon grew to include research into the history of contaminated sites. On her second research trip, Szumaski brought back information that was critical to victory for the firm's client. She also developed a fascination with environmental law, and a conviction that "we have to clean up these sites, and we have to get the responsible parties to pay."

With the encouragement of the partner who had hired her, Szumaski carefully drafted a proposal for a new job description. Two committees fine-tuned it. One of their greatest concerns was where to put the position in the chain of command. She remained part of the support staff, but functioned independently.

Szumaski's story shows that it's possible to create fundamentally new positions, even in fields as highly structured as the law. "This process was evolutionary," she says. "I didn't try to change things overnight. It was happening, and I helped give it form." And the job, in turn, gave form to her next step, into law school.

Three messages are shown by the cases above. There are innumerable ways to exert a positive influence in your workplace or industry. All these ways involve risks and unknowns. (Of course, so does passivity.) Finally, the opportunities to make a difference in an organization do not correspond in any simple way to the formal power you may have. Your status, budget, and job description are sources of power, but they don't necessarily outweigh the more subtle things like your working relationships, access to information, reputation and support system, or the unpredictable shifts in markets and regulations which determine what your supervisors may be worried about.

Co-creating your workplace can also take the form of co-creating your field of work. Jean Gardner, who teaches at the Parsons School of Design in New York City, is involved in a project to help schools of architecture become forces for sustainable development education by encouraging them to use solar energy in all their own new construction and renovation, making a powerful statement to entire student populations as well as surrounding communities.

Of course, your maneuvering room for innovation increases when you happen to have a budget, a staff, and some amount of a mandate. Even people who are nominally in charge may have trouble moving things in the direction they choose. But they certainly have wider options. And, in these times of flux, top jobs can be some of the highest-turnover positions around. In industry, government, and the nonprofit sector, the rule book of leadership is being rewritten continuously. There is hunger for new wisdom, and examples of it in the field are getting easier to unearth. Look, especially, in areas where there's a big need for transformation, and you will see interesting experiments in leadership. Two examples show the range.

Hazel O'Leary, the Clinton Administration's Secretary of Energy, earned one senator's nomination for a "Nobel Prize for guts in government" by admitting that military had performed radiation experiments on human subjects and endorsing the idea that the government owed victims and their families compensation. O'Leary also outlawed technospeak in the department; knocked down the bulletproof glass that surrounded her office area; replaced photos of missiles with others of wind farms and solar panels; froze contractor salaries and set standards for cost containment; started a large-scale project to declassify documents; and hired whistle-blowers and grassroots critics to positions of responsibility. Today she is on the speaking circuit talking about ways to create organizations that can handle change, starting with giving status and resources to people with diverging views. "When I first came to DOE, every other person I met was a nuclear engineer named Jim. You have to have different kinds of people sitting around the table or it simply won't work."

Today O'Leary is also on the board of a large and increasingly well-known company called AES Systems, a builder of power plants and a model for radically empowering workers to take responsibility. If you are looking to be an on-the-job innovator and you aren't enamored of pushing rocks uphill for the sake of the challenge, it is always possible to seek out and target organizations like this that encourage risk-taking. As Alex Markels writes in *Fast Company:*

> AES is big, rich — and unlike any company you've ever seen. It builds power plants by handing power to workers on the front lines. Its radical business model has worked wonders in the United States …

> "God made us all a certain way," says Dennis Bakke, 52, AES's cofounder and CEO. "We're all creative, capable of making decisions, trustworthy, able to learn, and perhaps most important, fallible. We all want to be part of a community and to use our skills to make a difference in the world." Adds Roger Sant, 66, AES's cofounder and chairman: "If Dennis and I had to lead everything, we couldn't have grown as much as we have. People would bring deals for us to approve, and we would have a huge bottleneck. We've shifted to giving advice rather than giving approval. And we've moved ahead much faster than we would have otherwise."

> Simple insights — but they have profound consequences for how AES operates. Lots of companies talk about pushing responsibility out from headquarters. Few companies push as hard or as far as AES. Just five years ago, it had fewer than 600 employees. Today it has nearly 6,000 employees (or more than 31,000, if you count those working in its joint ventures). Yet it has never established corporate departments for human resources, operations, purchasing, or legal affairs. Its headquarters staff includes fewer than 30 people.

> Lots of companies talk about grassroots teams. Few companies give teams more power than AES does. A few years ago, CFO Barry Sharp estimated that the company had raised $3.5 billion to finance 10 new power plants.

*But, he added, he'd secured only $300 million of that sum on his own. The
rest was brought in by decentralized teams. When AES raised £200 million
(about $350 million) to finance a joint venture in Northern Ireland, two
control-room operators led the team that raised the funds.*

*It sounds crazy — but it works. In 1990, the year before AES went
public, the company had annual revenues of less than $200 million and
profits of less than $16 million. In 1996, it had revenues of $835 million
and profits of $125 million. The company opened its first plant in 1986.
Today it owns or has an interest in 82 power plants, which generate nearly
22,000 megawatts of power for consumers in the United States, Argentina,
China, Hungary, and other countries.*

If AES blows the assumption that a certain amount of control and coordination is needed to
keep an enterprise from getting messy, a kindred limiting assumption is that consulting
with stakeholders like customers, shareholders, employees, and communities will constrain
rather than empower decision-making. In particular, it is unquestioned wisdom in some
business circles that shareholders only want to see profits maximized. But when shareholders themselves are consulted, their views are actually more complex and, in many cases, they
are perfectly capable of a longer-range vision.

A CEO who figured this out is Bill Hanley, Chief Executive Officer of the largest
publicly held military company to convert to civilian production. Galileo Electro-Optics, a
500-person high-tech firm in Sturbridge, Massachusetts, used to make night vision systems
for the military. Period. Now the company uses variations on the same core technology to
produce dozens of products: sensors on photocopy machines, medical and dental diagnostic
equipment. An engineer who worked his way up through the manufacturing ranks at
Corning Glass, he says, "I can tell people on the shop floor honestly that I know their jobs,
because I've done just about all their jobs."

Hanley is demanding as well as empowering. "What I run is a benign dictatorship,"
he admits. "Because that's what it takes to turn an organization around." All four of the
leaders I've highlighted here have risen in surprising settings — in the midst of highly resis-
tant organizations, or with no structure at all. All four have walked in with a set of assumptions about what is possible which might have been considered naive, and have proceeded,
with extraordinary effort, to realize the possibility.

Hanley's story challenges one article of faith about the capacity of corporations to
change. It is commonly held that the CEO of a publicly held corporation is powerless to do
anything but maximize short-term profits for shareholders who are clamoring for their dollars. This is sometimes true, especially when the investors are pension funds with inflexible
investment guidelines. But in 1985, when military contracting was booming and Galileo was
entirely dependent on that single customer, Hanley made a long-shot pitch to his board of
directors: "This isn't going to last. Either the world is going to get more peaceful, or the
world isn't going to last. We have to find other ways of earning a living here. It's going to
take some adjustment in the short term, but it will put us in a lot better position in the long

term." Some board members left; others were attracted; and the company has maintained a stable population of investors who are willing to wait for the payoff, financially and otherwise.

Not only in troubled old industries is there a need for transformative leadership. In some of the most promising new fields, people are discovering trade-offs and unanticipated consequences of their efforts, pointing to a need for activism to make a lot of good work better. For example, the groundswell of interest in oriental medicine is giving millions of people alternatives to surgery, new avenues for pain management, and an overall gentler set of tools for preventing disease and promoting wellness. At the same time, oriental medicine's toolkit includes a large number of endangered plant and animal products such as rhinoceros horn, a fact that concerns a growing number of practitioners. In the *Acupuncture Alliance Forum*, acupuncturist Elizabeth Call wrestles with this issue:

> *Since practitioners of Oriental Medicine believe that preventing or prolonging the onset of disease plays an important role in health care, it is clear that biodiversity plays a vital part in day-to-day clinical practice, from providing the source for herbal (and some allopathic) medicines, to protecting and inspiring humanity. We must expand our thinking from focusing on short-term issues to embrace solid solutions for the long-term survival of our profession, as well as our own species.*
>
> *The loss of biodiversity has emerged as one of the pressing environmental problems of our time. Addressing this problem requires a multidisciplinary approach from within the sciences, as well as the inclusion of policy-makers and consumers in creating solutions ... most importantly, though, it is the day-to-day behavior of all humans at home and at the workplace that will determine the ultimate survival of the human race (as well as our profession). Because the underlying philosophy of OM recognizes the interconnectedness of all things, we are in a good position to be role models for protecting biodiversity.*

While it's always possible to react to such a huge "opportunity" with terror, she makes it clear that there's much to be gained in terms of personal self-respect and professional credibility by making this stretch. While it is disingenuous to think you will do no harm, whatever your line of work, you can greatly minimize it. While it is customized for oriental medicine practitioners, Call's prescription for change illustrates some general principles every profession and trade needs to consider. She urges fellow acupuncturists to:

· Become informed about the issues affecting your professional practice;

· Support labeling bills;

· Support the Acupuncture Alliance's boycott of formulas that contain or claim to contain endangered species;

· Challenge herb companies to provide documentation that their products are obtained legally and cultivated in a sustainable manner;

- Reduce, reuse, and recycle whenever appropriate to alleviate pressure on natural resources;
- Devise ways to live and practice sustainably.

Sometimes, the innovation that makes all the difference is just to do one's job correctly, fairly, and without corruption. In a significant minority of workplaces, this is a path of bravery. For example, Karin Heimann, a botanist, was hired by the US Forest Service in western North Carolina to identify endangered plant species. In 1991, Heimann noticed that the only known species of water lichen in existence was living in the path of a major highway which was being built, over environmentalists' protests, through the Nantahala National Forest. She reported the discovery, in the process calling the highway Environmental Impact Statement "inadequate" and outspokenly criticizing the field work used to document the water quality of the area.

What happened next is reported in an environmental magazine article aptly headed "Combat Biologists." Four months after receiving a "fully successful" performance review, Heimann was given a negative review. It cited such lapses as missing three training sessions, two of which had been cancelled; and failing to meet a deadline which had not yet occurred. She was soon fired. When another respected local scientist, Charles Roe, Director of North Carolina's Natural Heritage Program, wrote a letter protesting Heimann's firing, he, too, lost his job. Ostensibly, he was fired for mailing a letter without clearance from his supervisor.

There are many workplaces where reporting problems and challenging inadequate performance are welcome behaviors. There are other workplaces where the same behavior draws swift retaliation; in the words of Claire Booth Luce, where "no good deed goes unpunished." While patient, thoughtful people can accomplish a great deal in their workplaces by the positive strategies of leadership and innovation, there are times when ethical resistance is legitimate and even necessary. The stories of whistle-blowers tend to arise as isolated cases. But their numbers are large, according to NASA whistle-blower Bill Bush, who lost his job and won it back through court action but was no longer assigned any work. Bush spent his idle hours on the payroll building a database of whistle-blowers in industry and government, and accumulated 8,500 names.

The inventiveness of the mischief which rewards unpopular truth-telling in the workplace is well known. A 1987 survey by Donald Soeken, a Washington area social worker serving whistle-blowers, and his wife Karen, a statistician, showed that 84 percent of those who worked in private industry had been fired. In government, 75 percent were demoted. A yearlong investigation by the *Houston Chronicle* of the nuclear industry and its whistle-blowers revealed that most of them were forced into a career change. Any individual who stands up to an organization on issues of credibility and ethics can expect a period of extended stress, often culminating in a career change. The average time it took for whistle-blowers in this survey to resolve their legal cases was three to five years.

The experience of whistle-blowing and related forms of public protest will change your life. However, some of those changes end up as highly positive steps, as lawyer Billie Garde can affirm. Years ago, as a temporary worker in the census bureau in Muskogee, Oklahoma, Garde reported her boss for sexual harassment. He was investigated, indicted and convicted of more serious improprieties, including conspiracy to defraud the government. The experience led Garde to go to law school, and she now specializes in the legal defense of whistle-blowers for a Houston law firm. In the short run, the episode was devastating. In the long run, however, it forced her to break through to a new level of strength. She says frankly:

> *My previous life was lost. I didn't have anything to go back to. I had worked closely with a public interest law firm in pursuing my case. Then they hired me as an investigator. As I got stronger, I got interested in a legal career. I think that's because I saw that I was good at pointing out corruption and advocating for the truth. In the process, I became a different person.*
>
> *Now, working with whistle-blowers who feel that their lives are falling apart, I say, "Let's review this. You lost your job. But it was in a corrupt organization that treated you like dirt. You lost your so-called friends. They ran away when your life got rough, so you didn't have much for friends anyway. What you lost was your illusions. What you do next is up to you."*

If you think you see serious fraud, abuse or illegality around you, take pains to document what you see and shore up your support system before you make a move. Consult the Government Accountability Project's manual, *Courage Without Martyrdom*, prepared by a team of experienced lawyers and counselors. Attorney Robert Backus, who works with whistle-blowers in the nuclear power industry, advises, "Keep careful records. First, they're going to say it's outside your area of concern. Then they're going to say it's not significant. You have to show why the issue is an issue."

Don't be dissuaded from asking questions just because things seem more strange than they could possibly be. In the words of one health care professional who was thinking of reporting possible research fraud, "I kept thinking, 'They couldn't be so transparent. They couldn't have gone so far.' The stunning part is how flagrant, how amateurish, it all seems."

In spite of resistance and harassment, 84 percent of the whistle-blowers who responded to the Soekens' survey said they would do the same thing again in the same circumstances. And an estimated 25 percent of whistle-blowers eventually see direct results from their action in the form of changes within the organization, and many others have a less direct impact in bringing about needed reforms. For example, in the aftermath of the Challenger disaster, Morton-Thiokol engineer Roger Boisjoly testified that he had reported faulty booster components to his superiors and tried to stop the takeoff. His testimony was one of the most powerful factors in reforming both the space program and federal laws to protect whistle-blowers.

Many whistle-blowers experience a double whammy: resistance and sometimes harassment by the employer; and reluctance on the part of other employers to risk hiring them. But this is a taboo that can be broken, and many people reading this book can help. Anyone who has hiring power, even for a tiny department, can play a role. What is needed is the equivalent of an Underground Railroad, or Oskar Schindler's factory in the great film,

Schindler's List — a commitment on the part of courageous employers to welcome courageous employees and reach out a strong hand to assist people who have told the truth at high cost.

This leads to the subject of organizational self-defense. The legal protections and social support systems which exist today for whistle-blowers have been built over decades, through tenacious and bitter battling, by whistle-blowers themselves and by activists, attorneys, legislators, and helping professionals who see these people as frontline defenders of democratic institutions. The same is true for labor and workplace law. Two valuable guidebooks for self-protection are Dan Lacey's *Your Rights in the Workplace*, and John D. Rappaport and Brian L.P. Zevnik's *The Employee Strikes Back*.

Court battles and appeals to regulatory agencies both tend to be nasty, brutish and long. Their payoff can be high, morally as well as financially, but so can the investment that is required. This fact has created a groundswell of interest in a win/win approach to self-defense.

At the same time, grassroots rebellions within organizations are becoming less and less surprising. For all the forces holding bad situations in place, there can be equal and opposite forces for innovation. Even changes which are not enough by themselves may bring unforeseeable ripple effects. Even the most toxic, unconscious, inconsistent, driven, nasty, neurotic organizations are still made up of human beings with at least a glimmer of desire for a better way to spend their days.

Sometimes an informed gamble pays off. At other times, wisdom dictates a conservative strategy. For example, according to organizational consultant Peter Block, it pays to be cautious when you're new or in an untested situation; when you or the organization are recovering from major change; when the survival of the organization (or your job) is threatened; and when you're in a zero-trust environment.

"No battle plan survives contact with the enemy."

— Clausewicz, *The Art of War*

We have been talking about promoting change. Before proceeding further, it's worthwhile to consider the fact that revolutions through the ages have brought with them nasty surprises in terms of unexpected consequences. What principles might guide change-agentry in a flexible and truly adaptive spirit? Here are a few to consider.

1. Accountability: identifying specific goals and people on whose behalf you're working (at least in your own mind, and preferably in your discussions with others who are affected), so that you get beyond ideology and have some concrete standards for evaluating your impact. When you take action on other people's behalf, make sure they know and support what you're doing.

2. Disclosure: being as open about your values and goals as you can in a situation, recognizing that there are limits to this but finding ways to build trust carefully over time and getting a grip on chronic secretiveness.

3. Start with an inside job. If you're pushing other people to deal with their "stuff," best deal with yours. How have your opinions on the issue been formed? Who have you tried to please over the years by the positions you've taken? It's easiest to see the issue through others' eyes — which you'll be called upon to do in countless ways — if you have some appreciation of your own blinders.

4. Responsibility. Taking risks to make change does not exempt you from responsibilities of your day-to-day job and working relationships. If you take an extra initiative, do so with grace and acceptance of the ways it may change your life. Having an agenda in an organization means carrying an added weight and setting yourself apart. Nobody is necessarily going to respond to your initiatives on your terms or timetable. Yours is the responsibility for meeting other people more than halfway, making the case and giving colleagues the resources to be helpful. This, in turn, requires tapping your own support system off the job for recharging and keeping perspective.

5. Follow-through and ongoing relationship. In Joanna Macy's words, "You can't change what you can't touch." Many of the best change agents root themselves deeply in the community they are trying to influence.

Linda Descano of Salomon Smith Barney sums up these principles: "If you're going to think of yourself as an internal innovator on any level — which is a great thing to do — first you have to really understand the workplace and the culture. That lets you identify opportunities that are very much consistent with the corporate culture, preferably in areas that you have some responsibility for. If you work in the print shop, start there, don't start calling for a building lighting audit. If you work in the cafeteria or an office, start there. If your ideas lead you to want to develop something commercial, then you have to do more than recommend something and believe in it. You must have strong financial skills, put the time into management and make a sound business plan so you will have stronger access to capital. Use networking, talk to people for feedback and to hone your own understanding. We often get so comfortable with our own views that we forget there's a world out there. Don't engage in eco-imperialism with your ideas."

A quintessential co-creator of his career is New Yorker Jeffrey Potent, who made the case within the city's Department of Environmental Protection for a new program to help small businesses comply with environmental regulations, and ended up running it. But that was 20 years into a career that illustrates a great deal about the twin skills of initiative and political sensitivity that will help you co-create the workplace you want. He started with a master's degree in environmental and energy policy, but unfortunately graduated during the 1980s, when government programs were being eviscerated. He ended up in business — to be exact, in the ITT regulatory affairs group. He recalls, "I felt I was a failure. But it was a fascinating time to be in telecommunications. AT&T was being divested. ITT was in flux after having had 40 percent of market share for 40 years. I saw a company that was in an incredibly sharp position disappear from the marketplace because it didn't have the ability to compete."

Potent stayed plugged into the environmental world by joining the Sierra Club and working his way up the organization's hierarchy, eventually winding up on the Club's national Clean Water Act Steering Committee, where he recalls:

> I lobbied on Capitol Hill, met members of Congress, and got appointed to the citizens advisory committee for the New York City Department of Environmental Protection with a focus on nonpoint water pollution problems. The agency decided to turn our little project into an agency-wide

program, and I was offered a position. Two weeks before I was about to be hired, the person who hired me was summarily discharged in a public, bloody battle. So there I was, taking a 40 percent reduction in salary to join an agency that had no idea what to do with me. They basically shoved me into a financial analysis unit.

I told a Deputy Commissioner my predicament. He responded by finding me a more interesting — and difficult — project, not much closer to what I wanted to do: implementing a "universal water metering" program. Our agreement was that, if I succeeded in that I could bring him another project to do. We had probably 200 people working on the project — some many levels above me, hardly any of whom I could actually direct, so it was a good opportunity to build consensus, to put it mildly. We proposed some radical changes that saved the city hundreds of millions of dollars.

By year's end, I had found an air pollution program employing 200 people that had no policy or planning arm attached. They just wrote rules. I recommended the establishment of a public policy unit, which ended up consisting of me and an engineer. We spent five years sorting out a bureau that had been drifting along for years.

Those five years were an opportunity to figure out a great deal more about state government's environmental mandates and realities.

Through that work, I began to be aware of pollution prevention as a major departure in how to conduct business. It was fascinating. Although I was a self-proclaimed radical tree-hugger, I found myself working effectively in industry and realized a lot of the roots of environmental problems were lack of information, plus the fact that the price structures didn't accommodate environmental issues then. I got a few grants for pollution prevention projects. But there was conflict between our enforcement role and the ability to gain companies' trust to do technical assistance.

Potent started looking around for an organization that had credibility and connections, and found Sarah Garrison, the head of the Industrial Technology Assistance Corporation. ITAC's goal is to assist small and medium-sized manufacturers to be competitive. Garrison was frustrated because environmental issues were playing heavy for a lot of her clients and she didn't know how to help them. She had the delivery vehicle, and he had the expertise. What they created was an outreach mechanism for pollution prevention using field engineers to help over 200 companies maximize efficiency. He was invited to step over to ITAC to run the program, which gave rise to a national initiative through the National Institute of Standards and Technology. The New York program became a primary model for 75 regional centers, and his job description became co-creating an entire organization.

Innovation has its risks. As Gifford and Elizabeth Pinchot write in their classic guidebook, *Intrapreneuring*, the First Law of the Intrapreneur is, "Come to work every day willing to be fired." But we have all lived through enough instability to put this in perspective.. Often, when taking a risk doesn't lead all the way to the hoped-for conclusion, it leads somewhere more interesting than previously imagined.

For example, Dan Ruben was a health care administrator with a giant HMO, [Health Maintenance Organization] Harvard Pilgrim, for years. He had been involved with a program to help households reduce resource consumption by forming "Eco-Teams," and he realized that the same basic vision and strategy could apply to his company. "We had a lot of opportunities for environmental improvement, and I suspected that they would carry significant benefits for the bottom line," he said. Ruben wrote a proposal to create a job for himself as Environmental Affairs Coordinator for the Harvard Pilgrim system of 70 buildings, with 10,000 employees, serving over a million members. Tying the proposal carefully to the HMO's mission — improving neighborhood health — he started with a broad scan of opportunities, from water conservation to beach cleanups to employee environmental projects. The company president OK'd the proposal and directed Ruben to focus on saving paper, the most visible change for most of the workforce. Ruben recommended a company intranet, which was implemented. He achieved a redesign of the organization's major publication, its physician directory, reducing an unbelievable 110,000,000 printed pages per year to a mere 69,000,000. He spent the year 1997 evaluating the company's practices and making recommendations for savings. The process brought him widespread recognition. "It was such a high," he reflects. "About every two weeks, somebody would ask me to give a talk, write an article, join a board. I did it all. It was a joy."

Ruben's efforts saved Harvard Pilgrim hundreds of thousands of dollars. But that was not enough to prevent the organization from going into a tailspin for unrelated reasons. And he knew the days of joy were numbered. "When you're an HMO and laying off doctors, it's hard to hang onto your environmental function, no matter how much money it's saving." He was laid off in 1998, then invited back in 1999, but not in his environmental role. Working as a project manager once again, he soon made a decision: to finish out his contract and then move into the environmental field. "Even if I end up taking a pay cut — which isn't guaranteed, but it's a possibility — the experience at Harvard Pilgrim made it abundantly clear where I need to move," he says. "What's more, it provided a bridge."

To be a co-creator of your career means gauging risks, building a safety net, and figuring out ways to land on your feet. If you have taken seriously the principles of creating a vibrant support system, stabilizing your life, and letting your steps be guided by emerging needs around you, then you will master the art of co-creating your career — in your present workplace or the one that comes next.

Appendix 1

A Note to Career Counselors: Gatekeepers of a Positive Future

Blown Sideways Through Life is Claudia Shear's manic performance piece about being one step away from Bag Lady, and learning to live there. For years. Sheer has been a waitress, proofreader, movie extra, receptionist in a whorehouse, and many other things, all of which she is seriously overqualified for. Vaguely sensing that she was not of this world in the way employers like us to be, she sought out undemanding gigs where she didn't have to dress up, and could eat and read on the job to her heart's content. Then one day she looked at herself and realized she was a very well-read two hundred pounds. "Writing this book is my 65th job," she admits. And it's the first one that she went after with some sense of her own potential.

Career counseling, or life-work counseling, is coming into its own as a profession because a lot of people are seriously weary of being blown sideways. While the shock waves of corporate and governmental restructuring have intimidated some of us some of the time, they have also shaken much of the workforce out of passivity. Changes upon changes have driven home the value of career entrepreneurship.

Whether they are in jobs or business ventures, whether nonprofit or for-profit or government or some hybrid, working people have to be entrepreneurial today as never before. They have to self-define, self-motivate, self-promote and self-defend. They have to find ways of going about these things that are consistent enough with their values that they can look at themselves in the mirror at the end of the day. In these times, it is more important than ever for our clients to bring their whole selves into the quest for work and the doing of it. More important for us, too, if we are going to be any help to them.

This means we all have to grapple with a set of questions that could be held at bay more easily during the era of the career ladder, when the options seemed relatively fixed. These are questions about the work that's out there and the capacities our clients are able to bring to it. They're also about the appropriate role for career counselors as gatekeepers of economic possibility. Is altruism the opposite of realism, or is there a convergence taking place between values and pragmatism? Are "environmental careers" and "socially responsible business" and "community service" destined forever to be niches for idealists, or are there deepening connections between these worlds and the economy as a whole? These questions are not going to go away, and our ability to deal with them directly can only help our clients muster courage for their own exploration.

In an era when both the future of work and the future of life on Earth are radically uncertain, our clients are faced with deeper levels of choice than conventional counseling methods are able to deal with. We must help them to hone their perceptiveness and critical thinking, so that they can carefully evaluate what's available now. We must also help them to name and sometimes bring into being what's important to them. Above all, we must help them to be brave.

There is a need for a new psychology of career development, one that is inseparable from the psychological and spiritual evolution of the individual and the culture. Such an approach must take aptitudes and skills into consideration, but focus on values and meanings — and, in particular, give legitimacy to social and environmental values which are the wellspring of the human being's ability to care about his/ her world. It amounts to recontextualizing every aspect of our lives, taking seriously that we are embedded within a cultural history and a living planet. For our clients and for ourselves, understanding our values and visions means knowing what we love enough to work hard for. It can be a source of a new level of resourcefulness in dealing with the stresses of any work situation, because it means shifting from "risk-management" to "opportunity-seizing" mode.

Aspiring to neutrality means risking irrelevance. At the same time, clearly, we cannot expect our own concerns and sensibilities to be mirrored by clients, or our own evaluation of the opportunities that make a difference to be a guideline for anyone but us. Somehow, we need to find a professional stance that is not value-neutral, but is not driven by a partisan or personal agenda either. The best language I've been able to come up with is Robert Lifton's term "disciplined subjectivity."

Several primary influences have shaped the model presented in this book:
- developmental psychologists, such as Robert Kegan and the researchers at Wellesley College's Stone Center, who have pointed out the importance of relationship as a context for growth (not just specific relationships, but the awareness of oneself as related, which is not as obvious as it may seem);
- the literatures of athletic peak performance and accelerated learning, which both rely on strong personal vision coupled with structured training and frequent feedback for achieving behavioral goals;
- gleanings from the fields of general systems theory and organizational learning, as applied to social and organizational change, popularized by such practitioners as Joanna Macy and Peter Senge.

The guiding principle for my work is supporting the client's SELF determination, but doing so with the clear awareness that the self is bigger than the ego and wiser than momentary impulse. I work as guide to help people invent working lives that maximize contribution, and minimize harm, in their own eyes. I agree with many of my colleagues that it is not the counselor's place to suggest conclusions, only to frame the exploration and provide a container for dealing with the complexity, difficulty, and full promise of the available options. To do this is to legitimate new levels of questioning that can lead to unexpected possibilities.

For every can of worms the counselor helps to open, however, it behooves us to understand the risks and challenges as well as benefits that may ensue. Thus, we need to have an expanded tool kit. If we're encouraging clients to be entrepreneurial, we need to know about entrepreneurial financing, business planning, self-employment insurance, zoning laws governing cottage industries, and more. If we're encouraging clients to consider "socially responsible" or "social venture" businesses, we need to do more than send 'em to Ben & Jerry's; there are hundreds of these enterprises on the national scene, and many more in our local communities, and we need to have a critical handle on how well they're meeting each one of their bottom-line goals. If we're encouraging clients to walk boldly into corporate or governmental jobs, considering what they can contribute as change agents, we need an in-depth, unromantic understanding of workplace rights and self-defense strategies. We need to know how to support clients when they take risks that bring repercussions.

Fundamentally, I suggest three ways to work with the principles outlined in this book. The first is to focus on facilitating the client's discovery of the social and environmental contexts that are important in his/her life, through the kinds of personal exploration that can be a rich part of the career development process. Second is to facilitate the client's discovery of the power to make a difference through interconnection and collaborative power. In fact, I prefer to use the book with committed groups rather than individuals one at a time. The third essential principle is to participate in the exploration with the client as a full human being, not a detached counselor-figure, owning your own biases and wishes and then letting them go.

My approach flips one common assumption on its head: that before taking strong stands in the bigger world, humans must grow strong as individuals. This new view affirms that we develop our strengths substantially by engaging with our surroundings, speaking our truths, stretching ourselves. Moreover, any definition of mental health, development and well-being must include the capacity to take responsibility for the impact of one's actions on individuals, social groups, and the ecological fabric of life.

No profession that is beyond its infancy has the luxury of staying value-neutral. Medical people have standards of health that they do their best to bring into patients' awareness and behavior. Psychologists have to hold out a vision of mental health, and their work is a complex interplay between their definition and their clients'. Career counselors, too, must grapple with a normative struggle revolving around the question, "What is a successful career?" Is it solely a matter of the client's personal preference? Do societal values figure in the conversation in a legitimate way?

Arguably, helping clients take a broader, longer view can also be in their financial self-interest. How many university placement staffers have colluded with the least reliable, least humane workplaces in the corporate culture and groomed their students to go after these options preferentially, without asking questions about these companies' commitment to work force or to place or even to a particular line of business? Complicating the process is demanding, for us as well as for our clients — but isn't it ultimately easier for our clients to deal with comparative risks and values at the front end of a decision about a job or business opportunity, rather than later, when they're shoulder deep in the enterprise?

By now, at least, you have seen my reasons for believing that values ought to be regarded as the primary driver in career choices, and that the social and environmental dimensions of values are among the most interesting areas of focus. After all, in the words of South African novelist Nadine Gordimir, a life divorced from any sense of social responsibility is a very lonely life. That is just one reason why it is in our clients' longer-term self-interest to rise to the challenges of the era — and in our longer-term self-interest to help them.

Appendix 2

Resources

There is a vast pool of rapidly changing information available on work that makes the world a better place. For additional information, please check the author's monthly column, "New World, New Work" on **www.SustainableBusiness.com.** Also check New Society Publishers' Web site, at **www.newsociety.com**, for information on related titles and future editions.

General Career Development, Job Search, and Workplace Issues

Basta, Nicholas. *Environmental Careers for Scientists and Engineers.* NY: Wiley, 1992.

Bellman, Geoffrey M. *Getting Things Done When You Are Not in Charge.* NY: Simon and Schuster Fireside, 1993.

Blasi, Joseph and Douglas Kruse. *The New Owners: The Mass Emergence of Employee Ownership in Public Companies and What it Means to American Business.* NY: HarperBusiness, 1992.

Bolles, Richard. *Job-Hunting on the Internet.* Berkeley: Ten Speed Press, 1998.

—. *What Color is Your Parachute?* Berkeley: Ten Speed Press, 1999.

Council on Economic Priorities. *The Corporate Report Card: Rating 250 of America's Corporations for the Socially Responsible Investor.* NY: Dutton, 1998.

Crystal, Graef. *In Search of Excess: The Overcompensation of the American Executive.* NY: Norton, 1992.

Duff, Carolyn S. with Barbara Cohen. *When Women Work Together: Using Our Strengths to Overcome Our Challenges.* Berkeley, CA: Conari Press,1993.

Earth Work: Advancing Your Conservation Career, magazine published by Student Conservation Association, Inc., 689 River Road, PO Box 550, Charlestown, NH 03603.

Edwards, Paul, Sarah Edwards, and Laura Clampitt Douglas. *Getting Business to Come to You.* San Francisco: Tarcher/Putnam, 1991.

Environmental Careers Organization. *The Complete Guide to Environmental Careers for the Twenty-First Century.* Washington, DC: Island Press, 1998.

Farr, Mike. *America's Top White-Collar Jobs*, 4th ed. Indianapolis: JIST Works, 1999.

Fox, Matthew. *The Reinvention of Work: A New Vision of Livelihood for Our Time.* San Francisco: HarperCollins, 1994.

Gale Research. *Job Seeker's Guide to Socially Responsible Companies.* Visible Ink Press, 1995.

Government Accountability Project. *Courage Without Martyrdom: A Survival Guide for Whistleblowers*. By mail from GAP at 810 First Street NW, Suite 630, Washington, DC 20002.

Hakim, Cliff. *We Are All Self-Employed*. San Francisco: Berrett-Kohler, 1994.

Handy, Charles. *The Age of Unreason*. Cambridge, MA: Harvard University Press, 1989.

Hawkins, Lori and Betsy Dowling. *100 Jobs in Technology*. NY: MacMillan, 1986.

Hodginson, Virginia A. and Murray Weitzman. *The Nonprofit Almanac, 1996-97: Dimensions of the Independent Sector*. San Francisco: Jossey-Bass, 1997.

In Business, the magazine of environmental entrepreneuring. Info: 419 State Ave., Emmaus, PA 18049. 1-800-661-4905.

Jackson, Tom and Ellen. *The New Perfect Résumé*. NY: Doubleday, 1996.

Jacobson, Deborah. *Survival Jobs: 154 Ways to Make Money While Pursuing Your Dreams*. NY: Broadway Books, 1998.

Jaffe, Dennis and Cynthia Scott. *Take This Job and Love It*. NY: Simon and Schuster/Fireside, 1991.

Janov, Jill. *The Inventive Organization: Hope and Daring in the Workplace*. San Francisco: Jossey-Bass, 1998.

Jarow, Rick. *Creating the Work You Love: Courage, Commitment, and Career*. Rochester, VT: Destiny Books, 1995.

Jebens, Harley. *One Hundred Jobs in Social Change*. NY: MacMillan, 1996.

Kaye, Kenneth. *Workplace Wars and How to End Them*. NY: AMACOM, 1994.

Kivirist, Lisa. *Kiss Off Corporate America: A Young Professional's Guide to Independence*. Kansas City: Andrews McMeel, 1998.

Krannich, Ron and Caryl Krannich. *Almanac of American Government Jobs and Careers*. Woodbridge, VA: Impact Publishers.

Krannich, Ron and Caryl Krannich. *Complete Guide to International Jobs and Careers*. Manassas Park, VA: Impact Publishers, 1992.

Lacey, Dan. *Your Rights in the Workplace*. Berkeley, CA: Nolo Press, 1994.

Mariotti, Steve. *The Young Entrepreneur's Guide to Starting and Running a Business*. NY: Times Business, 1996.

Mattera, Philip. *Inside US Business: A Concise Encyclopedia of the Leading Industries*. NY: Irwin Professional Publishing, 1994.

Meyer, Scott. *100 Jobs in Words*. NY: MacMillan, 1996.

National Directory of Nonprofit Organizations. Taft Group, 1991.

Internships 1998. Princeton, NJ: Peterson's Guides, 1998.

Quintana, Debra. *One Hundred Jobs in the Environment.* NY: MacMillan, 1996.

Riehle, Kathleen. *What Smart People Do When Losing Their Jobs.* NY: Wiley, 1991.

Reinhold, Barbara. *Toxic Work: How to Overcome Stress, Overload, and Burnout and Revitalize Your Career.* NY: Dutton, 1996.

Sacharov, Al. *Offbeat Careers: The Directory of Unusual Work.* Berkeley: Ten Speed Press, 1988.

Shear, Claudia. *Blown Sideways Through Life: A Hilarious Tour de Résumé.* NY: The Dial Press, 1995.

Sher, Barbara. *I Could Do Anything If Only I Knew What It Was.* NY: Delacorte, 1994.

Sher, Barbara with Annie Gottlieb. *Wishcraft.* NY: Ballantine, 1979.

Silbiger, Steven. *The Ten-Day MBA.* NY: William Morrow, 1993.

Sinetar, Marsha. *To Build the Life You Want, Create the Work You Love.* NY: St. Martin's, 1995.

—. *Work as a Spiritual Path.* 2 tapes. 1992. From Sounds True Recordings, 735 Walnut St., Boulder, CO 80302.

Smye, Marti, PhD *Is it Too Late to Run Away and Join the Circus?* NY: MacMillan, 1998.

Thrallkill, Diane. *Executive Temp: The Complete Career and on the Job Guide for the Interim Manager.* NY: Random House, 1999.

Toms, Michael and Justine. *True Work: Doing What You Love and Loving What You Do.* NY: Belltower, 1998.

Trzyna, Thaddeus C. and Roberta Childers, eds. *World Directory of Environmental Organizations.* Sacramento: California Institute of Public Affairs, in cooperation with Sierra Club and World Conservation Union. Annual.

Vaill, Peter B. *Managing as a Performing Art: New Ideas for a World of Chaotic Change.* San Francisco: Jossey-Bass, 1991.

Wagner, Stephen and the editors of *Income Opportunities* magazine. *Mind Your Own Business: The Best Businesses You Can Start Today for Under $500.* Holbrook, MA: Bob Adams Publishers, 1996.

Walton, Kimm Alayne, JD. *The Best of the Job Goddess.* Chicago: Harcourt Brace Legal and Professional Publications.

Weinstein, Miriam. *Making a Difference College and Graduate Guide.* Fairfield, CA: Sageworks Press, 1998. [PO Box 441, Fairfield, CA, 94978]

Winter, Barbara. *Making a Living Without a Job.* NY: Bantam, 1994.

Woodworth, David. *Vacation Work's Overseas Summer Jobs 1999.* Princeton, NJ: Peterson's Guides, 1999.

Magazines that Publish Annual or Frequent Special Issues on Careers and Salaries:

Adweek	*Monthly Labor Review (US Department of Labor)*
Advertising Age	*Personnel Administrator*
Cable Television Business	*Practical Accountant*
Chemical and Engineering News	*Public Relations Journal*
Datamation	*Purchasing*
Engineering News-Record	*Research and Development*
Federal Employees Almanac	*The Secretary*
Hotel/Motel Management	*Technical Communications*
Infosystems	*Traffic Management*
Lawyer's Almanac	*Training and Development Journal*
Mart (retail stores)	*US News and World Report*
Medical Economics	*Video Manager*
Meeting News	*Working Woman*
Money	

Personal Development Resources

Amen, Daniel. *Don't Shoot Yourself in the Foot: A Program for Ending Self-Sabotaging Behavior.* NY: Warner, 1993.

Armstrong, Thomas. *Seven Kinds of Smart: Developing Your Many Intelligences.* New York: Plume, 1993.

Baldwin, Deborah. "As Busy As We Wanna Be," *Utne Reader* (Jan./Feb. 1994) p. 52.

Bennis, Warren and Joan Goldsmith. *Learning to Lead: A Workbook on Becoming a Leader.* New York: Addison-Wesley, 1994.

Brown, Molly Young. *Growing Whole: Self-Realization on a Threatened Planet.* San Francisco: HarperCollins, 1994.

Collins, James C. and Jerry Porras. *Built to Last: Successful Habits of Visionary Companies.* San Francisco: HarperBusiness, 1994.

Dahle, Charyl. "Women's Ways of Mentoring," *Fast Company* (Sept. 1998) p. 187. [www.fastcompany.com]

Dominguez, Joe and Vicki Robin. *Your Money or Your Life?* NY: Viking, 1993.

Edwards, Paul and Sarah, and Rick Benzel. *Teaming Up: The Small Business Guide to Collaborating with Others to Boost Your Earnings and Expand Your Horizons.* Tarcher/Putnam, 1998.

Elgin, Duane. *Voluntary Simplicity: Toward a Way of Life That is Outwardly Simple, Inwardly Rich.* NY: Morrow, 1981, revised 1993.

Goldberg, Natalie. *Long Quiet Highway: Waking Up in America.* NY: Bantam, 1993.

Goleman, Daniel. *Vital Lies, Simple Truths: The Psychology of Self-Deception.* NY: Simon and Schuster, 1985.

Green, Tova and Peter Woodrow with Fran Peavey. *Insight and Action: How to Discover and Support a Life of Integrity and Commitment to Change.* Gabriola Island, BC: New Society Publishers, 1994.

Jackson, Phil and Hugh Delahanty. *Sacred Hoops.* NY: Hyperion, 1995.

Jaworski, Joseph. *Synchronicity.* San Francisco: Berrett-Kohler, 1998.

Kaufman, George. *The Lawyer's Guide to Balancing Life and Work: Taking the Stress Out of Success.* Chicago: American Bar Association, 1999.

Kelly, Jack and Marcia Kelly. *Sanctuaries* (series of books on monasteries and other spiritual retreats, organized by region). NY: Bell Tower.

Mander, Jerry. *In the Absence of the Sacred: The Failure of Technology and the Survival of the Indian Nations.* San Francisco: Sierra Club Books, 1991.

Nevis, Edwin. *Organizational Consulting: A Gestalt Approach.* Cleveland, OH: Gestalt Institute of Cleveland Press, 1987.

Pearson, Carol and Sharon Sievert. *Awakening the Heroes Within.* San Francisco: Harper, 1991.

—. *Heroes at Work.* Workbook available by mail from Mt. Vernon Institute on Women and Work, Mt. Vernon College, Washington, DC.

Pinchot, Gifford and Elizabeth. *The End of Bureaucracy and the Rise of the Intelligent Organization.* San Francisco: Berrett-Kohler, 1993.

—. *Intrapreneuring.* NY: Harper and Row, 1985.

Seligman, Martin. *Learned Optimism.* New York: Random House, 1990.

Shaffer, Carolyn R. and Kristin Anundsen. *Creating Community Anywhere: Finding Support and Connection in a Fragmented World.* Los Angeles: Tarcher/Perigee, 1993.

Simon, Sidney. *In Search of Values: 31 Strategies for Finding Out What Really Matters to You.* NY: Warner, 1993.

Sinetar, Marsha. *Developing a Twenty-First Century Mind.* New York: Villard Books, 1991.

Vaill, Peter. *Managing as a Performing Art.* San Francisco: Jossey-Bass, 1987.

Wurman, Richard Saul. *Information Anxiety: What to Do When Information Doesn't Tell You What You Need to Know.* NY: Bantam, 1990.

Sustainable Communities and Economies

Arnold, Matthew B. and Robert M. Day. *"The Next Bottom Line: Making Sustainable Development Tangible,"* report. World Resources Institute, 1998. **www.wri.org.**

Brandt, Barbara. *Whole Life Economics: Revaluing Daily Life.* Gabriola Island, BC: New Society Publishers, 1995.

Businesses for Social Responsibility
 609 Mission St., 2nd floor
 San Francisco, CA 94105-3506
 (415) 537-0888
 www.bsr.org

Co-Op America. *National Green Pages.* (annual) available from
 800-58GOGREEN / www.coopamerica.org

Frankel, Carl. *In Earth's Company: Business, Environment and the Challenge of Sustainability.*
 Gabriola Island, BC: New Society Publishers, 1998.

Frenay, Robert. "Biorealism: Reading Nature's Blueprints," *Audubon* (Sept.- Oct. 1995).

Goodstein, Eban. *The Tradeoff Myth: Fact and Fiction about Jobs and the Environment.*
 Washington, DC: Island Press, 1999.

Harman, Willis. *Creative Work; The Constructive Role of Business in a Transforming Society.*
 Indianapolis: Knowledge Systems, Inc., 1990.

Hawken, Paul. *The Ecology of Commerce.* San Francisco: Harper Business, 1994.

Meadows, Donella, Dennis Meadows and Jorgen Randers. *Beyond the Limits: Confronting Global
 Collapse, Envisioning a Sustainable Future.* Post Mills, VT: Chelsea Green Publishers, 1992.

Nonprofit Times
 240 Cedar Knolls Rd., Suite 318
 Cedar Knolls, NJ 07927
 (973) 734-1700

Schumacher, E.F. *Small Is Beautiful.* Harper Perennial, 1973.

Shuman, Michael. *Going Local: Creating Self-Reliant Communities in a Global Age.* NY: Free Press,
 1998.

Sirolli, Ernesto. *Ripples from the Zambezi: Passion, Entrepreneurship and the Rebirth of Local
 Economies.* Gabriola Island, BC: New Society Publishers, 1999.

Social Venture Network
 PO Box 29211
 San Francisco, CA 94029-0221
 (415) 561-6501
 www.svn.org

Students for Responsible Business (just renamed Net Profit)
 609 Mission St.
 San Francisco, CA 94105-3506
 (415) 778-8366
 www.srb.org

Work and the Environment: A Bibliography. Cornell University School of Industrial and Labor
 Relations, Ithaca, NY 14853-3901.

Industries and Occupations: Resources and Contacts for Further Research

Three environmental temp agencies on-line:

> ETI, Inc. **www.sni.net/envirotemps**
>
> Environmental Staff **www.envirostaff.com**
>
> Onsite Environmental **www.onsite.com**

Food:

Organic Trade Association

> PO Box 1078
>
> Greenfield, MA 01302
>
> (413) 774-7511
>
> **www.ota.com**
>
> soon to publish *The Organic Pages*

Urban Agriculture Network

> 1711 Lamont St. NW
>
> Washington, DC 20010
>
> (202) 483-8130
>
> Jack Smith, President
>
> **www.cityfarmer.org**
>
> 72144.3446@compuserve.com

Forestry:

Drengson, Alan and Duncan Taylor. *Ecoforestry: The Art and Science of Sustainable Forest Use.* Gabriola Island, BC: New Society Publishers, 1997.

Good Wood Alliance: 802-862-4448. **www.web.apc.org/goodwood/menu.html**

Motavalli, Jim. "The Forest Primeval," *E Magazine* (September/October 1997).

Travel/Transportation:

Association for Commuter Transportation

> 2 Wisconsin Circle
>
> Chevy Chase, MD 20815
>
> (301) 656-0555

Bicycle Federation of America

> 1506 21st St. NW
>
> Washington, DC 20036
>
> (202) 332-6986

DeCicco, John and Martin Thomas. *Green Guide to Cars and Trucks, Model Year 1999.* Washington, DC: American Council for an Energy-Efficient Economy, 1999. Lists best and worst vehicles, helping you figure out which automakers have a good thing going.

Surface Transportation Policy Project
1400 16th St. N, Suite 300
Washington, DC 20036
(202) 939-3475

Industry:

The Biocycle Guide to Maximum Recycling, from *Biocycle* magazine, 419 State Ave., Emmaus, PA 18049 (215) 96-4135

Journal of Cleaner Production, Elsevier Science.

Romm, Joseph. *Cool Companies: How the Best Businesses Boost Profits and Productivity by Cutting Greenhouse Gas Emissions.* Washington, DC: Island Press, 1999.

The built environment and land protection:

New Village
A publication of Architects, Designers and Planners for Social Responsibility
2721 Stuart Street
Berkeley, CA 94705 USA
(510) 845-2481
editor@newvillage.net

Austin Green Builder Program
PO Box 90008
Austin, TX 78709
(512) 264-0004
www.greenbuilder.com

American Planning Association
1313 E. 60th St.
Chicago, IL 60637
(312) 955-9100
APA Resources include:
Jobmart, job listing for members
Jobs Online
Planners' Support Task Force to help members with work-related issues
"It's Off to Work They Go," *Planning* (September 1998).

Boyce, Charles and Ralph Gakenheimer, eds. *Career Opportunities for American Planners in International Development.* Chicago: American Planning Association, 1997. Orders: APA International Division, c/o The Institute of Public Administration, 55 West 44th St., New York, NY 10036. **http://interplan.org.**

Land Trust Alliance
1319 F St. NW, Suite 501
Washington, DC 20004-1106
(202) 638-4725

Energy:

American Solar Energy Society

        2400 Central Ave., G-1

        Boulder, CO 80301

        (303) 443-3130

        ases@ases.org

        www.ases.org

American Wind Energy Association

        122 C St. NW, 4th floor

        Washington, DC 20001

        (202) 383-2500

        windmail@awea.org

        www.awea.org

Rocky Mountain Institute

        1739 Snowmass Creek Road

        Snowmass, CO 81654-4178

        (970) 927-3851

        Fax: (970) 927-3420

        http://www.rmi.org

American Council for an Energy-Efficient Economy

        1001 Connecticut Avenue NW, Suite 801

        Washington, DC 20036

        (202) 429-8873

        www.aceee.org

Directory of Energy-Related Graduate Programs in US Universities

        The Energy Foundation

        75 Federal St.

        San Francisco, CA 94107

        (415) 546-7400

        out of print but available in libraries

Solar Industry Journal

        122 C St. NW, 4th floor

        Washington, DC 20001-2109

        (202) 383-2600

Beauty and fashion:

Falconi, Dina. *Earthly Bodies and Heavenly Hair.* Woodstock, NY: Ceres Press, 1998.

PETA's *Shopping Guide for the Caring Consumer* also serves as a listing of cruelty-free consumer product companies. Order from PETA Merchandise, PO Box 42400, Washington, DC 20015.

Schoonover, Jennifer. "The Garment Industry Gets a New Foundation," *In Business,* (November/December 1993) p. 25.

Organic Fiber Council of the Organic Trade Association
　　PO Box 72424
　　Davis, CA 95617
　　(530) 750-2265
　　ofc@igc.org

The Organic Cotton Directory, produced by the Organic Trade Association in cooperation with the Pesticide Action Network, lists over 125 companies including growers, brokers, mills, manufacturers, and retailers. Also provides helpful overview of cotton growing ecology and economics. (413) 774-7511.

Wisconsin Hemp Growers Association
　　Jordan Grunow (715) 278-3937/Tom Fabjance (715) 682-8062
　　Industrial Hemp: Practical Products: Paper to Fabric to Cosmetics

Eco-tourism:

Eco-tourism Society
　　PO Box 755
　　North Bennington, VT 05257
　　(802) 447-2121

HVS Eco Services. *Ecotel Resource Guide: The Hotel Industry's Tool for Success.* $5.00 from: David Engledrum, HVS Eco Services, 372 Willis Ave., Mineola, NY.

Health care:

Case, Bette. *Career Planning for Nurses.* Albany, NY: Delmar Publishing, 1997.

Office of Alternative Medicine, National Institutes of Health
　　Executive Plaza South, Suite 450
　　6120 Executive Boulevard
　　Rockville, MD 20892-2466
　　(301) 402-2466 fax info system
　　(888) 644-6226
　　www.nccam.nih.gov

Lyons, Dianne J.B. *Planning Your Career in Alternative Health Care.* Garden City, NY: Avery Publishing Group, 1998. (800) 548-5757.

Holistic Health Directory
　　New Age Journal (annual)
　　42 Pleasant St.
　　Watertown, MA 02172

Health Care Without Harm: The Campaign for Environmentally Responsible Health Care, PO Box 6806, Falls Church, VA 22020. (703) 237-2249.

Physicians' Committee for Responsible Medicine
    5100 Wisconsin Ave., Suite 404
    Washington, DC 20016
    (202) 686-2210

Robotti, Suzanne B. and Margaret Ann Inman. *Childbirth Instructor Magazine's Guide to Careers in Birth*. NY: Wiley, 1998.

Sacks, Terence J. *Careers in Medicine*. VGM Professional Careers Service, 1997.

Zagury, Carolyn S. with Daniel S. Hochberg, Samuel L. Peluso, and John J. Brogan. *Nurse Entrepreneur: Building the Bridge of Opportunity*. Long Branch, NJ: Vista Publishing, 1995.

Psychology, social work, social services:

Sternbert, Robert J. *Career Paths in Psychology*. Washington: American Psychological Association, 1997.

National Association of Social Workers
    750 First Street NE, Suite 700
    Washington, DC 20002-4241
    (202) 408-8600/fax (202) 336-8311/TDD (202) 408-8396
    www.socialworkers.org

American Society of Training and Development
    1640 King Street
    Alexandria, VA 22313
    (703) 683-8100
    www.astd.org

Common Boundary Guide to Graduate Education
    Common Boundary Magazine
    4304 East-West Highway
    Bethesda, MD 20814
    (301) 652-9495

Coach Training Institute
    1879 Second Street
    San Rafael, CA 94901
    (415) 451-6007
    www.thecoaches@aol.com

National Association for the Education of Young Children
    1509 16th St. NW
    Washington, DC 20036-1426
    (800) 424-2460
    www.naeyc.org

American Association of Retired People
> 1909 K St. NW
> Washington, DC 20049
> (202) 434-2277

E.F. Schumacher Society
> 140 Jug End Road
> Great Barrington, MA 01230
> **www.schumachersociety.org**
> (413) 528-4472

Connie E. Evans, President
> Women's Self-Employment Project
> 20 North Clark St., 4th floor
> Chicago, IL 60602
> (312) 606-8255/fax (312) 606-9215

Education:

Alliance for Environmental Education
> PO Box 368
> The Plains, VA 22171
> (703) 253-5812

Association for Community-Based Education
> 1805 Florida Avenue NW
> Washington, DC 20009
> (202) 462-6333

Beyond Ecophobia: Reclaiming the Heart in Nature Education, V. 1 of the Orion Society's Nature
> Literacy Series, available from Orion Society, 195 Main St., Great Barrington, MA
> 02130. 413-528-4422. orion@orionsociety.org, **www.orionsociety.org.**

Center for Educational Renewal
> Box 353600
> University of Washington
> Seattle, WA 98915
> (206) 543-6230

Creighton, Sarah Hammond. *Greening the Ivory Tower.* Cambridge: MIT Press, 1998.

"Education for Life," special issue of *Yes!* magazine, winter 1998-99, available from Positive
> Futures Network, PO Box 10818, Bainbridge Island, Washington 98110.
> **www.futurenet.org.**

International Schools Service
> PO Box 5910
> Princeton, NJ 08543
> (609) 452-0990

Making a Difference College Guide (1998), $18 from Sageworks Press, PO Box 441, Fairfax, CA 94978. 415-258-9924. — A national directory of socially and environmentally oriented academic programs.

National Education Association
    1201 16th St. NW
    Washington, DC 20036
    (202) 833-4000

Second Nature, nonprofit developing methods of integrating sustainable practices and education into curricula, physical plant and management of higher education. 44 Bromfield St., Boston, MA. **www.secondnature.org.**

Teach for America
    20 Exchange Place, 8th floor
    New York, NY 10005
    (800) 832-1230

Teachers of English to Speakers of Other Languages
    1600 Cameron St., Suite 300
    Alexandria, VA 22314-2751
    (703) 836-0774
    (800) 329-4469 fax on demand (999 for index)
    www.tesol.edu

Catalysts for Change

Communication:

Society of Environmental Journalists
    PO Box 27280
    Philadelphia, PA 19118
    (215) 836-9970
    www.sej.org

Libraries:

American Library Association, Public Information Office
    50 East Huron St.
    Chicago, IL 60611
    (312) 944-6780
    Their web site — **www.ala.org** — offers copious resources on library education and training, plus a directory of master's degree programs in Library Science and Information Studies.

Advocates:

America@Work magazine for union activists
>AFL-CIO
>815 16th St., NW
>Washington, DC 20006
>(202) 637-5010
>**www.aflcio.org**

George Meany Center for Labor Studies
>10000 New Hampshire Ave.
>Silver Spring, MD 20903
>(301) 431-6400

Stainburn, Samantha. "Back to School: Where the Programs Are," (in nonprofit management and advocacy) *Who Cares?* (March/April 1998).

Mediation:

Society of Professionals in Dispute Resolution
>1527 New Hampshire Avenue NW, third floor
>Washington, DC 20036
>(202) 667-9700
>**www.spidr.org**

Law:

American Bar Association, Public Services Division
>1800 M St. NW
>Washington, DC 20036
>(202) 331-2276
>Publishes directory of public interest law programs in 180 US law schools, hosts local lecture series.

Arron, D. *What Can You Do with a Law Degree?* Niche Press, 1994.

Fox, Ronald W. *Lawful Pursuit: Careers in Public Interest Law.* Washington, DC: American Bar Association Career Series, 1995.

Munneke, G. and W. Henslee. *Nonlegal Careers for Lawyers.* American Bar Association Law Student Division, 1994.

National Association for Public Interest Law
>(202) 466-3686
>Has chapters in many law schools, provides fellowships and some stipends for attorneys taking on public interest projects at lower salaries.

Banking, Finance, and Investment:

Environmental Accounting Resource List **www.es.inel.gov/partners/acctg/acctg.html**

Environmental Capital Network
>(734) 996-8387
>**www.bizserve.com/ecn**

Enviroene: **http://es.inel.gov/index.html**

Epstein, Marc. *Measuring Corporate Environmental Performance: Best Practices for Costing and Managing an Effective Environmental Strategy.* Montvale, NJ: Institute of Management Accountants, 1995.

"Financing Environmental Technology: A Funding Directory for the Environmental Entrepreneur," which is also a list of entry points for working on the venture capital side, from Environmental Finance Center, a project of US EPA Region 9, at California State, Hayward (510) 749-6867

"Beyond Grey Pinstripes: Preparing MBAs for Social and Environmental Stewardship." A publication of the World Resources Institute and the Initiative for Social Innovation through Business of the Aspen Institute. Available on theWRI's web site, **www.wri.org/wri/bschools** or by mail order from:
>World Resources Institute
>10 G St NE, Suite 800
>Washington, DC 20002 USA
>phone (202) 729-7670
>fax (202) 729-7637

New York Society of Securities Analysts, Social Investment Security Analysts Group c/o Linda Descano, Salomon Smith Barney Asset Management Group. Annual conference: "Uncovering Value: The Links Between Environmental and Financial Performance" **www.nyssa.org**

US EPA. *Introduction to Environmental Accounting as a Business Management Tool: Key Concepts and Terms.* Washington, DC: USEPA 742-b-95-002, June 1995.

Ethics Officer:

Center for Business Ethics
>Michael Hoffman, Executive Director
>Bentley College
>175 Forest St.
>Waltham, MA 02154
>(781) 891-2981

Federal Career Directory. US Superintendent of Documents, Government Printing Office, Washington, DC 20402-9325. Order # 006-000-01339-2. US Employment Service (federal), 200 Constitution Avenue NW, Washington, DC 20210. (202) 535-0157. For United Nations work, there are four entry points:
>1. Technical Assistance Recruitment and Administration Service
>Room CD1-1208, Fax (212) 963-1272

2. Professional Staffing Service (nontechnical professionals)
Room S-2500, Fax (212) 963-3134
3. General Service Staffing Section (support and general staff)
Room DC1-0200, Fax (212) 963-3726
4. Internship Program (for graduate students)
Room S-2500E, Fax (212) 963-3134
All the above are at United Nations, New York, NY 10017.

National Ethics Officers Association
Ed Petrie, Executive Director
20 Church St., Suite 331
Belmont, MA 02178
(617) 484-9400

Endnotes

1. Paul Ray, *Integral Culture Survey*: A Study of the Emergence of Transformational Values in America," Sausalito, CA: Institute of Noetic Sciences (report), 1995.

2. I have been inspired and guided by many of them, including Joanna Macy, Tom Yeomans, Sarah and Lane Conn, Fran Peavey, Kevin McVeigh, Michael Cohen, Laura Sewall, John Seed, David Orr, James Hillman, Daniel Goleman, John Mack, Robert Lifton, Chellis Glendinning, Molly Brown, Gail Straub and David Gershon, Gale Warner and David Kreger.

3. *Audubon*, September-October 1995.

4. "Nonprofit Times' Annual Comprehensive Salary and Benefits Survey," *Nonprofit Times*, February 1997.

5. Rosabeth Kanter, "From Spare Change to Real Change," *Harvard Business Review* May/June 1999.

6. "3 in 10 Americans Work 'Non-Standard' Jobs," *Solidarity*, newsmagazine of the United Auto Workers, September 1997.

7. Michael Closson, "Fish Farming Frenzy: Can Aquaculture Become a Sustainable Industry?" in *Positive Alternatives*, summer 1998.

8. Joyce Miller, "Working in Environment: Skills, Expertise and New Opportunities," Chapter 15 in Walter Wehrmeyer, ed. *Greening People: Human Resources and Environmental Management*, 1995.

9. *Nature Conservancy* magazine, "Trust Us," Jan./ Feb. 1999.

10. Malcolm MacKinnon, "The New Health Pioneers," *New Age Journal*, May/June 1999; Diane Goldner, "6 Top Holistic Health Clinics," *New Age Journal* May/June 1999.

11. John Joss, "Stamping Out Breast Cancer," *Modern Maturity* March-April 1999.

12. This term is the title of Steven J. Bennett's out-of-print but worth-seeking guidebook for liberal arts graduates and other generalists, *Playing Hardball with Soft Skills*, NY: Wiley, 1986.

13. For contact information and details, see the Management Institute for Environment and Business's report, "Grey Pinstripes and Green Ties."

14. There are financial planners galore available to help you stabilize your life in this area. And they cover an incredible range, from sensitive counselors with degrees in psychology to securities salespeople working on straight commission. Interview potential helpers to learn the difference. Or get your hands on a very powerful book called

Your Money or Your Life? by Joe Dominguez and Vicki Robin. It presents a structured and tested program for people who are, in any sense, crazy about money — either addicted to accumulation or addicted to a scarcity mentality. It will help you:
- bring income and expenses into the same order of magnitude;
- separate needs from wants;
- develop more resourcefulness in meeting your needs; and
- free yourself from the psychological hold of money in order to reclaim an even more valuable resource, your time.

15. Clinical burnout is more than high stress. It's a chronic, decreased capacity of body and mind, often with symptoms such as fatigue, irritability, lack of enjoyment, difficulty in focusing and decision-making, and a sense of hopelessness. If you are suffering the symptoms, psychologist Neil Wollman suggests these approaches:
- living one day at a time;
- prioritizing activities and focusing on quality rather than quantity;
- letting go of the need to control everything;
- claiming time for renewal;
- celebrating yourself for the values and commitments you hold;
- exercising, resting, playing, laughing, touching, breathing deeply, having time alone.

     Creating this kind of "space," of course, means limit-setting with clarity and confidence. As my friend Sally Crocker, a Rhode Island career counselor, points out, "'No' is a complete sentence."

16. Jeff Reid, "Networking Overtime," *Utne Reader*, Sept./ Oct. 1993.

17. Thanks to Boston career counselor Kendall Dudley for this very useful question.

18. Adapted from "Spiritual Exercises for Social Activists," in Joanna Macy's *World as Lover, World as Self*, Berkeley: Parallax Press, 1992.

19. Used by permission.

20. SCANS: Secretary's Commission on Achieving the Necessary Skills, US Department of Commerce: 992. *Skills and Tasks for Jobs: A SCANS Report for America 2000*, Washington, DC: NTIS PB92-181379.

21. This doesn't mean King didn't have a strategy, and didn't spend untold hours refining and testing it. He just knew that vision is what gives rise to strategy, and what motivates people.

Index

About the Author

MELISSA EVERETT has facilitated career change support groups and counseled individuals in transition since 1992, working with a diverse population that includes MBA candidates, seminarians, environmentalists, social service professionals, and artists. She has brought workshops and lectures on socially responsible career planning to campus, adult education, and professional audiences throughout the United States and in Europe. Melissa received training in counseling and group leadership through the Concord Institute in Massachusetts, and is currently at work on a Ph.D. in Sustainable Development through the off-campus program of Erasmus University in Rotterdam.

Melissa's previous books include *Bearing Witness, Building Bridges: Interviews with North Americans Living and Working in Nicaragua* (New Society Publishers, 1985), and *Breaking Ranks* (New Society Publishers, 1989), winner of the Olive Branch Award from the New York University Center on War, Peace and the News Media. Her articles have appeared in many publications including the *Boston Globe, Boston Phoenix, Earthwatch* and *Business Ethics*. She is Executive Director of Hudsonia, an environmental research institute in the Hudson Valley of New York.

If you have enjoyed *Making a Living While Making a Difference*, you might also enjoy other

---

BOOKS TO BUILD A NEW SOCIETY

New Society Publishers' mission is to publish books that contribute in fundamental ways to building an ecologically sustainable and just society, and to do so with the least possible impact on the environment, in a manner that models that vision.

We specialize in

sustainable living
ecological design and planning
environment and justice
nonviolence
resistance and community
the feminist transformation
progressive leadership
accountable economics
conscientious commerce, and
educational and parenting resources

For a full catalog, call 1-800-567-6772, or visit our web site at
www.newsociety.com

NEW SOCIETY PUBLISHERS